Children of Wrath

Children of Wrath

*New School Calvinism
and Antebellum Reform*

Leo P. Hirrel

THE UNIVERSITY PRESS OF KENTUCKY

Publication of this volume was made possible in part
by a grant from the National Endowment for the Humanities.

Scholarly publisher for the Commonwealth,
serving Bellarmine College, Berea College, Centre
College of Kentucky, Eastern Kentucky University,
The Filson Club Historical Society, Georgetown College,
Kentucky Historical Society, Kentucky State University,
Morehead State University, Murray State University,
Northern Kentucky University, Transylvania University,
University of Kentucky, University of Louisville,
and Western Kentucky University.

Editorial and Sales Offices: The University Press of Kentucky
663 South Limestone Street, Lexington, Kentucky 40508-4008

02 01 00 99 98   5 4 3 2 1

Library of Congress Cataloging-in-Publication Data

Hirrel, Leo P., 1952–
    Children of wrath : New School Calvinism and antebellum reform /
Leo P. Hirrel.
        p.   cm.
    Includes bibliographical references and index.
    ISBN 0-8131-2061-6 (cloth : alk. paper)
    1. New Haven theology.   2. Calvinism—United States—History—19th
century.   3. Congregationalist churches—United States—History—19th
century.   4. Presbyterian Church—United States—History—19th century.
5. Reformed Church—United States—Political activity.   6. Church and social
problems—Reformed Church—History—19th century.   7. Church and social
problems—United States—History—19th century.   8. United States—Politics
and government—1815-1861.   9. United States—Church history—19th
century.   I. Title.
BX7252.N5H57   1998
285'.0973'09034—dc21   98–12157

This book is printed on acid-free recycled paper
meeting the requirements of the American National Standard
for Permanence of Paper for Printed Library Materials.

Manufactured in the United States of America

For my mother
Evelyn Hirrel
with appreciation for all that she has done for me
and for the memory of my father
Michael A. Hirrel
for all that he has taught me

Contents

Illustrations

Acknowledgments

So many people helped and encouraged me throughout the course of this project that this list will be a long one. Of all those who contributed to this project, three friends and mentors were essential to my efforts. Without their assistance this work probably would not have been completed. Robert D. Cross has patiently guided my work through the beginning of my dissertation, and he has continued to support my efforts well after completion of my graduate work, always challenging me to produce the best work possible. Stuart Rochester provided some critical advice and encouragement during the dissertation phase and has been a stalwart source of support throughout my professional career. Richard Shiels has provided the friendship and intellectual stimulation needed to preserve my interest in American religious history even after I began working in public history.

During my studies at the University of Virginia Michael F. Holt, D. Alan Williams, and Gerald Fogarty all guided the dissertation to its completion, in addition to Robert Cross. William King first introduced me to religious history with his insightful course on American religious thought. Certainly all the faculty members who taught me contributed in some way to improving my skills.

The Society for Historians of the Early American Republic (SHEAR) has been a constant source of friendship, encouragement, and intellectual stimulation. In addition to Richard Shiels, I am especially indebted to Marc Harris, Mitchell Snay, Rosemarie Zagarri, Mark Hanley, Curtis Johnson, Daniel Walker Howe, Paul Bushnell, James Bradford, and James Broussard for all of their efforts on my behalf. Virtually all of the other participating members of SHEAR are to be thanked for their friendly atmosphere of support to new scholars.

Most of the research was performed at the Library of Congress, where the librarians not only assisted my research but provided an enjoyable atmosphere for my work. I am also grateful to the librarians at the University of Virginia, the University of Maryland, George Mason University, and the Presbyterian Historical Society.

I would also like to express my appreciation to the anonymous readers who contributed so much to this work.

Through her careful proofreading of the dissertation, Joyce Savage has helped me more than she realizes. Michael Mahoney has been not only a good friend but also an excellent commentator on the dissertation. I have a long-standing debt to Michael Henry for his early encouragement and support of my interest in American history. Other friends have always been available when I required encouragement or support. The list includes all of my immediate family: Evelyn Hirrel, Michael Hirrel, Shannon Hirrel, Helene and John McCabe, Timothy and Rosangela Hirrel, Marc and Eydie Hirrel, the Davidsons (Terese, Bruce, Julia, and Kurt), Charlotte Hirrel, Christine and Michael MicKnick, Surisa Hirrel, Rudy Nuissl and all of the Mitrano family. Other friends who have given me support and encouragement include Celia Adolphi, Katherine Grandine, John Ounan, Tom Davis, Norman St. Amour, Julianne Mueller, Cathy McConville, the Fadden family, Lillian Lowery, Mich elle Moran, Deborah Johnston, Elizabeth Crowell, the Murthas (Veronica, Michael, Meghan, and Anne), Aino Pulles, Paula Renshaw, and Jerry Robb. Lynn Stoner has been an especially valuable source of advice and support.

Margaret Townsend stands out among all of the others for her unfailing counsel, support, and friendship.

I am sincerely grateful to these people and to everyone else who has contributed to this project.

Introduction

On September 10, 1828, members of Connecticut's Congregationalist clergy assembled at the chapel of Yale College to listen to a traditional *Concio ad clerum*, or "advice to the clergy." The occasion itself was not unusual. This time, however, the selection of Nathaniel William Taylor as speaker should have caused the audience to suspect that the address would be controversial. Taylor and his fellow theology professors at Yale were at the center of theological arguments about the fundamental nature of New England Calvinism.

That day Taylor showed that his controversial reputation was well deserved. Taking his text from Ephesians 2:3, "and were by nature the children of wrath," Taylor began the sermon with the customary remarks on the biblical passage selected as the text. "The Bible is a plain book. It speaks, especially on the subject of sin, directly to human consciousness, and tells us beyond mistake what sin is and why we sin. . . . The text then teaches; THAT ENTIRE MORAL DEPRAVITY OF MANKIND IS BY NATURE." Yet he soon changed the tone of his sermon as he argued that humans had at least the theoretical option of rejecting sin. The suggestion that sin was voluntary caused conservatives among Connecticut's Congregational clergy to denounce Taylor and his "New School" theology.[1]

Taylor's protestations of orthodoxy, combined with assertions of the importance of human standards of reason and justice, characterized New School, or New Haven, theology. Essentially, New School theologians attempted to reconcile traditionalist Calvinist language of such terms as original sin or human depravity with the intellectual trends toward a more rational religion prevalent in the eighteenth and nineteenth centuries. They did so by sacrificing the theocentric orientation of traditional Calvinism while preserving the vocabulary of sin and depravity.

Whereas the traditional Calvinists had used such terms to emphasize man's dependence on God, New School adherents sought to demonstrate that such terms were in keeping with human concepts of reason and justice. They insisted that all humans were totally depraved from the moment of their first moral act until their regeneration, yet they also insisted that this depravity was a willful choice of sin.

This combination of Calvinist terminology with rationalist ideas produced a religious outlook that combined a strong fear of human depravity with a belief in human ability to overcome sin. New School Calvinists believed that people were capable of obeying God's law but that men and women refused to do so. They further believed that there were clear distinctions between good and evil, or between truth and error.

During the years prior to the Civil War, New School Calvinists engaged in the broad variety of activities now labeled as "antebellum reform," while carrying the presuppositions of New Haven theology with them. These ideas provided the intellectual grounding and moral frame of reference for a prominent range of antebellum reform movements. New School adherents understood their world within a backdrop of beliefs that included the depraved nature of humanity, the objective validity of moral and religious truths, the coming of the millennium, and similar issues. Historians who seek to interpret antebellum reform within the late-twentieth-century meaning of reform can be puzzled by the distinct intellectual climate of antebellum reformers. The purpose of this book, therefore, is to examine the beliefs of these people, especially within the context of their antebellum reform activities.

New School Congregationalists and Presbyterians constituted an exceptionally important component of the movements that we now call antebellum reform. These men and women were at the forefront of reform movements within what is generally termed the "evangelical Protestant" tradition. They provided critical leadership to anti-Catholic, temperance, antislavery, missionary movements, and other religious enterprises. Indeed, some of the largest reform organizations, such as the American Temperance Society, were overwhelmed by New School Calvinists. Others, such as the American Board of Commissioners for Foreign Missions, were exclusively Congregationalist and Presbyterian.

In order to preserve an intellectual coherence to this work, I have consciously excluded other reformers who may merit inclusion in a general history of antebellum religion or reform. Movements such as women's rights, utopian communities, or radical pacifism attracted comparatively few followers in antebellum America, especially within the Presbyterian and Congregational communities. These movements are interesting to subsequent generations of historians, yet their impact on nineteenth-century society was less obvious. The number of Americans who participated in utopian communities was small, and they had little effect on the remainder of American society. Women's movements remained in their seminal state during the antebellum era, and even the small number of advocates of women's rights aroused fierce opposition. The mutual antagonisms between these various types of reformers further restrict the application of broad generalizations to these disparate movements. Therefore, I have focused my attention on issues that were important to the New School community.

Another category of reformers generally excluded from this study is American Protestants outside of the Presbyterian and Congregationalist denominations. Certainly other denominations, such as Baptists and Methodists, were growing at an astonishing rate during these years, and their remarkable proliferation has been the subject of superb recent historical scholarship. Yet these studies of other denominations further underscore the need to recognize denominational distinctions. Other Protestant denominations shared many of the philosophical and religious assumptions of New School Calvinists, especially the commitment to Common Sense realism. Yet other denominations differed from the Presbyterians and Congregationalists both in theology and in socioeconomic status. Rivalries between denominations often limited the extent of interdenominational cooperation. As Nathan Hatch has so vividly demonstrated, other religious persuasions vigorously pursued their own agendas, often in defiance of Presbyterian and Congregational claims to leadership.[2]

In general, I have tried to avoid the terms "evangelical" and "evangelical Protestant." Although the terms are popular with historians describing nineteenth-century American Protestantism, they lack a clear definition. The *Oxford English Dictionary's* first definition of evangelical is "of or pertaining to the Gospel," which was a common use of the word during the nineteenth century. The term "evangelical religion" was frequently used to describe virtually all trinitarian Protestants. In fact, Robert Baird uses "evangelical" to include virtually all Protestants except Unitarians and Mormons. At other times, the word could be used to denote a religious style that emphasized an immediate relationship with God, especially with Jesus.[3]

In view of the importance of antebellum religion to contemporary reform movements, it is not surprising that the topics of religion and reform have attracted considerable scholarship. In general, while scholars have recognized the role of organized religion in advancing some reforms, they have not analyzed the correlation between theological concepts and reform rhetoric within the framework of New Haven theology. The result has been schools of interpretation that can be divided into reform as a means of social control and reformers as optimists.

Historians who favor the social control interpretation—notably Clifford S. Griffin, Charles Cole, Charles I. Foster, Joseph Gusfield, and David Donald—have explained antebellum reform as a means of social control by displaced elite classes. These historians have pointed out that many reformers came from established families whose comparative social standing had declined in the early nineteenth century. Reform activities were one method of reasserting their leadership.[4]

Beginning with Lois Banner in 1973, other historians have questioned the use of social control as an explanation for antebellum reform. Banner pointed to the diversity of reform efforts and noted that many reformers came from upwardly mobile families. In 1985, Lawrence Kohl argued that historians have not used sufficient rigor in applying or defining the term "social control."[5] Other scholars have questioned the social control explanation of religious benevolence by pointing to the phenomenal growth of evangelical religion among less affluent groups, who joined Methodists, Baptists, or other denominations.[6]

Other historians emphasize the importance of American churches, while pointing out the alleged optimism that resulted from the supposed passing of Calvinist orthodoxy. In 1933, Gilbert H. Barnes linked New School Calvinism and antebellum revivalism with reform activities, especially abolitionism. Barnes was most interested in demonstrating that religious, not economic, factors motivated antislavery activists. He did not discuss the nature of New School theology in detail. He considered that New School beliefs constituted an overt rejection of traditional Calvinism.[7] In 1944, Alice F. Tyler produced a classic account of antebellum reform that blended secular and religiously oriented reforms while proclaiming the optimistic spirit of the early republic.[8]

Interpretations of historians such as Timothy L. Smith, Ronald G. Walters, and John L. Thomas amplified Tyler's theme by describing antebellum reformers as being exceptionally optimistic, clearly repudiating Calvinism, adopting nineteenth-century romanticism, and being forerunners of the Social Gospel. They correctly stressed the importance of what they termed "evangelical Protestants," or "evangelicals," including Presbyterians, Congregationalists, Baptists, and Methodists. In essence, they asserted that nineteenth-century Protestants rejected a dour Calvinism in favor of a romantic faith in humanity.

In a 1978 overview of antebellum reform movements that was revised and republished in 1997, Ronald Walters argued that "Beecher's generation softened Calvinism still further and Finney, nominally a Presbyterian, overthrew it." Later Walters stated that the "evangelical faith in the heart was extremely significant. Like Finney's disinterested benevolence and perfectionism, it belonged to the nineteenth-century repudiation of Calvinism."[9]

Promoters of the optimist interpretation have asserted that the New School's repudiation of Calvinism is evident in a vibrant optimism among American Protestants. Timothy L. Smith, one noted proponent of the optimist interpretation, commented, "It is difficult, indeed, for those who have lived through the 1960s to realize how expansive was the optimism, how confident the hopes that American Christians shared in the 1830s." Walters reiterated this characterization when he observed that "Evangelical Protestantism released people from some of the old Calvinist suspicions about human nature and gave them an outlet for emotional and reformist enthusiasm."[10]

John L. Thomas added another dimension to the optimist interpretation in 1965 when he asserted that nineteenth-century romanticism pervaded the latter phases of antebellum reform. Thomas used Charles G. Finney and Perfectionism as examples of the spread of romanticism in American religion.[11]

To be sure, proponents of the optimist interpretation will admit that antebellum Protestants still believed in man's sinfulness. Yet they have failed to appreciate how deeply the New School feared human depravity. Furthermore, the description of reformers as optimists appears plausible only if one accepts the assumptions that traditional Calvinism was pessimistic, and that New School theology was a clear repudiation of Calvinism. New School Calvinists were more complicated than such descriptions suggest.

Robert H. Abzug has described antebellum reformers as motivated by a belief that they live in an era in which the divine will might affect human affairs. He begins with descriptions of conventional reformers, emphasizing Lyman Beecher, and then moves to unconventional topics, including dietary reforms, radical abolitionists, and women's rights. He finds a common thread in the concern of all reformers with promoting the Kingdom of God. Abzug expresses some interesting ideas about the cosmic perceptions of reformers, especially some of the radical reformers.

Abzug's analysis is confined to the cosmological perceptions of his subjects, in that the subjects of his book shared the perception that they could assist in the achievement of God's plans for this world. This limitation enables him to extend his analysis to divergent categories of reformers, but it leaves unanswered questions about other religious or philosophical perceptions of antebellum reformers.[12]

Most recently, Steven Mintz has produced an overview, which argues that, despite their tendency toward moral judgments, antebellum reformers were precursors to modern liberalism. He suggests that they sought "to place limits on acquisitiveness and exploitation, establish basic standards of human dignity and justice, and renew the ideals of the Declaration of Independence."[13] Whatever validity his argument may have on other categories of reformers, it cannot be applied to the New School Calvinist community. New School adherents operated in an intellectual environment in which late-twentieth-century concepts of liberalism would have had little meaning. These men and women were primarily interested in protecting what they perceived to be universally valid morality in the face of a sinful, depraved world.

George Marsden's study of New School Presbyterians is by far the best history of that subject. Marsden was among the first to modify descriptions of the New School as a precursor of modern religious liberalism, by pointing to some aspects of their theology that would later appear in fundamentalist religions. In spite of this fact, his focus was on the events of the movement, and he therefore did not assess the impact of New School ideology on reform rhetoric.[14] Other historians of New Haven theology have emphasized how Taylor's departures from traditional Calvinism led to greater departures in later years. Sidney Mead's description of Taylor as "a Connecticut liberal" seems to be an appropriate summary of these histories.[15]

This study will turn to the Presbyterian and Congregational communities to develop a perspective on this one component of antebellum reform. For these men and women, their religion provided a structure to comprehend their world and to understand their role in promoting God's will. For the late-twentieth-century historian, an enhanced understanding of the perceptions and beliefs of these reformers will contribute to a comprehensive interpretation that accounts for the profound differences among the various movements that we now call "antebellum reform."

Part One / Religion

The first part of this book is devoted to explicating the origins and development of New School Calvinism. This endeavor includes an analysis of the underlying philosophical and theological assumptions, concurrent trends within the major Calvinist denominations, and the social and political setting for the appearance of New School Calvinism.

Accordingly, chapter 1 is an overview of New England theology prior to the 1820s, while chapter 2 is a study of the New Haven theology of Nathaniel William Taylor and his contemporaries. Chapter 3 explores the reactions to the growth of New Haven theology by conservative Calvinists and more radical innovators. In chapter 4, I briefly describe the religious community of the two major Calvinist denominations. The role of religion within a republican government is the subject of chapter 5.

🌺 1
The Challenge to Orthodoxy

At the close of the colonial period of American history the American people retained a strongly religious orientation. This interest in religion exerted a formidable influence on the American character, particularly in the northern colonies. Americans were not only a religious people, but their beliefs tended toward a Calvinist Protestantism. In Massachusetts, Connecticut, and New Hampshire the Congregational churches were established by law. Although there were no legally established churches in the middle colonies, the Presbyterian and Dutch Reformed denominations had achieved a remarkably strong following. American clergy, who had improved their stature through their support of the Revolution, enjoyed the esteem of their communities.

In spite of this deep religiosity, American Calvinist clergy faced a new challenge to the very fundamentals of their religion. Until the second half of the eighteenth century, few people questioned Calvinist orthodoxy. After that time a new challenge to Calvinist supremacy, which may be loosely described as rationalist influences, acquired sufficient popularity to threaten the Calvinist ascendancy. Despite wide disagreements among themselves, rationalists asserted that God's ways must conform to human standards of reason, morality, and justice. In response to this challenge to orthodoxy, certain clergymen revised their theology in ways that would reshape American religious, social, and political history.

In order to understand this challenge to Calvinist orthodoxy, it is necessary to appreciate the highly theocentric nature of traditional Calvinism. Calvinist religion involved more than a restatement of doctrinal formulas. Religion was a profound experience of man's absolute dependence on God, and of the infinite glory of God. Calvinism resisted an easy expression of man's relationship with God in human language. The traditional Puritan doctrinal terms such as "total depravity," "inability," and "predestination" were only poor attempts to express in a systematic manner a feeling of God's glory and man's dependence.

The Calvinist experience was based on a conviction that God was the end and the measure of all things. Whereas the chief purpose of man was to glorify God, the end of God was His own glory. Moreover, in His omniscience God had so arranged all events within the universe in a way that would promote His own glory. Even the fall of man had been foreseen and allowed by God.

As creatures of God, humans existed for the sole purpose of glorifying their Creator. Yet, because of the fall of Adam, all mankind was utterly disabled from fulfilling this obligation. Men and women selfishly pursued their own gains without a thought to the glory of their Creator. In their preference for the good of the creature to the Creator, humans committed their first sin, and all subsequent sins arose from their obstinate pursuit of their own welfare.

This calamitous state of affairs could be traced directly to Adam's first sin. God had appointed Adam as the federal head of the human race and had decreed that Adam's deeds should determine the fate of his posterity. If Adam had not offended God, the fate of mankind might have been different. In defying God's commands, however, Adam condemned subsequent generations to a state of sinfulness.

Calvinists further asserted that an omniscient God knew and foresaw all events. Thus, God realized that Adam would sin before He created the first man. Despite this knowledge, God allowed Adam to fail the test for the purpose of His own glory. Nonetheless, Calvinists denied that God was in any sense the author of sin. God had merely arranged a situation in which Adam would succumb to temptation. Although this doctrine of decrees was mysterious, the *Westminster Confession* asserted that the doctrine should "afford matter of praise, reverence, and admiration of God; and of humility, diligence, and abundant consolation to all that sincerely obey the Gospel."[1]

Even though all humans were totally depraved after Adam's fall, they were not necessarily as criminal as they could be. The doctrine of total depravity meant that corruption extended to every part of a person's being, but it did not necessarily mean that every part of a person's being was entirely corrupt. The larger Catechism taught that humans were opposed to all that is "spiritually good," while not mentioning the temporal good. Most people could adhere to normal standards of morality. Even the most sinful of individuals could obey the letter of God's law through such practices as church attendance.

The unregenerate worshipped to secure his own salvation, however, not to glorify God. Thus good works by themselves could not be pleasing to God unless these works were performed in order to glorify the Deity. Even the repentance of sin could not please God if the sinner merely felt a "legal" repentance, in that he wished to escape punishment for his offenses.[2]

In this wretched condition, every person fully deserved God's condemnation. The duty of man was to glorify God, but Adam's fall had so utterly corrupted humanity that all people selfishly and obstinately pursued their own interests. Even an outward conformity to the letter of God's law could not be pleasing to the Creator, because humans obeyed God in order to escape from His wrath. The force of sin was so strong that the *Westminster Confession* described the human condition as one of bondage, or slavery, to the power of sin.[3]

To the traditional Calvinist, the wonder of Christianity was that God did not punish all humanity, even though He might have served His glory by doing so. Instead, He devised a method to save at least a part of mankind. The Son of God (who was part of a single God in a triune form) assumed a human state in the person of Jesus of Nazareth. While a human He allowed Himself to be sacrificed in propitiation for the sins of mankind. Because of this Atonement, God was pleased to account men and women righteous for Christ's sake. God would do for humans what they could not do for themselves, to the greater praise of His mercy and glory.[4]

In order to profit from the Atonement, a person needed to have faith in its efficacy. A real "saving faith" involved more than merely a belief in God, or even in the divinity of Jesus. Rather, a genuine saving faith required the conviction that one's salvation came through the sacrifice of Jesus Christ, not through one's own merits. Without such faith a person would persist in attempts to placate an offended deity with selfish works and a legal repentance, which would not be pleasing to God.[5]

To the true believer, however, a saving faith enabled him to serve God with unfeigned devotion and gratitude. The sacrifice of Christ did not free humans from the law, but it did free them from the curse of the law. Once men and women put aside their fears for their own salvation, they could respond to Christ's sacrifice by praising the mercies of their Creator. Obedience to God's law would cease to be a burden; instead, the believer would wish to please God for the sake of His glory. Certainly the believer would relapse into sin, and he might have moments of doubt, but, if the faith was genuine, he would repent with sincerity and return to his God. As the person grew in faith, the devotion to God would increase proportionally.[6]

Humans could never acquire a real saving faith through their own efforts. In this respect too, men and women depended entirely on God to assist them in their helplessness. True faith only came as a free gift of God's grace. Normally God bestowed this gift through the workings of the Holy Spirit while the person was attending the means of grace (such as Scripture reading or worship services). Even the most diligent use of means, however, would be useless unless God chose to bless the effort with the aid of the Holy Spirit. Faith was an unmerited gift from the grace of God. Unworthy humans had no right to demand this gift from their Creator.[7]

In His omniscience God knew from all eternity who would receive this gift of faith and who would not. The people so favored could be described as predestined to eternal life without respect to their own merits. God simply withheld His grace from the rest of humanity. The *Westminster Confession* described their unfortunate fate. "The rest of mankind, God was pleased, according to the unsearchable counsel of His own will, whereby He extendeth or witholdeth mercy as He pleaseth, for the glory of His sovereign power over His creatures to pass by, and ordain them to dishonor and wrath for their sin, to the praise of His glorious justice."[8] Calvinists argued that God did no injustice to humans in damning them, for He merely judged them according to their deserts.

True Calvinists considered their religion antithetical to legal religion. That is, they denied that humans could claim salvation as a right through the performance of works. Eternal life was possible only because of the Atonement of Christ. Faith in the Atonement came to people only through the gift of God's grace. Moreover, God granted or withheld this grace without regard to human merit, as all mankind were equally unworthy in His eyes. Although Calvinists certainly did not neglect obedience to God's law, they held that true devotion was possible only through faith. The emphasis of their religion was on the glory of God, not human behavior.

Similarly, traditional Calvinists limited the application of human reason. They devoted considerable effort to the study of logic and to metaphysics derived from medieval scholastics and the Reformation philosopher Petrus Ramus. While they believed that logic was an essential tool in the discovery of God's works, it could not replace faith or revelation. Indeed, faith was necessary to go beyond the possibilities of human reason.[9]

Certainly, man's dependence on God is an essential theme of Christianity, and in one sense the Reformed theology was an elaboration on the Augustinian or Pauline traditions.[10] The Catholic Church, at the Council of Trent, also affirmed the absolute necessity of grace in converting the sinner. The Council of Trent, however, also asserted the ability of the person to respond to God's grace, either positively or negatively. It further stressed the role of the church as a sacramental means of grace.[11] Reformed theology differed from Catholic theology in its emphasis on the unlimited sovereignty of God and in the starkness of man's dependence on his Creator.

In practice, New England Puritans modified the strictness of Calvinism with their covenant theology and strictures on the means of grace. They held that God had offered Adam a covenant of works, making salvation dependent on conformance to the law. After Adam's failure, God mercifully provided a covenant of grace, saving His favored people. God normally chose to dispense His saving grace through such means as preaching, Bible reading, and religious services. Although the gift of grace remained at God's sovereign pleasure, human attendance on the means might indicate a better chance of receiving salvation. Here New England clergy perceived of themselves as crucial to the salvation of their communities. By teaching Christian doctrines, they helped the sinner prepared to receive God's grace. The perception of New Englanders as God's chosen people further amplified the expectation that their system of churches and society was best designed to fulfill the divine plan of redemption.[12]

With its highly theocentric bias, strict Calvinism remained a vibrant intellectual tradition in New England. It is true that there were differing degrees of emphasis on man's duty to pray for grace, but no one would openly deny the right of a sovereign God to grant or withhold His mercy at His own sovereign pleasure. Any suggestions to the contrary were carefully qualified.

The theocentric orientation of Calvinism received one of its strongest expressions in the works of Jonathan Edwards. In a determined effort to make God the absolute center of his theological system, Edwards relied on his Puritan heritage for his theological foundations, to which he added his own insights and his visions of the infinite beauty of God. Because Edwards's work would be so important in the nineteenth century, it merits some discussion. In later years, Edwards would be widely cited by all parties in theological disputes.

As a Calvinist, Edwards held that the chief end of man was to glorify God and to delight in the perfection of the Deity. To fulfill this obligation, however, required certain supernatural impulses that mankind had lost with the fall of Adam. Humans, therefore, willfully and sinfully pursued their own interests despite their obligation to worship their Creator.[13] To be sure, most men and women would adhere to a certain natural code of ethics that covered normal social intercourse, but this natural morality had a foundation in self-love, in that humans saw others as extensions of themselves. Because men and women did not delight in the excellence of God for His own sake, they slighted their Creator.[14]

Man's obligations to God were the most vital aspect of his existence. Edwards reasoned that as the magnitude of an offense was proportional to the majesty and dignity of the offended party, so an offense against God was infinitely heinous. Even in his well-known denunciation of the unregenerate as more loathsome in the sight of God than the spider that one might cast into the fire, Edwards did not mean that people were incapable of obeying normal social mores. He was reminding his audience that human standards of morality and justice were woefully insufficient in God's eyes.[15]

With his highly theocentric orientation, Edwards denied that humans could change their behavior merely out of a desire to escape the pains of Hell. As the sovereign ruler of the universe, God would dispose of all events for His own purposes. To argue that mere humans could thwart the divine will was unthinkable. In one of his more original contributions to Calvinism, Edwards argued that, even in their freedom, humans would adhere to the divine will.

In his dissertation on *Freedom of the Will*, Edwards proposed a very limited definition of human freedom. Men possessed a natural ability to fulfill their obligations to God, but they were restrained by an equally powerful moral inability. Human freedom consisted in the natural ability to follow one's own volitions or choices. Nonetheless, the scope of this freedom was severely limited because of a moral inability, which prevented the contents of these volitions from being holy.

Edwards adhered to the common eighteenth-century psychology of dividing the mind into two faculties, the understanding and the will. The will (which for Edwards included any act of choice, desire, or inclination) would always be determined by the greatest apparent good, or the strongest motive. Here the understanding played a critical role by processing information arising from the sensations. Nevertheless, Edwards held that the sensations that determined the understanding arose from a source outside of the self. Hence, the strongest motive was determined by a cause outside of the self. He concluded this argument by applying this principle of causality. Any motive must have a cause. All causes could be traced to a prior cause and ultimately back to God. The only real human freedom consisted in the ability to follow one's desires, not to determine the content of those desires.[16]

Despite the apparent severity of Edwards's works, there was another side to his theology. There was a visionary quality that was most apparent in his concept of the nature of true virtue. Edwards's concept of true virtue as a benevolence to being in general becomes most comprehensible in terms of a reflection of God's glory. He believed that it was in the nature of God to emanate His attributes to His creation and that God's glory would be most pronounced when His creatures reflected some measure of that glory back. When an individual gave his assent to the beauty of the entire system, then God would receive at least some reflection of His emanated glory. Benevolence toward being in general could be described as an aesthetic appreciation of the entire system of being, including the salvation or damnation of humans through divine action. "True virtue most essentially consists in benevolence to Being in general. Or perhaps to speak more accurately, it is that consent, propensity and union of heart to Being in general." To the truly virtuous person, this entire arrangement had an excellence or sweetness that the unregenerate could not even begin to comprehend. Of course, the person who possessed this vision of God's excellence would anxiously await the time when he or she could praise God in heaven.[17]

This visionary quality of the beauty and excellence of God's system characterized Edwards's theology as much as his works on *Freedom of the Will* or *Sinners in the Hands of an Angry God*. In all facets of Edwards's works there is a common theme of God as the end and the measure of all things.[18] Mere humans were not to question God's ways or to seek to impose their own standards on Him. It was only the perversion of mankind by the Fall that prevented them from appreciating the beauty and majesty of this arrangement.

Although strict Calvinism remained a viable religious system in colonial America, developments in Europe threatened to undermine its fundamental assumptions. Philosophers of eighteenth-century Europe termed their era the "Enlightenment," or the "Age of Reason" because they conceived of their age as a time when human reason might replace the darkness and superstition of previous ages. Despite their differences, men of the Enlightenment held common assumptions about their age and the use of reason. They believed that their age was more enlightened than previous ages. They further asserted that humans understand nature and mankind best by using their natural faculties.[19]

When judged by these standards, orthodox Christianity contradicted human ideas of reason, morality, and justice. Deism, the most radical form of rationalism, was an effort to substitute human concepts of reason and morality for the Calvinist belief in a sovereign, omnipotent God. In order to understand the effects of Deism in the United States, it is necessary to discuss briefly the European background of the rationalist challenge to Calvinist orthodoxy. Deism originated in the late-seventeenth and early eighteenth centuries with such writers as John Toland and Matthew Tindal. It reached America much later, most notably through the writings of Thomas Paine.

To the Deists the purpose of all religion should be to inculcate morality by offering a system of rewards and punishments in the afterlife. Their own religion consisted of a belief in God and an afterlife and the necessity for good behavior while on earth. They assumed that all humans were fully capable of obeying God's laws. The idea of men and women sharing in Adam's guilt or mankind's bondage to the power of sin made no sense, because they believed that God would judge each person on his or her own merits. Whereas the Calvinists denied that salvation depended on adherence to God's law, the Deists deliberately applied the principles of law to religion.[20]

Deists believed that the doctrines of man's bondage to sin and redemption through Christ were inconsistent with the basic principles of human law. Since man's original sin came as a result of Adam's act, his descendants should not be held accountable for a deed that had occurred long before their births. God had no right to demand that humans glorify Him if they were unable to do so; an inability to perform a duty canceled the obligation.

Even if humans were truly sinful, Christianity did not offer a plausible plan of salvation, for God could not impute the righteousness of Christ to the elect any more than He could impute the guilt of Adam to mankind. According to the fundamental principles of law, a ruler could not punish an innocent party for the misbehavior of a guilty party. To do so would destroy all standards of justice. The doctrine of the Atonement led Thomas Paine to describe Christianity as "'the strangest system of religion ever set up' because it committed a murder on Jesus in order to redeem mankind for the sin of having eaten an apple."[21]

Deists pressed their attack on Christianity by questioning the logic of scriptural revelation. The Bible was available only to a comparatively small group of people. A just God could not require humans to be familiar with Scripture unless He had ensured that all people could learn of His revelation. Even those people who possessed a Bible might be excused for questioning its divine origin. Jesus appeared personally to a very few disciples, and He did not even take the trouble to write or dictate the Gospels. Instead, He left this task to four writers who could not even agree on the details of their Savior's life.[22]

Stories of miracles performed by Christ did not convince anyone who did not already accept Christianity. Any account of a miracle depended on the testimony of witnesses, not the observations of the believer. Relying on David Hume's critique of miracles, they claimed that delusions and deceptions were within the experience of mankind, whereas miracles were contrary to the experience of mankind. Therefore, it was more reasonable to assume that witnesses to a miracle were wrong than to believe that a violation of the laws of nature had occurred.[23]

Even the Bible itself seemed to contradict any assertions of inspiration. The stories of the Old Testament contained so many incidents where God apparently sanctioned immoral acts, such as the conquest of Palestine from the Canaanites, that the Deists would not admit to its divine origin. Although most Deists professed a respect for the person of Jesus of Nazareth, Thomas Paine also thought that the story of His birth was immoral. "The story, taking it as it is told, is blasphemously obscene. It gives an account of a young woman engaged to be married, and while under this engagement she is, to speak plain language, debauched by a ghost."[24]

This analysis is worse than ridiculous to the Christian, with its characterization of the Virgin Birth as carnal misconduct. Yet Paine and other Deists could not understand the Virgin Birth because they could not understand why men and women should depend on a divine redeemer for their salvation. Humans were not so depraved that they could not attain salvation through their own acts. Therefore there was no need for a redeemer. Once they had rejected the concept of man's dependence on God, other aspects of Christianity appeared irrelevant. The Incarnation and the Trinity lost their function, and without the Incarnation there was no need for the Virgin Birth. Saving faith was unnecessary because eternal life did not come through the Atonement. Special revelation was unjust because all men should have equal access to the essential truths of religion. The Bible seemed to be little more than a compendium of errors.

In place of Christianity, Deists devised a religious system based on reason and natural revelation. They asserted that God existed as the creator and governor of the universe. He governed humans through the moral law that all humans could discern and obey. The most important part of the moral law included a duty to love one's neighbors and to be just with other people. God would reward or punish men and women in the hereafter on the basis of their adherence to this law during their lives on earth. The Deists conceived of God as a lawgiver and judge rather than as the infinite being the Calvinist worshipped.

Deism did not appear openly in the United States until after the American Revolution, and Deists were never more than a tiny minority of the population, yet they distressed the orthodox ministers by their sudden appearance. American clergy were unaccustomed to any open opposition to their religion, so even a few professed skeptics were alarming to them. Furthermore, Deists could appeal to the unexpressed doubts that even orthodox ministers might harbor about the justice of God.

Calvinist writers had always recognized that some people would not accept their theology. Eighteenth-century Calvinist clergy might have dismissed their opponents as unfortunate men and women who had not yet received the gift of faith. Nevertheless, they seemed to feel a desire to establish that God was being fair to His creatures. Consequently, they began making "improvements" on traditional theology in order to make Calvinism more acceptable to their audience. One of the most important revisions of Calvinism came from a group of ministers commonly termed "New Divinity" or "Hopkinsian." Samuel Hopkins, a student of Jonathan Edwards and prominent minister, was the best known member of this movement, although other men, especially Joseph Bellamy, readily joined Hopkins in his theological speculations. Lacking the visionary quality of Edwards, New Divinity ministers wanted to preserve the structure of Calvinism while reassuring their readers that the glory of God would coincide with the greatest good of humanity.[25]

Throughout the late-eighteenth and early nineteenth centuries, Hopkins would exert an influence that was, perhaps, more formidable than that of his mentor. Because Hopkins was a student of Edwards, readers might assume that his work was an accurate reflection of Edwards. His two-volume study of systematic theology provided a readily accessible guide to divinity students. Probably most important, it was Hopkins's very lack of Edwards's visionary quality that contributed most to his ascendancy. Whereas Edwards's theology was often too lofty to be comprehended easily, Hopkins's writings were more readily understood by clergy and lay readers.

As Edwards's disciples, the New Divinity ministers asserted that they were upholding his teachings. In the sense that they preserved Edwards's restricted definition of freedom of the will, they were correct. Like Edwards, New Divinity ministers relied on a distinction between natural and moral inability, granting humans the natural ability to comply with God's law but insisting on a moral inability. Similarly, they held that freedom comes through choosing. The fact that the content of that choice is governed by a cause outside of the self does not alter the freedom on men's part. A sovereign God still ruled the universe, and men fulfilled His will.[26]

Indeed, their ardent adherence to Edwards's position on freedom of the will led to some of the controversial features of New Divinity theology. Because God's sovereign pleasure determined who would or would not receive divine grace, New Divinity ministers denigrated the traditional role of the church as the means of grace. Samuel Hopkins went so far as to assert that attendance on the means of grace made the sinner more loathsome in the sight of God, because the person now had a better understanding of God's law. Questions about the precise mechanism for man's sinfulness and moral inability led to an arcane debate between two schools known as the tasters and the exercisers. The former argued that depravity was an inherent taste or relish for sin, whereas the latter held that sin consisted in exercises, for which God was responsible.[27]

Even while they preserved Edwards's teachings on freedom of the will, New Divinity ministers began to compromise on the more visionary aspects of Edwards's theology, especially such works as *The End for Which God Created the Earth*, or *The Nature of True Virtue*. Edwards firmly held that the purpose of God was His own glory. Unregenerate humans were incapable of judging the divine plan. While New Divinity ministers maintained that their system advocated the glory of God, they held that the honor of God was best reflected in the happiness of the greatest number of humans. In so doing they sacrificed an essential tenet of Edwardsean piety.[28]

Hopkins based his system on the principle of benevolence, which for him meant a calculated regard for the greatest good of all beings and a conscious effort to promote that good. Here Hopkins altered Edwards's theology in two crucial respects. Edwards had used "being in general" to describe a difficult metaphysical or ontological concept. Hopkins used "all being" to mean the total of all self-cognizant entities (i.e., God and humans). Moreover, Edwards's idea of benevolence was an abstract appreciation of beauty, whereas Hopkins saw benevolence as a practical desire to do good.[29]

As intelligent entities, both God and men were obligated to promote the greatest good of all other beings. Of course, any being might have a proper concern for his or her own good but only when one's own good was consistent with the greatest general good. Whenever a conflict existed, a being must be prepared to sacrifice his or her own welfare for the sake of the whole. In other words, to be genuine, benevolence must be disinterested.[30]

Because he also believed in God's omnipotence, Hopkins faced the problem of reconciling this sinful world with God's omnipotence and benevolence. He boldly responded that God actually caused Adam's fall and mankind's subsequent sins so that, in overcoming men's sins, He could create a better world than one that would have existed without the first sin. God would bring honor to Himself and happiness to those creatures whom He had determined to save. Hopkins did not doubt that "God does superintend and direct with regard to every instance of sin; He orders how much sin there shall be, and effectively restrains and prevents all that which He would not have take place."[31] Later he explained that "God, infinitely wise and good, has determined that evil should exist, as necessary to the highest perfection, beauty, happiness, and glory of the system which was to be formed by His hand. . . . God has foreordained all this, and all that ever will take place for His own glory and the greatest good of the universe; He . . . brings good out of all this evil; infinitely greater good than could have been without the evil." This assertion was a departure from the *Westminster Confession*, which merely assigned God a negative responsibility for permitting Adam's fall. Even so, Hopkins would not admit to any wrongdoing on God's part, for God brought good out of evil.[32]

As evidence that this creation was truly a benevolent system, Hopkins argued that God would probably save thousands of souls for every one that He damned, so God's glory would be manifested in the happiness of the greatest possible number of His creatures. Believing that this world had existed for approximately six thousand years, he asserted that the next thousand years would be the time of the millennium. Just as one day in seven was the Lord's day, so one thousand years out of seven thousand years would be the time of triumph of the kingdom of the Lord. Hopkins further reasoned that an absence of disease, famine, and war would cause the earth's population to multiply frequently, whereas during the years before the millennium, these factors had limited the population growth. Assuming that virtually every person living during the millennium would be saved, then thousands of souls would be saved for every one lost. Although Hopkins did not give an exact figure, his colleague Joseph Bellamy calculated that at least 17,456 souls would be saved for every one lost.[33]

For these comparative multitudes of fortunate people, a world in which evil existed was preferable to a world without evil. Seeing that they might have perished, these souls would be that much more grateful for their salvation. "While they [the elect] see others perish under the same advantages which they had enjoyed, they see what they should have done, had they not been distinguished by sovereign grace. . . . They see all this, and give all the glory to sovereign grace, and in a greater degree, are happy in the enjoyment of the love of God."[34]

Benevolence was also the test of all human virtue in this system, and it led to Hopkins's well-known assertion that the true Christian ought to be willing to be damned for the glory of God. All men and women were obligated to desire the greatest good for the total of all beings. A person might wish to act in his or her own behalf, if there were no conflict between his or her welfare and the greater good of the whole. True benevolence, however, required a disinterested assessment of the greatest good, even at the cost of one's own gain. Within the Hopkinsian theological framework a certain amount of evil was a necessary means to the greater good, and the damnation of some souls was necessary for the greatest happiness of the elect. Therefore, true benevolence required humans to accept this system with the realization that God would arrange for the greatest degree of happiness among His creatures. Even if an individual was to be consigned to eternal perdition, he or she should willingly accept this terrible fate.[35]

Hopkins made another departure from the *Westminster Confession* by denying the imputation of Adam's guilt to his posterity. Humans were judged guilty because they freely consented to Adam's act, and in so doing joined with their first parent in his rebellion. By entering into Adam's rebellion, humans made Adam's sin their own.[36]

Joseph Bellamy, another New Divinity minister, used the concept of law and God's moral government to justify God's ways. Bellamy asserted that God manifested His goodness through His law. As the perfect creator God had created a binding law, which was eternal and immutable. God's moral government operated according to predictable principles that were just and beneficial to mankind. Although God was sovereign, the benevolence of His essence defined the government of the world. He further argued that the excellence of God's law reflected the benevolence of His nature. Even the punishment of sin was a manifestation of God's benevolence because it upheld the authority of God's moral government.[37]

Bellamy also used a moral calculus to demonstrated that God's omnipotence would result in the greatest degree of happiness for the largest number of people. He provided an example of angels, where one-third of the angels would fall from grace, and the remaining angels would experience a tenfold increase in happiness, recognizing the precious nature of God's saving grace. Through some intricate calculations, he concluded that the happiness of the saved angels would rise by a factor of 32. As noted above, Bellamy reasoned that the onset of the millennium would result in such frequent multiplications of the population that more than 17,000 souls would be saved for every one damned. Therefore, humans might rest assured that God's decrees would work to the greatest advantage for most of humanity.[38]

In many respects the New Divinity was a remarkable achievement. While retaining the doctrines of divine decrees, human bondage to sin, and man's dependence on God, New Divinity ministers devised a system that defended the ways of God to mankind. Even though humans might have difficulty in comprehending God's system, Hopkins, Bellamy, and the other New Divinity ministers reassured their followers that God would promote the best interests of the greatest number of His creatures.

More important, New Divinity ideas would reappear during the nineteenth century. Hopkins' concept of benevolence as a disinterested calculation of the greatest good of all beings provided a rationale for antebellum reform thought. Bellamy's definition of God's eternal laws and of the moral government of God also helped to shape the theology of Nathaniel William Taylor and other New School adherents.

Despite its following, Hopkinsianism failed as a permanent defense of reformed theology. Whereas Edwards might have consistently argued that humans were incapable of judging the divine plan, Hopkins and Bellamy implicitly conceded that God's ways might be evaluated by human standards. In saying that thousands would be saved for every soul damned, they unwittingly converted the sublimeness of Puritan theocentrism into a question of numbers. Even if God were more benevolent, He still appeared to violate human standards of justice. It did little good to preserve Edwards's teachings on the will while compromising the visionary quality that motivated him.

Hopkins's denial of the imputation of Adam's guilt did little to defend the justice of God, because Hopkins used such a restricted definition of freedom that humans were still condemned for an unavoidable condition. Indeed, to deny the imputation of Adam's guilt was a dangerous concession to the opponents of Calvinism, because Hopkins was once again admitting that God's justice could be explained by human standards. Hopkins compounded the problem by teaching that God is responsible for sin. Eventually, Hopkinsianism would be caricatured as consisting of two propositions: God is the author of sin, and men ought to be willing to be damned for the glory of God.

Although a powerful movement within the late-eighteenth century, the New Divinity did not encompass all Congregational clergy. Led by such men as Yale's Ezra Stiles, many clergy still adhered to the traditional covenant theology. These Old Calvinists, or Old Lights, preferred to attenuate the starkness of Calvinism with an emphasis on the church and the means of grace. Lacking the Hopkinsian penchant for speculation, they ministered to their congregations while reacting against the more extreme positions of the Hopkinsians. With the passage of time, their numbers diminished compared to the New Divinity, even though they remained a substantial portion of the New England Congregationalists.[39] Of course, like all distinctions within intellectual history, the division between Old Calvinists and Hopkinsians works better for some ministers than for others. It would be left to men such as Timothy Dwight to employ portions of both branches of New England theology.

With the beginning of the nineteenth century, the Unitarians also became part of the New England religious community. Frustrated by the New Divinity and the Old Calvinist failures to provide a reasonable justification for Christianity, liberals coalesced into a respectable movement that rejected many principal Calvinist tenets while searching for a plausible form of Christianity.

Like the Deists, the Unitarians insisted that faith must be subject to reason. They also believed that revelation might supplement reason, so they remained within the Christian community. Yet they altered the nature of Christianity by denying the Incarnation of God and man in Jesus. Their denial of the Incarnation could be traced to their rejection of the idea of man's total depravity and of slavery to the dominion of sin. A just God would not punish humans for their helplessness. Therefore, people must be at least no more inclined to vice than to virtue. As such, God would judge people according to their behavior while on earth, rewarding the good and punishing the wicked. Because individuals could expect to earn salvation through their own merits, there was no need for an Atonement. Without an Atonement, there was no need for the Incarnation or the Trinity. In place of a God with three persons, Unitarians posited a God with only one person.[40]

Nonetheless, Unitarians strongly disapproved of the Deists' rejection of Christianity. They saw a value in revelation and in the person of Jesus of Nazareth. As long as revelation did not contradict human reason, it might go beyond reason by clarifying questionable points. Even miracles were quite plausible, since God might interrupt the settled order of nature if He so desired.[41]

Within this context, Jesus of Nazareth played a central role in Unitarian theology. He was not the redeemer or the Incarnation of God and man, but He was a divinely ordained teacher, who may or may not have been more than human. While on earth, He taught God's requirements for love to God and to one's fellow man. If humans listened to Jesus and followed His precepts, they might expect salvation. Even though the self-evident wisdom and beauty of Jesus's message ought to have convinced people of His divine mission, God gave Jesus the ability to perform miracles in order to establish His credentials beyond question.

Deists and Unitarians differed on many crucial issues, and adherents of either persuasion would have vehemently denied an affinity with the other side, yet each system reflected the assumptions of the Age of Reason. Both believed that God must act in accordance with human concepts of justice and morality. God would only expect compliance with His reasonable requirements for love of God and one's neighbors, which all men are quite capable of fulfilling. Thus these two varieties of religious thought emphasized the moral or legal aspects of the religious experience. The focus of their religion was conformity to God's law. In this crucial point, these new religions differed significantly from the orthodox position that dependence on God's grace enabled the individual to go beyond mere observance of the law to a joyful praise of the Lord.

A Unitarian party had been growing, especially in eastern Massachusetts, during the late-eighteenth century. The first confrontations between Unitarians and conservatives came in the beginning of the nineteenth century. In 1805, Henry Ware, the Unitarian candidate, became the Hollis Professor of Divinity at Harvard. A few years later, the conservative controversialist, Jedidiah Morse, published his scathing attacks on Unitarianism, which led William Ellery Channing to deliver his sermon entitled *Unitarian Christianity*. In this address Channing completed the rupture among the New England Congregationalists by making a forthright statement of Unitarian views.

Disagreements became increasingly bitter after the so-called Dedham case in 1821. At that time the Massachusetts law provide for a publicly supported church and allowed the majority of the town to select the minister for the parish. Between 1818 and 1821 the Unitarian majority of Dedham township obtained control over the church and its property. They installed their own minister, relegating the Trinitarians to an outsider status. The Massachusetts Supreme Court sustained the Unitarians in 1821, alarming Trinitarians over the future of their church, and hastening the end of publicly supported religion.[42]

Trinitarians responded with attempts to defend their religion. The most notable exchange between the two sides came when the orthodox minister Leonard Woods of Andover engaged Harvard's Henry Ware in an inconclusive pamphlet debate. Woods allowed himself to be trapped into discussing such irrelevant issues as the moral propensities of small children. At the same time he tried to avoid the issue of divine responsibility for sin, while Ware pressed the issue. At best the "Woods 'n Ware" debate was indecisive, although even some Trinitarians felt that Ware had the better part of the argument.[43]

Fundamentally, Woods and other Trinitarians had difficulty in defending their religion because they had difficulty with the highly theocentric orientation of traditional Calvinism. Despite their professions of orthodoxy, they wanted a religion that would agree with their standards of justice. To many people, God ought not punish men and women for their helplessness, and humans ought to expect some recognition of their behavior in the afterlife. Although Woods clung to his beliefs, others sought a better accommodation with the rationalist tendencies of the age.

In these circumstances a new theological movement, known as the New Haven theology, achieved an important place in American thought. Led by new ministers such as Nathaniel William Taylor of Yale, this movement appealed to those people who wished to preserve the outward structure of Calvinism while justifying the reasonableness of their religion. Relying heavily on the English apologist Joseph Butler, Taylor and others refashioned traditional Calvinism to make the old religion compatible with the times. While retaining the Calvinist vocabulary with such terms as "depravity," "the Atonement," "the Trinity," and "regeneration," they placed the emphasis of their religion firmly on human behavior and the moral government of God.

2
Theology at New Haven

In the 1820s, a new theological system emerged from the Yale Divinity Department as a rebuttal to Deism and Unitarianism. The revised system acquired substantial popularity in antebellum America because it appeared to refute skepticism while adopting the rationalist premise that God's ways must be compatible with human ideas of morality and justice. In thus answering the challenges to their religion, the new defenders of Calvinism made moral human behavior and the moral government of God the most important aspect of their religion.

Because of its association with Yale College this new system of divinity was termed the "New Haven theology," or "New School Calvinism." Nathaniel William Taylor, Yale's professor of didactic theology, was the major architect of the new system, and he had the support of other faculty members such as Chauncy Goodrich, and Eleazar Fitch, who concurred in Taylor's theological innovations. Although not a faculty member at Yale, Lyman Beecher maintained a close association with that school. In time, the theology would spread far beyond the university. It spread throughout the North, with only minor inroads within the South; within the North, New Haven ideas were strongest within New England or among transplanted New Englanders. Eventually almost half of the Presbyterian ministers and a larger portion of Congregationalists adopted the New Haven view, either entirely or partially. The seminary at Andover eventually employed faculty members who sympathized with the New School, such as Moses Stuart, Calvin Stowe, and Thomas Skinner.

Yale's leadership in revising Calvinist doctrines is not surprising, considering the school's history under Timothy Dwight. As President of Yale from 1795 until his death in 1817, Dwight distinguished himself through his vigorous attacks against any opposition to Calvinist orthodoxy. Although Dwight was a grandson of Jonathan Edwards, he did not share other post-Edwardsean Calvinists' interests in speculative theology on such issues as divine responsibility for sin. He wanted a workable Calvinism, which would stress the sinner's responsibility for his salvation and the need for the sinner to repent.[1]

Dwight's major work, *Theology Explained and Defended in a Series of Sermons*, displayed his preference for a practical theology. He simply declined to enter the theological speculations that occupied so much of Hopkins's or Edwards's energies. Instead, he focused his efforts at encouraging his readers to employ the means of grace and to believe that they could be justified through God's grace and Christ's Atonement. He did not openly question Calvinist doctrines, but he did place less emphasis on the finer points of Calvinism. Without employing Edwards's elaborate argument on moral inability, he simply noted that humans are universally disinclined to obey God until they receive the gift of grace from the Holy Spirit.[2]

Dwight's favorite student, Nathaniel William Taylor, was more interested in speculative theology than his mentor; but Taylor was even more committed to a rationally defensible theology than was Dwight. To Taylor the glory and majesty of God were comprehensible only when God acted according to man's ideas of morality and justice. Taylor asserted that the two greatest influences on his theology were Jonathan Edwards and the English Bishop Joseph Butler. From Butler, Taylor derived the concept that there must be an analogy between natural religion and the revelation of Christian tradition.[3]

Because he emphasized the means of grace, historians such as Sidney Mead and Allen Guelzo have place Taylor within the Old Calvinist tradition.[4] While there is some truth to this characterization, Taylor borrowed liberally from many traditions, including the moderate Calvinists, Jonathan Edwards, Hopkinsians, and contemporary English theologians such as Butler. He then contributed his own ideas and his own interpretations of other theologians to create a distinctive theology. For example, the New Haven theology modified Hopkins's concept of disinterested benevolence to remove any suggestion of a willingness to be damned. From Bellamy, New Haven theologians discovered the possibilities of applying concepts of law and God's moral government to Calvinist theology.

In later years, Taylor asserted that Edwards was a determining influence on his theology, and he believed that he was preserving Edwards's theology with only minor variations and improvements. Nevertheless,

Taylor made a significant departure from Edwards, even while he used Edwardsean terminology. In particular, Taylor employed Edwards's terminology on freedom of the will, while altering the intent. He relied heavily on the term "moral inability," yet he vastly softened the impact of the term by teaching that moral inabilities could be removed. In later years, one of Taylor's students actually asserted that Jonathan Edwards had preached the importance of human ability in order to arouse New Englanders from a stupor caused by Calvinist determinism.[5]

At the heart of the New Haven theology lay an assumption that, when properly understood, reformed theology was completely compatible with human standards of reason, morality, and justice. Taylor had insisted that the ability to reason correctly was essential to all theological inquiry and that "he who deserts the altar of reason abandons the altar of his God."[6] The New School adherents used traditional Calvinist terminology, but their emphasis on unaided human reason to justify these doctrines went beyond the traditional tenet that faith did not depend on reason.

New School Calvinists did not conceive of a God who glorified Himself through man's dependence. Their God was a more rational figure who governed His creation through intelligible moral laws. They believed that people were quite capable of discerning and obeying God's demands, even if humans consistently rebelled against their Creator. Their religious system emphasized the enforcement of moral behavior through rewards and punishment, at the expense of God's glorification through man's dependence.

To advance his contention of human freedom, Taylor added a third faculty to Edwards's psychology. Whereas Edwards divided the mind into the understanding and the will, Taylor included another faculty termed the "affections." This additional faculty was capable of assessing motives and affecting the will.[7]

New Haven theologians asserted that Christianity demonstrated the moral government of God over His creatures. God governed mere objects through physical laws; but He ruled accountable creatures through a perfect moral government, which Lyman Beecher defined as *"the influence of law upon accountable creatures*. It includes a law-giver, accountable subjects, and laws intelligibly received, and maintained by rewards and punishments."* This statement implied that in order to be accountable under God's moral government a person must have a knowledge of God's commandments and an ability to comply with God's demands. If men could not obey His law, God would be required to assist helpless men as a matter of equity; thus divine grace would be no more than divine justice. God condemned humans for violations of His law only because they had both a knowledge of Him and the ability to obey Him.[8]

Under the New Haven system, all beings were required to obey the law of benevolence, which resembled a Hopkinsian concept of a calculated regard for the greatest good of all beings. God adhered to this rule, and He expected all men to comply. Humans were expected to direct their energies to promoting the greatest good of God and His creatures. Unlike Hopkins, New Haven theologians did not believe that men should be willing to be damned for the glory of God. The glory of God would be best secured through men's salvation.

In some respects, New School Calvinists resembled Unitarians more than traditional Calvinists, because they portrayed a God who judged humans according to their obedience to a moral law. New School theologians differed radically from the Unitarians, however, in their assessment of man's actual compliance with God's law of benevolence. They believed that ever since Adam's sin, and because of that act, all humans willfully and obstinately pursued their own selfish gain at the expense of every other good. New Haven assertions of human ability to act benevolently were always followed by the qualification that no person ever did obey God's law.

New School Calvinists further argued that any moral behavior by an unregenerate person was motivated solely by the thought of rewards and punishments. Unregenerate people always acted selfishly whenever they believed the opportunity existed. Even the worst crimes on earth were but imperfect exhibitions of human depravity.[9] The text of Taylor's famous *Concio ad clerum*, "and were by nature the children of wrath, even as others" (Ephesians 2:3) was deliberately selected to emphasize that human depravity and sin were fundamental tenets of New School theology. (By contrast, Old School Calvinists held that most people would obey normal social mores and that total depravity consisted in the failure to glorify the Creator.)

God chose such a system out of His benevolence because He knew that a moral government was the best possible system for His creatures. Taylor insisted that "*a moral system is the best conceivable system. . . .* Moral beings alone can contrive, design, and produce good to any extent worthy of notice. How imperfect would be a system in which mere animal sensation should take the place of holy affections and holy activity." In His infinite wisdom God knew that humans would abuse the freedom necessary to a moral system; still, a moral system was the best of all conceivable worlds.[10]

If God did choose this system out of benevolence, New School writers needed to explain the invariable human depravity. They admitted that there was some relation between Adam's fall and the present human condition, but they could not agree on the precise nature of that connection. Like the Hopkinsians, they rejected the concept of imputation of Adam's sin as inconsistent with the justice of God, without an alternative theory. Eventually, men like Lyman Beecher would vaguely argue that Adam's descendants suffered from the "social liabilities" of their ancestor's actions, in much the same manner that citizens felt the social consequences of the actions of their rulers.[11]

New School Calvinists experienced a similar difficulty in reconciling human freedom with invariable human depravity. If humans were truly free to choose between good and evil, why did they always choose evil? To explain this problem, they adopted Jonathan Edwards's distinction between physical ability and moral inability while significantly altering Edwards's intent. To the New School Calvinists, men possessed a physical ability to fulfill God's demands. They sinned because of a moral inability, which consisted of a tremendous bias or inclination against God and favoring this world. This bias existed prior to a person's first moral act and remained so powerful that no one would ever obey God's law without divine aid. The New School magazine, *Presbyterian Quarterly Review*, described the moral inability of a sinner by stating that the sinner "is *indisposed* to comply with . . . [God's] commands, we assert what has been termed his *moral inability*. His indisposition, or unwillingness, to obey the law of God, is the voluntary perversion of his faculties, or their wrong exercise." Edwards used the terms moral and physical ability, but he explicitly denied that moral inability was a correctable condition.[12]

One Yale faculty member, Chauncy Goodrich, provided an even more detailed explanation. He suggested that habits of self-gratification, which developed in infancy, shaped the person's behavior. An infant would become accustomed to self-indulgence from the time of its first act, well before he or she could make an informed moral decision. "A child enters the world with a variety of appetites and desires, which are generally acknowledged to be neither sinful nor holy. . . . Under such circumstances it is, that the natural appetites are first developed." By the time the child is old enough to make a moral decision, these selfish habits would be so strong that his first choice would always be self-centered. "*[S]elf indulgence* becomes the master principle in the soul of every child." Thereafter, these habits would be reinforced with successive repetitions, until the individual developed such powerful selfish inclinations that no person would ever fulfill God's law. Even though this explanation for human depravity was not universally accepted among

New School Calvinists, it did reflect a concern with the power of habit among nineteenth-century Americans.[13]

Moses Stuart, another New School adherent, relied on his personal sense of freedom to support his assertion that human sinfulness was voluntary. "I cannot philosophize [*sic*] about it, nor make a verbal diagram of it, . . . but *I can and do feel it*, every conscious moment of my life. My soul is sovereign over all the objects which surround it. It has an ultimate *moral* control." Stuart did not attempt to explain why all humans failed their probation or why God allowed humans to stand probation knowing their uniform sinfulness. He simply admitted that some questions were beyond human understanding.[14]

Whatever explanations for human depravity New Haven theologians employed, they firmly asserted that all men and women were fully culpable for their transgressions. Humans sinned freely and did possess at least a nominal ability to obey God's law of benevolence. Therefore, all people fully deserved eternal damnation.

New School rationalist biases also are apparent in their explanations for the Atonement. They held that the principle of benevolence, as a calculated regard for the greatest good of all beings, required God to enforce His sanctions on humanity in order to protect His laws. He simply could not extend a free pardon to sinners without destroying the effectiveness of His law and producing anarchy. Taylor explained:

> This right to give law, which imposes an obligation to obey, can not be sustained a moment unless the king shows that in giving his law and in punishing its violation he acts on the principles of eternal rectitude. . . .
> Now the subject who violates this law, pronounces it unworthy of regard, tramples on the authority of the lawgiver, and virtually treads the whole Moral Government of God into the dust. If God does nothing His designs are defeated, and all that infinite wisdom and goodness have done, or ever can do to secure their high purpose is in ruins.

Any unconditional forgiveness of sins by God would not be true disinterested benevolence, because God would be destroying His moral government merely to avoid the painful duty of punishing transgressors. Thus, simple forgiveness would be a misguided gratification of selfish impulses by God.[15]

In order for God to forgive men's sins, He needed a method of preserving His moral government. This method must demonstrate God's displeasure with sin so that humans would understand that His moral government was still intact. Here, the Atonement of Christ served a governmental function, for it displayed God's abhorrence of sin and His willingness to impose the penalties of the law. (New School writers argued that the law could be upheld if an innocent person willingly accepted the punishment of the guilty.) Albert Barnes summarized the purpose of the Atonement by commenting that the "unchangeable God *may* consistently offer pardon to the sinner now that an Atonement has been made, though there would be insuperable difficulties in such an offer if *no* Atonement had been provided."[16]

Even with the Atonement there was no automatic forgiveness to any individual. The rebellious sinner still needed to act in such a way as to show that he intended to obey God's commandments. Once the sinner indicated that he was willing to accept this offer of a pardon, the Atonement would become effective.[17] Gratitude by itself was insufficient to move the sinner. Humans must realize that their eternal happiness depended not merely on accepting God's offer of pardon but in adhering to God's law in the future. Indeed, according to Beecher, "the idea that gratitude will restrain, without fear of punishment, where the confidence of pardon precedes sanctification, is at war with common sense."[18]

Conformity to God's law required adherence to the principle of benevolence. Like Hopkins, Taylor and the other New Haven theologians conceived of benevolence as an "elective preference of the highest happiness of all." They refined Hopkins's teachings by making a distinction between self-love and selfishness. Self-love was legitimate because all people naturally seek their own happiness. The distinction between selfishness and benevolence came with the manner of seeking one's happiness. The individual who delighted in promoting the glory of God and the welfare of his fellow humans exhibited benevolence. The person who merely sought earthly pleasures was selfish and in opposition to God. Benevolence and selfishness could not exist in the same individual at the same time.[19]

Taylor specifically denied that any spontaneous emotions could constitute true benevolence. His position was in contrast to the attitude of traditional Puritans, who described the impulsive gratitude of the elect. Jonathan Edwards had described benevolence as a visionary appreciation of God's excellence. In contrast, Taylor insisted that benevolence must be an elective preference in that it involved a deliberate choice. He insisted that if love to God is not an elective preference, or if it does not involve an act of the will, then it can possess no moral quality. "If it is not such an act, it must merely be a necessary *constitutional* affection; and can no more possess moral quality than the circulation of the blood, or the beating of the heart."[20]

While retaining Calvinist terminology such as depravity, the Trinity, and the Atonement, the New School displayed a substantial shift in emphasis away from the traditional Calvinist emphasis on God's glory and man's dependence. They made morality the basis of their religious system with God serving to distribute the rewards and punishments. Beecher succinctly described the fundamentals of religion as "the being of God, the accountability of man, a future state of rewards and punishments without end, and a particular providence taking cognizance of human conduct in reference to future retribution."[21] The historian Richard Rabinowitz has noted how the emphasis of the individual religious experience during the 1820s changed from what he termed "devotionalism" to "moralism." As the New Haven theology increased in importance, individual New Englanders became more concerned with moral behavior as central to the religious experience.[22]

New Haven theology contained a similar rationalist bias in accounting for the process of regeneration. According to the orthodox Calvinist position, a person received a saving faith when the Holy Spirit enlightened his mind. Normally the Spirit worked in conjunction with the means of grace, such as Scripture or preaching. Yet it was still the Spirit who turned the sinner's mind toward evangelical truths. Traditionalists further believed that, once the Spirit began working on an individual, the person could not resist God's power. They termed this doctrine "irresistible grace."

New School Calvinists did not deny the working of the Spirit, but they maintained such a strong faith in the power of the means of grace that they all but ignored the role of the Spirit. For them, the means of conversion were the expressions of the word of God in such forms as the Bible, sermons, or religious literature. These expressions of God's word contained such a self-evident exposition of the essential truths of Christianity that any person ought to accept its veracity once he or she confronted God's word. Beecher commented that "it is by the *truth* that the Spirit of God Converts the soul and sanctifies the heart." Taylor further clarified this observation by noting that "Truth presents the things to be done; the objects, the motives, the reasons, in view of which the mind must act." This faith in the self-evident nature of evangelical truths once again reflected their bias toward an age of reason. They believed in the ability of humans to recognize and accept fundamental truths.[23]

Even though he maintained that the Spirit was active in regeneration, Taylor denied that the Spirit would overcome human obstinacy. For the Spirit to be effective the individual must acquiesce in its operations. If a sinner resisted the Spirit, its efforts might be frustrated. "*This influence of the Spirit when effectual, is unresisted.* Obedience to truth cannot be produced by compulsory power." He explained that those people who give their attention to the subject of religion are converted, and those sinners who ignore God's work remain in their iniquity. He derided the idea of irresistible grace. "According to this scheme, the sinner would be a volunteer *dragged* to his duty. Would this be holy obedience to God? God, by the mere force of omnipotence, crushes the moral agency of the sinner in producing moral action."[24]

Within this framework there existed an implicit encouragement to revivalists. The periodic conversion of substantial numbers of men and women had been a standard feature of American religion ever since the Great Awakening of the eighteenth century. Indeed the revivals of the eighteenth century extended through England, Scotland, and the American colonies. To the traditional Calvinist revivals came about solely at the sovereign pleasure of God, who chose to dispense His grace according to His own design. Although New School adherents did not deny the importance of God's Spirit, their emphasis on the presentation of truth as the impetus to conversion encouraged them to greater exertions. Many of the most prominent New School ministers, including Beecher, Barnes, and Duffield, achieved reputations as important revivalists. The distinction should not be overemphasized, however; conservatives also believed in the power of revivals, and many Hopkinsians, such as Asahel Nettleton, were also important revivalists.[25]

By its presentation of truth, the Bible was the single most important means of converting the sinner. Like most Protestants of their time, New School Calvinists conceived of Scripture as a direct communication from God. As such, the Bible possessed a unity and coherence, with every part serving to illuminate God's desires for humanity. The book was historically and factually correct. It also contained divine precepts and an understandable moral law. Furthermore the divine decrees were revealed clearly enough for all people to be capable of understanding them and reaching the single correct conclusion. "To say that the doctrines of the Bible are so obscurely revealed as to supersede the possibility and the obligation of understanding them, is blasphemy. It is ascribing to Jehovah folly, or injustice, or both."[26]

New School Calvinists refused to admit that there could be any legitimate doubt about the authenticity of scriptural revelation. To them God would not insist on faith in the Bible unless the external evidence for revelation was so compelling that people had no excuse for disbelieving the Bible. David Hume notwithstanding, they held that testimony about miracles constituted conclusive evidence about the divine origin of Scripture. They asserted that the large number of witnesses to

Christ's miracles could not have been deceived and that other contemporary observers would have corrected any false statements in Scripture. Beecher made the argument that if someone wrote a fanciful account of the American Revolution, the book would be discredited by authentic histories of that event. Prophecy provided even more evidence of the Bible's divine origin. They believed that parts of the Bible such as the Book of Revelation and the Book of Daniel contained such accurate accounts of future events that the prophet must have been guided by God. Indeed, it seemed as if God had caused the prophecies for the purpose of validating Scripture.[27]

Just as the New School asserted that the external evidence of Biblical inspiration was conclusive, they also asserted that the light of nature was sufficient to lead any person to the essential religious truths without scriptural revelation. To them faith must be a rational decision based on sufficient evidence, or else God would have no right to command faith. All men and women must have the capacity to discern the features of God's moral government without the aid of scriptural revelation. Only man's stubborn refusal to accept the truth caused God to produce additional revelation as an act of mercy. To authenticate His scriptural revelation, God ensured that the Bible contained miracles and prophecy.

Natural revelation, which included the human faculties of observation and reason, would enable all humans to discover the same truths that New Haven theologians discovered in the Bible. New Haven theologians asserted that all men and women could discover the existence of a supreme being largely by reasoning that an effect must have a cause and that all causes could ultimately be traced to God.[28] Once they accepted the existence of a God, people should see that He is both benevolent and just. As such He desires good behavior and punishes bad behavior. Because humans are free moral agents, it is apparent that God rules through a moral government.[29]

If they reached this point in reasoning, men and women might be driven to despair. If God ruled through a moral government, He would certainly punish transgressions, and all humans ought to recognize their own sinfulness. Still, it was possible for a person to reason that God had made some provision for the pardon of penitent offenders. Without a knowledge of the Atonement, however, it was extremely unlikely that any person would see how God could pardon sin without destroying His moral government. Humans probably would not repent and ask for God's forgiveness. Therefore, God mercifully provided for Biblical revelation in order to clarify points humans probably would not have discerned by using their own reason.[30]

To the New Haven theologians, this line of argument decisively answered Deists' objections to revelation. It demonstrated how God could be just, while offering scriptural revelation to only a portion of mankind. This argument also showed that New School Calvinists shared more ground with Deists and Unitarians than they may have realized. They agreed with their opponents that human reason was sufficient in itself to guide men to the essential religious truths. New School Calvinists differed from their rationalist adversaries primarily in their belief that people would not use reason correctly. Deists and Unitarians held that humans could and did discern the divine will through the use of their reason. New School Calvinists insisted that despite a nominal ability to determine religious principles, humans would never use their reason correctly without divine revelation.

This reliance on religious truth to convert the sinner suggests how heavily New School Calvinists depended on Common Sense realism as a philosophical basis for their religious thought. This school of philosophy originated in the work of Scottish philosophers such as Thomas Reid and Dugald Stewart. According to Common Sense philosophers, we know objects in the external world in their real sense, not merely as ideas or copies. Although Scottish philosophy pervaded all varieties of American religion in the early nineteenth century, it was especially influential among New School Calvinists. To them, truth existed independently of the observer, as an objectively valid phenomenon. Taylor stated that

> Truth also may be distinguished from the knowledge and belief of it. Contrary to a favorite conceit of all skepticism, truth exists in absolute independence of all knowledge and all belief. No doubting, no ignorance, no sincerity of unbelief can alter it. We know that two and two are four, and so it would be whether we knew it or not. We believe that the earth revolves around the sun, and so it is, believe it or disbelieve it, as we may. Things are what they are, independently of all assertion, of all evidence, of all knowledge, of all belief, and of all unbelief. Whether it be known or not, asserted or not, believed or not, there is a reality of things.

People could trust their senses or reason to recognize the truth. Even religious and moral questions could be resolved by logical demonstrations that would lead to a single correct truth.[31]

To the New Haven theologians, such a fixed concept of truth was essential to their entire system. This was the case because they believed that faith must have a foundation in immutable truths. Taylor explained: "What is common sense? It is the competent, unperverted reason of the human mind, whose decisions . . . are to be relied upon as infallible.

Man must know *some things* beyond the possibility of mistake, or there is an end to all knowledge and all faith. Otherwise all his deductions and all his faith have no sufficient basis." Once again, Taylor asserted that faith must be subject to the dictates of reason.[32]

Such a Common Sense conception of truth helps to explain why New School Calvinists could place considerable faith in the efficacy of means. Once a person received and acknowledged the truth, he or she would naturally follow that truth. Doubts or skepticism could not withstand a convincing demonstration of the true religion. One of Beecher's daughters even remembered how he assumed that he might have converted the profligate English poet Lord Byron, if only he had a chance to reason with him. The daughter then added that "though he [Beecher] firmly believed in total depravity, yet practically he never seemed to realize that people were unbelievers for any other reason than for want of light, and that clear and able arguments would not at once put an end to skepticism."[33]

When applied to moral and religious problems, the New School variation of Common Sense philosophy produced a fixed concept of truth. Moral and religious truths possessed a universal, objective validity. "This fitness of things [moral principles] then is independently and eternally the same; and is a part of that reality of things by which the acts and doings of God are determined, and which we call truth."[34] Questions of right and wrong were not affected by time or circumstances. "When God pronounced the moral law on Mount Sinai, He did not then originate its obligations, but only proclaimed those which had existed from the beginning; and He did this as their political lawgiver, that they might understand His civil and political statutes were based upon the moral law."[35] Not surprisingly, these fixed and universal truths often bore a striking resemblance to traditional New England values.

This belief in a fixed, objectively valid truth indicates that, philosophically, New School Calvinists should be categorized with the eighteenth-century rationalists rather than the nineteenth-century romantics. The foundation of romanticism in theology and philosophy has been the insights of such German philosophers as Immanuel Kant and G.W.F. Hegel, with their emphasis on the subjectivity of knowledge. New School adherents fervently held to their belief in objectively valid nature of all truths, including moral and religious truths. As will be discussed in part two, New School adherents frequently went to extreme lengths to uphold their universal, objectively valid truths.[36]

Such an ardent faith in the power of truth may also appear as an indication of an optimistic outlook among New School Calvinists. Yet this approach contained some difficult implications. If truth existed independently of the observer and possessed an objective validity, there could be no room for disagreements. New School Calvinists assumed that they were expounding the only true faith. (Of course they accepted denominational differences within what is generally termed the "evangelical Protestant" tradition, but they gave no credit to non-Protestant religions.)

The New Haven emphasis on human depravity led them to use the Gospel of John (3:19-20) to explain why men failed to accept their truth. "Men loved darkness rather than light, because their deeds were evil. For every one that doeth evil hateth the light, neither cometh to the light lest his deeds should be reproved." This approach contributed to a rigid style in antebellum religion and reform. Beecher could proclaim that "erroneous opinions are criminal because they falsify the divine character, and destroy the moral influence of the divine law, because they are always voluntary, the result of criminal negligence to obtain a correct knowledge, or of a criminal resistance of evidence, or perversion of the understanding through the depravity of the heart."[37]

When large numbers of people failed to see the same universal truths, New School Calvinists frequently assumed that some wicked and designing men must be conspiring to suppress the light of truth. A complicated phenomenon that the historian Richard Hofstadter has labeled the "paranoid style" was an important aspect of antebellum reform, especially when desired reforms fell short of success. Although "paranoid" may not be appropriate in psychological language, New School Calvinists were often willing to attribute their opposition to conspiratorial forces. The belief in a self-evident truth, with the concurrent rejection of perceived errors, was one contributing factor to this pattern.[38]

The two most important antebellum manifestations of a conspiratorial mentality, the "Catholic conspiracy" and the "slave power conspiracy," seemed to rest on the assumption that an informed person would not remain a Catholic or a slave owner. New School Calvinists therefore assumed that someone must be suppressing the truth. Daniel Walker Howe has suggested that perhaps the terminology about conspiracies was a method of rallying Americans against competing interests. New School Calvinists, however, viewed these alleged conspiracies as promoting illicit objectives. They did not regard their opposition as merely competitors but as part of a concerted effort to perpetuate the reign of darkness.[39]

For a time, the New Haven reformulation of Calvinist doctrine appeared to its adherents as the decisive rebuttal to Deism and Unitarianism. New School proponents proved, to their own satisfaction, that the Calvinist doctrines did not conflict with the justice and morality of God. They further demonstrated that God acts to promote the moral welfare of His kingdom. In their system, God acted as the moral governor of His accountable agents (humans). As a moral governor, God endowed His creatures with a real capability to discern His law and to obey or disobey His demands. People invariably chose to revolt from God's government. Because God desired the moral improvement of humans, not merely their punishment, He used the Atonement of Christ as a means of pardoning men's transgressions while upholding His government. Humans might accept God's amnesty with the promise of future good behavior. Thus, the vocabulary of Calvinism remained unaltered. The themes of man's dependence on God and the glory of God, however, became obscured in the emphasis on God's moral government and human behavior.

As Taylor and his fellow New Haven divines were developing their theology, they were also utilizing their new system as a tool for promoting their definition of evangelical Christianity. Early in the 1820s, New Haven adherents using the New Haven theology, and led by Taylor and Beecher, launched a vigorous counterattack against the Unitarian criticisms of Calvinism. As the Unitarian challenge diminished in importance during the 1820s, New School adherents assumed that their arguments had successfully averted the Unitarian assaults on Calvinism. In time, New School advocates would consider their theology the most effective apologetic for trinitarian Christianity.[40]

For these reasons, the New Haven position attracted a strong following among those people who wished to reconcile the features of orthodoxy with an assurance of the reasonableness of their religion. The new theology offered a way to attain salvation through adherence to God's laws. New Haven theology offered its adherents a chance to believe that they were not slaves to the power of sin and that they had the ability to determine their own fate. This affirmation of men's sense of freedom appealed to a society that valued political and social freedom.

Throughout the antebellum era, the New Haven theology helped its adherents to interpret their world, especially their reform efforts. New School adherents believed that, despite a universal depravity, all humans were capable of recognizing correct moral truths. This belief in the pernicious extent of human depravity led them to view unregenerate men and women as a danger to the community. Their Common Sense metaphysics, with its stress on an objectively valid truth, produced a tendency to deny the legitimacy of differing views, especially with regard to moral and religious questions. It would be an overstatement to assert that New Haven theology caused its adherents to engage in reform movements, but for those New School Calvinists who were active in reform efforts, this theology provided the intellectual grounding and moral frame of reference for their activities.

Even with its rising popularity, however, the New Haven theology could not gain complete acceptance within the Congregational or Presbyterian communities. Conservatives protested that Taylor and his fellow ministers changed the essential features of Calvinism, whereas radicals went beyond the innovations of New Haven. These disagreements helped to define the New School position with regard to both religion and reform.

3

Theology at Princeton and Oberlin

The New Haven response to the rationalist challenge sparked a vigorous debate within the Congregational and Presbyterian communities. Other theologians either reasserted their conservatism or moved forward to a more radical departure from Calvinist orthodoxy. Conservatives, led by the faculty at the Princeton Seminary, feared that the new theology undermined the concept of divine sovereignty in order to emphasize human behavior and the moral government of God. The so-called Princeton theology became renowned for its adherence to the theocentric orientation of classical Calvinism. While the conservatives were defending Calvinist doctrines, Charles Finney and other members of the faculty at Oberlin College openly repudiated Calvinist doctrines. The Oberlin theology carried the innovations of New Haven even further by asserting that obedience to God's law, even perfect obedience, was a real possibility.

Even as the New Haven theologians were developing their doctrines concerning human freedom and responsibility for sin, conservatives were expressing their doubts about the departures from the theocentric orientation of traditional Calvinism. Initially some conservatives welcomed the New Haven defenses against Unitarianism and other attacks on orthodoxy. As the implications of Taylor's innovations became apparent, however, conservatives began to fear that the New Haven theology had compromised the essential spirit of Calvinism. Their anxieties were accentuated by the Unitarians, who eagerly pointed to the discrepancies between traditional Calvinism and the New Haven doctrines.

The first signs of opposition to the New Haven theology came from the Hopkinsian ministers of Connecticut and Massachusetts. Men such as Bennett Tyler, Leonard Woods, Asahel Nettleton, and Joseph Harvey had once been allies of Taylor and Beecher in their efforts to preserve Connecticut's Congregational tradition. Later, the Hopkinsians complained that this new theology had compromised the essential tenets of God's sovereignty and omnipotence. They charged that Taylor's insistence on a moral system implied that God was helpless to prevent sin. Taylor responded with a vigorous defense of his own orthodoxy, and the dispute became increasingly bitter. At one time, Taylor ridiculed Tyler's Hopkinsianism with the comment that "Dr. Tyler will have it that a benevolent God could not be satisfied with the perfect holiness and perfect happiness of those who are saved, they must owe it, in no stinted measure, to the eternal agonies of the damned!" The fact that the principal opponents had once been friends only exacerbated the animosity of the arguments.[1]

Presbyterians had traditionally adhered to a strict Calvinism, without the Hopkinsian "improvements." In time, however, Presbyterians also felt the impact of rationally oriented criticisms of Calvinism. When the New Haven theologians offered a seemingly plausible defense of orthodoxy, some Presbyterian clergy accepted these innovations, either entirely or partially. Other clergy vehemently denounced any departures from traditional Calvinism.

By the mid-1820s the two educational institutions at Princeton, New Jersey, emerged as the leading defenders of traditional Calvinism. The older of the two institutions, the College of New Jersey (later Princeton University), received its charter in 1748 during the height of the first Great Awakening. Its first presidents included some of the most illustrious clergy of the era, such as Jonathan Edwards, the elder Aaron Burr, Samuel Davis, and Samuel Finley. Unfortunately, they all died shortly after assuming office, creating an instability within the college. In 1768, John Witherspoon arrived from Scotland to assume the presidency. From then until 1794, the influence of his personality contributed to the growth of the college. Witherspoon energetically obtained support for expanding the school. He became an ardent supporter of American independence, and the school achieved a reputation for supporting the American cause, despite the disruptions caused by the war.[2]

Witherspoon's most important intellectual contribution to the college came with his introduction of Scottish Common Sense philosophy. In Scotland, Witherspoon had studied at the University of Edinburgh, where he first studied Common Sense. In America, he persuasively propagated the metaphysics of Thomas Reid and other Scottish philosophers. At the same time that the New England churches accepted Common

Sense realism as their metaphysical foundation, the Presbyterians of the middle and southern colonies were moving in that direction.[3]

Witherspoon's successor, Samuel Stanhope Smith, was also committed to Common Sense realism. In fact, Smith envisioned an institution where the natural sciences and moral philosophy would work in harmony with the Presbyterian theology. Unfortunately, Smith's administration was characterized by disruptions among the students until he was replaced by Ashbel Green in 1812.[4]

Green's inauguration as president coincided with a decision by the Presbyterian General Assembly to create a theological seminary under its own control. The seminary was also located at Princeton, and the geographic proximity of the two institutions contributed to a sense of cooperation by their respective faculty members. Members of the college faculty, such as Albert Dod and John MacLean, wrote articles for the seminary's principal publication the *Princeton Review*.[5]

Princeton Seminary's first president, Archibald Alexander, determined the direction that the institution would follow for the remainder of the nineteenth century. As a highly orthodox Calvinist, Alexander turned the institution into the nation's foremost proponent of classical Calvinist theology. Under his direction, Princeton students studied the early reformed theologians. Perhaps the most influential theologian was the seventeenth-century writer François Turretin, whose exposition of justification by faith became a standard feature of the curriculum at Princeton.[6]

Alexander's student and successor, Charles Hodge, displayed an even greater devotion to the principles of classical Calvinism than did his mentor. Hodge had traveled in Europe and was familiar with the theological speculations of Friedreich Schleiermacher and the church history of Johann Neander. Yet he still looked to Turretin and the classical reformed tradition for direction in his theology.[7]

Although Hodge is often remembered for Perry Miller's derisive remark that he boasted about not having broached an original idea in fifty years, the Princeton theologians made a highly credible defense of Calvinist orthodoxy. Having observed how any concessions to any opposition merely created more difficulties than they solved, Hodge and the other strict conservatives took the position that once theologians tried to justify God's ways to men, the entire structure of Calvinism was open to question. If the Princeton theologians did defy the nineteenth-century tendencies to modify Calvinism, they made an informed decision. They chose the classical reformed theology because they preferred it to any alternative. The conservatives protected their religious heritage with exceptional intellect and vigor.[8]

Although Princeton theologians disagreed with almost any innovation in religion, they were willing to accommodate some differences. Hodge and other members of the Seminary held that a minister who accepted the "substance of doctrines" contained in the *Westminster Confession* fulfilled the church's requirement and that nonessential points of doctrine could be debated within the church. They opposed demands for a strict subscription to all aspects of the Westminster standards as a condition for ordination. In particular, they could accept Hopkinsian ideas as conforming to the essential points of the *Westminster Confession*. On this issue, they were opposed by an influential clique of ultraconservatives who insisted on a strict interpretation of the *Westminster Confession*.[9]

Princeton theologians did not extend their toleration to the New Haven theology. They complained that the New Haven theologians adopted a Pelagian or semi-Pelagian theology. Named after Pelagius, the early Christian adversary of Augustine, the term "Pelagianism" was used in the nineteenth century to describe any theology that taught salvation depended on human works instead of God's grace. To the conservatives, the New Haven emphasis on human freedom and God's moral government minimized the orthodox tenet of man's dependence on God. Even if New School theologians retained much of their Calvinist vocabulary, they qualified and redefined their terms so heavily that the New School lost the theocentric spirit of traditional Calvinism. To the Old School adherents, this defense of Calvinism posed a danger equal to the outright opposition to reformed theology.[10]

Of course, it is important to realize that the distinction between New School and Old School was not as precise as the terms suggest. Some New School ministers could adopt the New School position without accepting all of Taylor's innovations. New School ministers could believe that they were merely improving Edwardsean or Hopkinsian ideas. Even the Old School Presbyterians may have unknowingly placed a greater stress on the importance of moral behavior than they might have done without the influence of the New School. More important, Old School Calvinists also used Scottish Common Sense realism as a philosophical foundation for their religion. Like the New School, they conceived of an objectively valid, demonstrable truth, but they normally added that men accepted evangelical truths only when aided by the Holy Spirit.[11] New School and Old School Calvinists had more in common than they may have realized.

Furthermore, any generalizations about the dominance of the Princeton Seminary need to be qualified. As the leading defenders of conservative Calvinism, the professors at Princeton Seminary enjoyed the esteem of their contemporaries and exercised a formidable influence over Old School members. Nevertheless, one should not assume that the Princeton professors represented a monolithic Old School population. Old School members did not hesitate to disagree with the Princeton professors. A clique of ultraconservatives constantly berated the Princeton professors for any sign of a conciliatory attitude toward the New School. Although the Princeton Seminary was the leading institution of the Old School, it could not command unanimous assent to all of its teachings.

Princeton theologians, and other conservatives, feared that the innovations of the New Haven theologians might lead to even greater departures from orthodoxy. Having observed how Hopkins's "improvements" on Edwards's theology had contributed to Taylor's formulations, Hodge and others feared that another person might advance beyond Taylor to an open repudiation of the *Westminster Confession*. As if to confirm the conservatives' fears, Charles Grandison Finney emerged from northern New York as a prominent revivalist minister who flagrantly challenged orthodox theology. His controversial career, which culminated in the formulation of the Oberlin doctrine of perfectionism, accentuated the disputes within the two Calvinist denominations.[12]

As a young man, Finney studied to be a lawyer rather than a minister. He decided to become a clergyman only after an intense personal conversion experience during his legal career. Because he joined the religious profession comparatively late in his life, he did not attend a seminary. Instead, he studied for the ministry by reading under the supervision of George Gale, his local minister. Later in life, he recalled studying divinity by reading the Bible and interpreting it as he would interpret a law book. During his examination for the ministry, Finney responded to a question on the *Westminster Confession* by admitting that he had never read the work.[13] This background accounts for the pattern of legalism that remained in his theology. His eclectic education produced a theology that blended—or juxtaposed—Hopkinsianism, New Haven theology, and Finney's own observations. Undoubtedly Finney was very much influenced by the growing numbers of Methodists that he encountered. During his early years, however, he remained a Presbyterian, at least in name.

Finney's initial successes came as a result of his extraordinary abilities as a revivalist. Early in his new career, he achieved an admirable reputation in the far northern section of New York State around the St. Lawrence valley. From there, he began to preach in the upstate portion of New York, covering what Whitney Cross described as the "burned over district."[14]

Because he was a revivalist, Finney wanted to produce tangible results, preferably in the form of persons affected during his visits. His favorite devices included the protracted meeting, which might last several days; the anxious bench, where prospective converts sat at the front of the Congregation; promiscuous prayer, where women prayed publicly with and for men; and praying for sinners by name. Finney placed such intense emotional pressure on a prospective convert that he would not resist the revivalist's entreaties. More conventional Calvinist clergy argued that such emotionally charged meetings produced spurious conversions, which were experienced by people who had no real change of heart.[15]

Traditional Calvinists feared that these tactics diminished the importance of divine influence in working regeneration. These novel techniques appeared to make conversion depend on the skill of the revivalists, not the sovereign will of an inscrutable Deity. Both Old School and New School adherents firmly believed in the importance of revivals, although they viewed Finney's methods with skepticism.

Finney dismissed his critics by pointing to his results. Under his direction, revivals could produce large numbers of professed converts. He further strengthened his argument by accentuating the New Haven emphasis on the importance of the presentation of truth to the sinner. Even in the earliest phases of his career, he developed this practice further than Taylor would have approved.[16]

Not content with defending his own techniques, Finney responded by attacking the opponents of his revivals. He described his opposition as cold, or as a time-serving, hireling ministry. Then, in 1826, he shocked the orthodox community with his sermon "Can Two Walk Together Except They Be Agreed." After defending the importance of revivals, Finney advised dissatisfied Congregations to shake off their sleepy ministers if the clergymen could not produce a revival. Even moderately liberal clergy were scandalized by this direct threat to a system of settled ministry. A standing, educated ministry had long been a tradition of the two primary Calvinist churches. Its members usually regarded attacks on the clergy as a sign of a dangerous enthusiasm. Here Finney was inviting a removal of the settled clergy with little regard for the consequences.[17]

In order to counter this new danger to ecclesiastical stability, a group of Connecticut ministers, led by Beecher and Asahel Nettleton, traveled to New York and met with this disruptive new minister. The Connecticut clergy arranged to confer with Finney and several other itiner-

ant revivalist ministers in New Lebanon, New York. At times, the acri-
mony of the council reached new heights, and Beecher went so far as to
threaten to oppose Finney with cannon if the western revivalist should
attempt to preach in Boston.

Nonetheless, the meeting ended with an inconclusive declaration
of mutual principles, passed as a series of resolutions. At one point,
Beecher and his colleagues proposed a resolution condemning any revivalist who criticized a settled minister as cold or dead in the faith.
Finney and his friends amended the resolution to include a denunciation of any attacks on itinerants as enthusiasts. Thus phrased, the in-
nocuous declaration passed with one abstention. Nettleton departed from
the conference believing that Beecher had not responded forcefully to
Finney's new measures and later drifted toward the conservative Congregationalists.[18]

For a short time after the New Lebanon conference, Finney appeared to have modified his techniques to make himself more respectable. He achieved his greatest success in his 1831 campaign at Rochester, where he dominated city life with his presence. In many respects,
the Rochester revival marked the pinnacle of Finney's influence within
the Calvinist community. He came to the city as the population was
adjusting to the changing social structure of a growing manufacturing
center. It was a time when the respectable portion of the community
was concerned over the breakdown of traditional social structures, with
the concurrent rise of drink and disorder among the working classes.
Arriving at the invitation of a Presbyterian minister, Finney brought a
measure of sobriety and unity to the city.[19]

By 1832 he was delivering his revival message in Boston. Instead
of opposing him with artillery, Beecher allowed Finney to preach in
his Boston parish. For a short time, it seemed as if Finney would be
accepted within the two major Calvinist denominations. Finney, however, continued to create consternation among the conventional Congregationalists and Presbyterians. After Rochester, subsequent revivals
were notably less successful. Finney's preaching in Boston, Philadelphia,
and New York City achieved only modest results. Later he accepted the
pastorship of the Broadway Tabernacle Church in New York City. From
there he allowed his lectures and sermons to be transcribed and published. These written opinions created new controversies as the Old
School Calvinists discovered evidence of the heresies that they had
long suspected.[20]

The publication of his speeches, *Lectures on Revivals of Religion*, pur-
ported to instruct ministers on methods of producing mass conversions.

He opened the work by baldly proclaiming that a revival depended on the forceful presentation of truth, even to the point where a revival was "a purely philosophical result of the right use of the constituted means," and that God "found it necessary to take advantage of the excitability there is in mankind . . . before he can lead them to obey." It is true that Finney did allow a role for the Spirit of God as a personal being in leading men to conversion, but he qualified these assertions by teaching that the individual could "grieve away the Spirit." To the traditionalists, this appeared as resistible grace.[21]

Finney finished antagonizing the conservatives by comparing the alleged success of his revivals with the traditionalists' formality. Amid abundant denunciations of settled ministers as cold formalists, he argued that under their care hundreds of thousands of souls were lost. "No doubt more than five thousand millions have gone down to hell, while the church has been dreaming and waiting for God to save them without the use of means." His remark that "no doubt there is a jubilee in hell every year, about the time of the meeting of the General Assembly," appeared particularly inappropriate for an ordained Presbyterian minister.[22]

In the July 1834 issue of the *Princeton Review*, Albert Dod, a professor at the College of New Jersey, vented an uncommon degree of fury on Finney's *Lectures on Revivals*. Finney had not yet left the Presbyterian Church, and Dod could not comprehend how a minister of that church could publicly proclaim doctrines so contrary to the Westminster standards. To Dod and the other conservatives, Finney's discussion of human means in creating revivals was little more than a resurrection of the Pelagian errors of the fourth century. By arguing that the success of a revival depended on the proper use of means, Finney had downgraded the importance of God so much that conservatives complained that he had ignored the doctrine of the Holy Spirit. Dod concluded with a sarcastic expression of gratitude to Finney for revealing the errors of the new theology, "We tender him our thanks for the substantial service he has done the church by exposing the naked deformities of the New Divinity. He can render her still another, . . . by leaving her communion and finding one within which he can preach and publish his opinions."[23]

Shortly afterward, Finney would leave the Presbyterian ministry and enter the Congregational fold. In 1835, he accepted a position as Professor of Theology at the recently founded Oberlin College. Even after going to Oberlin, he continued to create new discord for the orthodox Calvinists. In 1837, he joined Asa Mahan and other Oberlin faculty members in espousing the doctrine of perfect obedience to God's law. Undoubtedly influenced by the resurgent perfectionist or holiness movement within the Methodists, the Oberlin professors created their own version of perfectionism. In his *Lectures to Professing Christians,* he first advanced the idea that perfect obedience to God's law in this life was a real possibility. He further developed this perfectionist ideology in 1846 with his *Systematic Theology.*[24]

The perfectionism of Finney and other Oberlin faculty members was consistent with their emphasis on adherence to God's law. Like Taylor, Finney had argued that the Atonement of Christ had served a governmental purpose, making a pardon of repentant sinners consistent with God's moral government. He specifically denied that justification by faith could be accomplished unless accompanied by good works and personal holiness.[25] He confused faith with works in asserting that the knowledge that one's sins could be pardoned created an obligation to comply with God's law in the future. "And here let me say, that we receive this grace by faith. . . . Faith is the voluntary compliance on our part, with the condition of the covenant."[26]

To be sure, Finney lectured against what he termed "legal religion." Yet his description of legal religion as merely outward conformity to God's law left the responsibility for salvation to the individual not the grace of God. He adopted an Hopkinsian definition of true virtue as a disinterested benevolence, or a calculated regard for the greatest good of all beings. Unlike Hopkins, he denied that any person ought to be willing to be damned for the glory of God, for the glory of God required men's salvation. Finney did assert that any person who performed good deeds merely for the sake of his own salvation gained no merit. Two people might outwardly praise God, but inwardly they might act for different reasons: "The true saint because he loves to see God glorified, and the deceived person because he knows that is the way to be saved. The true convert has his heart set on the glory of God, as his great end, and he desires to glorify God as an end, for its own sake. The other person desires it as a means to *his* end, the benefit of himself." The orthodox Calvinist believed that such an interest in God's glory would come from the elect as a result of the knowledge that they were justified. Finney reversed the traditional order by making this disinterested benevolence a precondition for justification. He seemed to believe that such clear distinctions between selfish and benevolent motives were quite feasible.[27]

Having blurred the distinction between faith and works, Finney faced the same problem that Martin Luther had confronted. How can a human possibly perform sufficient good works to merit salvation? Whereas Luther concluded that justification depends on faith and faith alone,

Finney reasoned that a perfect God demands perfect obedience to His law. "God cannot discharge us from the obligation to be perfect. . . . If He were to attempt it He would give a license to sin. He has no right to give any such license. . . . And if he cannot discharge us from the whole law, he cannot discharge any part of it, for the same reason."[28]

Finney also made perfection a more realistic possibility for humans. He pointed out that the Gospels command men to love God with one's whole heart and no more than one's whole heart. The person who loved God to the most of his abilities fulfilled the law perfectly. He further clarified this doctrine by making all morality dependent on the ultimate intention, which would be either entirely selfish or benevolent. Thus, a divinity student who entered the ministry in order to save souls was entirely benevolent, while one who wanted to earn a living was entirely selfish.[29]

Even the desire to save other people from Hell might be based on selfish motives. Finney explained why a Christian ought to concur in the damnation of an obstinate sinner.

> They [false Christians] pray for sinners, not because they have such a sense of the evil of sin which the sinners are, as because they have such a sense of the terrors of hell to which the sinners are going.

> True friends of God and man feel compassion for sinners too, but they feel much more for the honor of God. They are more distressed to see God abused and dishonored than to see sinners to go to hell . . . just as certainly as they love God supremely, they will decide that sinners shall sink into endless torment sooner than God fail of His due honor.

In these passages there is further evidence of a Hopkinsian influence on Finney. He still believed that a true Christian ought to accept the damnation of sinners.[30]

In practice, Finney measured benevolence according to a variety of minor issues. The historian Melvin Vulgamore has concluded that Finney's concern for revivals was more important than his interest in other reform issues. To the extent that he did address reform movements, Finney concentrated much of his attention on the theater, novel reading, fashionable dress, coffee, tea, tobacco, and similar items. According to his principles, all true Christians must not only avoid these small pleasures, but they should admonish their neighbors to abstain also. Perhaps many of Finney's admonitions reflected the concerns of the lower middle classes about the luxuries of the upper classes.[31]

Finney's most noteworthy contribution to the cause of reform came with his opposition to chattel slavery. He was one of the first ministers to denounce slavery as a national sin and to demand its termination. In fact, he even allowed his church to be used for abolitionist meetings at a time when anti-abolitionist mobs presented a serious danger.[32] Even so, his opposition to slavery had its limitations. He believed that the solution to the slavery problem would come with the growth of revivals, not abolitionist agitation. When Theodore Weld tried to persuade Oberlin students to leave their studies to become abolitionists, Finney earnestly pleaded with his students to remain at Oberlin. In his dissertation, Vulgamore found no evidence that Finney devoted a single sermon to the antislavery cause.[33]

Because Finney emphasized the ability of men to work their own regeneration and because he advanced the idea that humans might be perfect in this life, he has often been described as optimistic and human oriented. In this respect, he has been contrasted with the Old School Calvinists, with the conservatives being described as pessimists because of their emphasis upon man's dependence on God. There is some truth to these characterizations. Finney's theology did place more emphasis on human abilities, and he did appeal to a sense of self-confidence of the early national era. Nonetheless, Finney should not be classified as an optimist merely on the basis of his theology. Like the New Haven theologians, he firmly believed that from the moment of their first moral act until the moment of their conversion, all men are fully and culpably depraved. He had no difficulty believing that the unregenerate person was capable of the most flagrant transgressions. Even his perfectionism had a darker side, for any person not perfect must be willfully violating God's laws.[34] By contrast, the Old School Calvinists would have rejected the label of pessimists. They believed that it was more comforting to believe that the fate of mankind rested in the hands of an infallible, although inscrutable, Deity than to think that the future of the world depended on sinful humans.

Finney's perfectionism has also been described as an expression of nineteenth-century romanticism. Perhaps the word "romanticism" might be used in a very general sense. Philosophically and theologically, however, Finney resembled the eighteenth-century rationalists far more than the nineteenth-century romantics. His metaphysics, especially his epistemology, was derived from the Scottish Common Sense school. He believed in a discernible, objectively valid truth and in a clear distinction between subject and object. He was unaware of Kantian and post-Kantian metaphysics, with their emphasis on the subject. His assertions of man's freedom and independence contrasted sharply with the teachings of man's dependence on God by Friedreich Schleiermacher and other German romantics. Indeed, Old School Presbyterians ridiculed Finney's work as rationalism taken to an extreme.[35]

Furthermore, it is easy to overstate the contribution of the Oberlin theology to the antebellum Presbyterian and Congregational communities.[36] By 1837 Finney's influence was already diminishing, and the publication of perfectionist opinions hastened the decline of his stature within the two major Calvinist denominations. After their separation from the Old School, the New School Presbyterians flatly refused to allow Oberlin perfectionism within their communion.[37] Only a few Congregationalists accepted a perfectionist ideology. The kindest words about Oberlin from within the Presbyterian and Congregationalist communities came from the New Haven magazine the *New Englander*, which stated that the terrors of "Oberlinism" had been greatly exaggerated.[38]

One important indication of the very limited acceptance of the Oberlin theology within the Presbyterian and Congregational community is the curriculum at northern colleges and theological seminaries. The principal Congregational seminaries—Andover, Yale, and East Windsor—excluded Finney's perfectionism from the curriculum. Instructors at New School Presbyterian seminaries, such as Auburn and Lane, also avoided any association with Finney's perfectionism. Of the colleges and universities associated with Presbyterians and Congregationalists, only Oberlin taught perfectionist theology, and it was a center of controversy within the Congregational and Presbyterian communities. The school's historian has commented that Oberlin was accused of a variety of heresies and unsound doctrines. "Oberlin was by many believed to be 'a kind of *Sewer* into which all the filth & froth gathers of all *sorts & colours*.'" The *New York Observer* displayed a particularly strong hostility toward Finney and Oberlin.[39]

Finney's own memoirs further suggest the controversial nature of his later career. Although he discussed his successes within the villages of upstate New York in great detail, he moved through the later years quite rapidly. He also complained that Oberlin did not receive financial or other support from the Ohio religious community. Finney's memoirs reflect a distinct bitterness about his ostracism by his fellow ministers, especially Beecher's opposition to Oberlin. In one episode, Finney recounted the story of how a woman told him that she had been led to believe that a sentence to prison would be preferable to study at Oberlin.[40]

Princeton and Oberlin represented different responses to the New Haven theology. The faculty of Princeton Seminary achieved a reputation as the most articulate defenders of Calvinist orthodoxy. The Oberlin doctrine of entire perfection marked the most extreme departure from the traditional Calvinist themes of men's dependence on God. Finney and his colleagues at Oberlin went beyond the careful qualifications of the New Haven theologians and repudiated openly any association with Calvinism. As the New School adherents advanced their ideas on theology and reform, they also contended with the disagreements of conservatives and radicals.

To be sure, these disagreements occurred in an environment that was influenced by factors other than religious ideas. Within the Presbyterian and Congregational communities, ethnic diversity and geographic variations affected the way in which New Haven ideas spread. Within the American religious environment in general, this was a time of revivals and growing interest in evangelical religion.

4

The Antebellum Congregational and Presbyterian Communities

New School Calvinism grew within the Presbyterian and Congregational communities, eventually reaching about 44 percent of the Presbyterians and a much larger portion of the Congregationalists.[1] As such, its history reflected the traditions and mores of these two churches, especially the commitment to an educated and settled clergy, an emphasis on the intellectual aspects of the religious experience, and a generally tempered pastoral style. Ethnic and geographic factors also affected the history of the New School within both churches. Despite some striking similarities, these two churches also differed in important respects. These differences would influence the spread of New Haven theology and its eventual rejection by Old School adherents.

As the older of the two communities, the Congregationalists had practiced in America since the Puritan settlers first arrived in Boston Harbor. During the ensuing years, the descendants of the Puritans established their religion throughout New England, but with only sporadic settlements in the middle and southern colonies. By the close of the colonial period, Congregationalism had become firmly associated with New England "Yankees."

The basis of Congregational order in Massachusetts, the Cambridge Platform, had existed since the mid-seventeenth century. In it the ministers professed adherence to the Westminster standards in theology. They further provided for a system of congregational autonomy and ministerial associations in church affairs. In essence, each congregation possessed final authority over its own government. Associations of ministers could advise and admonish individual ministers or congregations. In extreme cases they might refuse communion with a particular congregation, but even this action had no coercive power. In the earliest colonial times, the government might act against serious disruptions of church discipline. Although this system served to protect New England Calvinism for one and a half centuries, it proved to be ineffective in preventing the growth of Unitarianism in Massachusetts.[2]

Connecticut's system of consociations, as expressed in the Saybrook Platform, allowed greater oversight of individual congregations by the ministers of the region. Under this arrangement, the ministers of each county formed a consociation in order to hear cases involving scandal or heresy. Groups of ministers could oversee the ordination and installation of ministers. The agreement also provided for annual meetings of all the state's ministers in a general association. The collective oversight of Connecticut ministers over their brethren did symbolize a greater commitment to orthodoxy by Connecticut Congregationalists, yet the distinctions between Connecticut and Massachusetts should not be over-emphasized. In both states, the most extreme sanction against errant congregations was noncommunion.[3]

New Englanders had traditionally regarded their clergy as an essential component of their religious system. During the nineteenth century, however, the patterns of relationships between the congregations and their ministers were changing. In the eighteenth century, a minister normally remained in a single location for his entire career, but during the opening years of the nineteenth century, ministers became increasingly mobile, sometimes seeking larger parishes to improve their salaries, other times being dismissed by dissatisfied congregations.[4]

Prior to the appearance of Nathaniel William Taylor and the New Haven theology, New England Calvinists could be divided into the Hopkinsians, or New Divinity, and the Old Calvinists. Old Calvinists, such as Yale's Ezra Stiles, were less interested in doctrinal speculations than in serving their congregations. Although upholding the sovereignty of God, they reassured their audience that diligent attendance on the means of grace would probably result in their salvation. The more aggressive Hopkinsians applied their improvements on, and explanations of, Jonathan Edwards's works to justify New England theology, despite Unitarian ridicule. In time, Taylor's innovations achieved the preeminent position in New England. Taylor's justifications of God's ways seemed to offer a more plausible rebuttal to Deism and Unitarianism than did Hopkins's works.

Nevertheless, it would be a mistake to apply these generalizations too strictly. Despite their differences, Old Calvinists and Hopkinsians were capable of working together during the conflicts with Unitarians, such as the creation of Andover Seminary. Quite probably, many minis-

ters could borrow selectively from both schools. Even the growth of
Taylor's theology was more subtle than a simple renunciation of Hopkinsianism. People who accepted Taylor's innovations could still believe that
they were within the Edwardsean tradition. Taylor had always considered his ideas to be refinements on Edwards and other Puritans, not
radical departures from his predecessors. New Haven theologians believed that as long as they maintained the language of traditional Calvinism, especially human depravity, they were remaining faithful to their
religious heritage.[5]

Lyman Beecher provides a unseful example of how New School
adherents could proclaim their fidelity to New England Calvinism.
When, during the 1830s, he was accused of heresy by an Old School
critic, Beecher vehemently denied that he had departed from the education of his youth. "All that I hold is the old approved New England
divinity; it is that and nothing else. . . . There is nothing new in my
creed. I learned it under Dr. Dwight; and my preaching is as sound as
was the preaching of that illustrious man." Beecher buttressed his defense by relying heavily on the Edwardsian distinction between moral
and natural ability. He refused to concede any substantial differences
between his theology and that of the conservatives.[6]

The experience of Andover Seminary illustrates how New Haven
theology spread slowly throughout New England. Created in 1808, after Harvard had drifted into Unitarianism, Andover became a preeminent institution for New England Congregationalists. It was the product of an agreement between the Old Calvinists and Hopkinsians that
provided for cooperation between the two schools. Both Old Calvinist
and Hopkinsians were to serve on the faculty, and all members were to
subscribe to a confession of the basic Calvinist tenets. The initial faculty
included the Old Calvinist Eliphalet Pearson and the Hopkinsian
Leonard Woods. Jedidiah Morse, another prominent Old Calvinist,
performed a crucial role in creating the seminary.[7]

Following the articulation of Nathaniel William Taylor's theology,
New Haven ideas also infiltrated into Andover. Moses Stuart, another
student of Timothy Dwight who joined the faculty in 1810, expressed
his agreements with Taylor as the controversies developed. Stuart's open
partiality toward New Haven theology led to disagreements between
the New Haven adherents and the Hopkinsians. One history described
the situation: "Professor Stuart . . . would flash out one set of views on
the lower story; Dr. Woods would reply with rumbling thunders in his
lecture room on the second story; and good Professor Emerson would
draw off both lightning and thunder in the third story, and tell the se-

niors that there was no real cause for alarm-the brethren evidently did not quite understand each other." By the time of Justin Edwards's presidency, from 1836 to 1842, New School tendencies at Andover were increasing. Edwards appeared personally sympathetic to New Haven ideas. He accepted an honorary Doctorate of Divinity from Yale and encouraged his children to study in New Haven. He also maintained friendly relations with the strongly New School organization, the American Home Missionary Society. The passage of time brought important New School ministers such as Calvin Stowe, E. P. Barrows, and Thomas Skinner into the faculty at Andover.[8]

Nevertheless, Andover never became completely dominated by New Haven adherents. The most formidable Hopkinsians was Edwards A. Park, who succeeded Leonard Woods as professor of theology from 1847 to 1868. Although his Hopkinsianism was slightly moderated by a brief study at Yale, Park retained his essential Hopkinsian orientation. He used his position to defend his ideas even in the face of an increasingly popular New Haven emphasis.[9]

Elsewhere in New England, a vocal minority of dedicated Hopkinsians bitterly protested against the ascendancy of Taylor's ideas. Bennett Tyler, Asahel Nettleton, and Joseph Harvey led attacks on the progress of New Haven theology. In 1834, Taylor's opponents, including Tyler and Nettleton, concluded that they required their own educational institution. Consequently, they established the East Windsor school, with the avowed purpose of counteracting New Haven teachings. The tradition of congregational autonomy ensured continued diversity in New England churches.[10]

Beyond New England, Presbyterianism was the most important Calvinist religion. Of the many denominations that used the word "Presbyterian," the most important was the Presbyterian Church in the United States, which is the exclusive focus of this study. Like their Congregationalist brethren, the Presbyterians also affirmed their commitment to the Westminster standards. Because of their common doctrinal standards, the two denominations were considered almost identical except in church government. The generalization was substantially correct, yet it should not be overstated. Presbyterians also differed from Congregationalists in their history and ethnic composition. Furthermore, there was a stronger tradition of strict adherence to doctrinal standards among a large portion of the Presbyterian community.[11]

The most obvious difference between the two denominations was in church government. In contrast to the Congregationalists, the Presbyterians created a hierarchy of ecclesiastical bodies, with explicit rules for church discipline. At the base of the structure were the presbyteries. These bodies could examine ministerial candidates and hear cases involving scandal or heresy. Synods existed above the presbyteries, and decisions of the lower bodies might be appealed to the synod. The General Assembly, which met annually, was the highest body within the nation. The Assembly could hear appeals from the synods, issue advisory statements on church policy, and appoint standing boards. The Presbyterian *Book of Discipline* prescribed rules and procedures for individuals to follow when pursuing a charge of scandal or heresy. These procedures for resolving heresy charges allowed the church to maintain a greater doctrinal uniformity and gave its members a reputation for contentiousness.[12]

A Presbyterian organization first appeared in America in 1707, and almost from the beginning the church contained two distinct factions. One side, composed of both New Englanders and Scots-Irish immigrants, favored revivals and a liberal interpretation of the *Westminster Confession*. The other faction, composed almost exclusively of Scots-Irish immigrants, was skeptical about revivals and favored a strict interpretation of the *Westminster Confession*.[13]

From 1741 to 1758, the tension between the two factions was so strong that the church was divided into two separate bodies, the New Side and the Old Side. To a large degree, this schism reflected disagreements about the revivals of the Great Awakening, with the New Side favoring the revivals. Moreover, New Side Presbyterians favored a "substance of doctrine" approach to the *Westminster Confession*. That is, they believed that a minister who accepted the essential points of the Confession was qualified to be a minister, and there was room for interpretation on minor points of doctrinal standards.[14]

In 1758, the two factions were reunited, on terms largely favorable to the New side. The terms of the reunification sanctioned revivals and provided for some latitude in interpreting the *Westminster Confession*. In spite of the rapprochement, the factors that contributed to this schism remained within the Presbyterian community. In the nineteenth-century, questions about revivalism and doctrinal standards, as well as antagonisms between Scots-Irish and Yankees, would reappear as divisive issues for the Presbyterian community.[15]

After the reunification, the conservative, Scots-Irish faction grew in power. An influx of Scots-Irish immigrants added to the numerical strength of the conservatives. The two educational institutions of Princeton Seminary and the College of New Jersey became leading proponents of conservative theology. The hierarchical structure of the church further discouraged doctrinal innovations or improvements.[16]

One other institutional agreement of the early national period affected the future of both the Congregational and Presbyterian Churches. This arrangement was the 1801 Plan of Union. In that year, the Presbyterian General Assembly and the General Association of Connecticut reached an agreement to combine their efforts in the frontier regions. A Congregational community could choose a Presbyterian minister and vice versa. Disagreements might be resolved through an appeal to either the Congregational or the Presbyterian forms of church government. The agreement further provided for committees of laymen to help resolve disputes in communities that contained both Congregationalists and Presbyterians.[17]

The practical effect of this plan was to increase the numerical strength of the Presbyterians through the addition of New England emigrants. As New Englanders moved westward, they either joined existing Presbyterian churches or formed Presbyterian churches under the Plan of Union. The results of this arrangement pleased neither New England Congregationalists nor conservative Presbyterians. New Englanders regretted the loss of their congregational form of church government. Conservative Presbyterians feared the introduction of Congregationalist influences into their community. Traditional animosities of the Scots-Irish Presbyterians toward New England Yankees did not improve the situation.[18]

The misgivings of Presbyterian traditionalists were amplified by the fear that the Plan of Union enabled New Haven theology to enter their community. Their concerns contained a substantial basis in fact. As a rule, the churches within the areas where the Plan of Union operated were more receptive to the New School theology. Joshua L. Wilson, one ultraconservative minister from Cincinnati, expressed his disdain for New Englanders and their theology with the comment that "neither the 39 articles . . . nor the Westminster [Confession] . . . nor even the Bible alone could satisfy them! Every Congregation must be an independent society, forming its own creed and Covenant . . . and the same lawless inventions and artifice which have characterized the Sons of the Pilgrims in pecuniary affairs . . . has led to the discovery of the NEW DIVINITY and *new measures* for its widest circulation." Wilson's opinions were extreme, yet he expressed a common hostility toward the Congregational influence within the Presbyterian community.[19]

Geographically, the plan was most evident in western New York. Three synods, Utica, Genesee, and Geneva, rapidly developed reputations as "Plan of Union" synods. During the first part of the nineteenth century, large numbers of New Englanders migrated to this region, along with New England ministers. Once in New York they united with Presbyterians under the Plan of Union, thus becoming part of the Presbyterian Church, while retaining many of their Congregational prerogatives. By 1822 the last Congregational Association in New York had dissolved. All but a few Congregational churches had joined the Presbyterians.[20]

Within New York State, Auburn Theological Seminary became an important educational institution for Presbyterian clergy. The institution accepted its first students in 1821, and throughout the antebellum era it instructed prospective clergy within the Finger Lakes region. Its faculty contained eminent New School ministers such as Luther Halsey or Baxter Dickinson. During the schism of 1837, New School clergy convened at Auburn to plan their actions.[21]

Northeastern Ohio had traditionally been Connecticut's Western Reserve area. As such, it attracted a sizable number of New England emigrants, who entered the Presbyterian Church under the Plan of Union. In 1825 the Presbyterian General Assembly created the Synod of the Western Reserve, composed primarily of churches formed under the Plan of Union.[22]

Lane Seminary in Cincinnati, Ohio, also became a principal New School institution because of the influence of Yankee emigrants. The school had been endowed by the Lane brothers and presented to the Presbyterian Church. When the institution's trustees encountered financial difficulties, they decided that they could attract more support by inviting Lyman Beecher to become the president. On Beecher's arrival, the institution became embroiled in theological controversy, as Joshua Wilson accused him of heresy. After Beecher defended himself against the charges, Lane Seminary became firmly associated with the New School. When the church divided in 1837, Lane became an important New School institution.[23]

Developments in Illinois followed a pattern similar to that in New York and Ohio. The earliest pioneers in that state had migrated from the southern states and had settled in the southern regions of Illinois. To the extent they belonged to either the Congregationalist or the Presbyterian Church, they were conservative Presbyterians. Beginning in the 1830s, however, Yankee settlers from New England and western New York moved into the northern portions of Illinois, especially the area between the Illinois and Mississippi rivers. At first they organized Presbyterian churches according to the Plan of Union, with only a handful of Congregational churches. As late as 1840, only twenty-two Congregational churches existed in Illinois. Congregationalists did not appear in large numbers until the mid-1840s.[24]

Thus, with some important exceptions, the progress of the New Haven theology was strongly influenced by these ethnic and cultural patterns. Taylor's theology received its widest acceptance among the New England Congregationalists and those portions of the Presbyterian Church that employed the Plan of Union. Conservatives were strongest among the Presbyterians within the mid-Atlantic region, especially among the Scots-Irish. The pattern of controversy that was established in the schism of 1741 remained, as ethnic suspicions, revivals, and doctrinal disputes continued to create tensions within the Presbyterian Church. By 1837, slightly less than half the Presbyterians sided with the New School.[25]

Certainly there were exceptions to this pattern. Some of the most important New School ministers, including Albert Barnes and George Duffield, practiced in the mid-Atlantic region, and they enjoyed the support of their congregations. They also held the support of a substantial minority of the Presbyterian community in this region. Moreover, the New Haven theology had not received unanimous acceptance in New England. Yet the general tendencies of Presbyterians and Congregationalists conformed to these social and geographic patterns.

These patterns can be observed in some of the more important New School leaders. Within the New School community, some ministers distinguished themselves by their energy or intellectual ability. Six of these leaders—Nathaniel William Taylor, Lyman Beecher, Albert Barnes, George B. Cheever, George Duffield, and Moses Stuart—are emphasized in this study. Two of these six—Taylor and Stuart—remained in New England throughout their careers. Another two—Beecher and Cheever—were native New Englanders who later joined the Presbyterian Church. Barnes and Duffield practiced in the mid-Atlantic region throughout their stormy careers.

Nathaniel William Taylor (1786-1858), the foremost New School theologian, developed his ideas while serving as Professor of Didactic Theology at Yale. His principal contribution to the New School community came through his theological ideas. He was the primary architect of the theological system discussed in chapter 2. He did not participate in the numerous reform activities that engaged the attention of other New School Calvinists. Presumably, he agreed with the reform activities of other New School Calvinists, especially his friend Lyman Beecher. Yet he confined his written opinions to theology.

As the grandson of a Connecticut minister, Taylor held a lifelong concern for the condition of the Congregational ministry within Connecticut. After his graduation from Yale in 1807, he worked directly for

Nathaniel William Taylor. Courtesy of the Library of Congress

Timothy Dwight. In 1812, he accepted a call to New Haven's Center Church, where he replaced Moses Stuart as minister. His tenure at Center Church was noteworthy for his sermons, which moved the audiences with an inexorable logic. Even after he was replaced by Leonard Bacon, Taylor continued to preach at Center Church.

In 1822, he returned to Yale to begin his long service in the Theology Department. Until his death in 1858, he remained in this position,

Lyman Beecher. Courtesy of the Library of Congress

training hundreds of prospective ministers in theology. His students respected his earnest interest in their welfare, which was most evident in his willingness to continue discussions and questions throughout lengthy sessions.[26]

Lyman Beecher (1775-1863) complemented Taylor's interest in theology with his own energy in advancing reform causes. As a close friend of Taylor, Beecher shared his ideas on the nature of religion. Partly because of his intimacy with Taylor, Beecher came to be considered a leading spokesmen for the New Haven theology. Eventually, his well-recognized association with Taylor and New Haven theology would lead to accusations of heresy by conservative Presbyterians.

Following his mother's death, Beecher was sent to live with his uncle. The young Beecher proved to be too absent minded for farming, and his uncle sent him to Yale for further education. Beecher commenced his studies at Yale just as Timothy Dwight became president of that institution. Beecher's admiration for Dwight undoubtedly contributed to his conversion while at Yale and his decision to enter the ministry.[27]

Beecher's remarkable personality played an important role in America's religious history. He was passionately involved in the welfare of the Congregational and Presbyterian Churches, and he relished his role as a leader among the ministers. Whether in leading the campaigns to preserve Connecticut's standing order or converting the western states, Beecher could be found persuading, cajoling, or advising his fellow ministers for the sake of Protestant Christianity.

Throughout both their lives, Beecher and Taylor remained close friends. The two ministers first met while Taylor was working for Timothy Dwight and Beecher made a call. Mistaking Beecher for a local farmer, because of his plain clothing, Taylor directed Beecher to wait for Dwight. After Dwight introduced the two men, they began a lasting friendships based on shared interests. Together they worked to protect the Congregational system in Connecticut and to propagate the New Haven theology. Following Taylor's death, Beecher requested that he be buried beside his lifelong friend, and the request was granted by Taylor's widow.[28]

Beecher's interests were more practical than Taylor's. He devoted his intense energy to propagating religion throughout the United States. His popularity among fellow clergy and laymen caused him to be placed in formal and informal leadership positions within the New School movement, including membership in most major benevolent organizations. He devoted himself to spreading and nurturing evangelical Christianity throughout the United States, and he embraced the New Haven theology because he believed that it effectively answered the doubts of the skeptics.[29]

Beecher's influence was multiplied through his remarkable family. Three of his children, Henry, Edward, and Harriet Beecher Stowe, achieved a prominent place in the antebellum religious community. Edward, Lyman's second son, quickly developed a reputation as an important New School minister in his own right. He became president of

Illinois College and later became affiliated with Knox College, in Illinois. He wrote considerably, and was later charged with heresy for propagating New School theology. During the antebellum era, Henry Ward Beecher had already begun to achieve the renown that would characterize his post–Civil War career. Harriet became a distinguished novelist and antislavery activist. In addition, her husband, Calvin Stowe, was a noted New School minister and Biblical scholar. Calvin Stowe had taught at both Lane and Andover Seminaries and had assisted Lyman Beecher when the latter was accused of heresy.[30]

Albert Barnes (1798-1870) was a Princeton graduate who became an important New School minister. He was born in Rome, New York, to New England emigrants who may have converted to Methodism during Barnes's youth. Barnes father was a tanner, and his son appeared likely to become an artisan until a schoolmaster persuaded him to seek an education. Barnes then entered Hamilton College, where he experienced a conversion and decided to enter the ministry. He won a scholarship to Princeton Seminary and commenced studying at Princeton in 1820. After graduation, he accepted a call at the Presbyterian church in Morristown, New Jersey. In 1830, he moved to the First Presbyterian Church in Philadelphia.[31]

During his ministry, Barnes gradually moved toward a New School theology, until his personal influence and his extensive writings caused him to be considered a leading New School spokesman. As the disputes between the New School and Old School grew more intense, Barnes was twice accused of heresy. His published works included an extensive set of Biblical commentaries, theological writings, and appeals for reform efforts. Biographers have commented on his quiet demeanor, even during his heresy trails and the contentions that surrounded his life.[32]

Another important New School Presbyterian from the mid-Atlantic region was George Duffield (1794-1868). Duffield preached in Carlisle, Pennsylvania, until his New School views caused a division within his congregation. He then moved to Detroit, where he continued to play a prominent role in the New School community.[33]

George B. Cheever (1807-90) achieved an important position among the New School Calvinists, despite his tendency to engage in bitter personal quarrels. He was born in Hallowell, Maine, along the Kennebec River, at a time when this region was still a part of Massachusetts. After his education at Bowdoin and Andover, Cheever progressed from minister in Salem, Massachusetts, to pastor at a New York City Presbyterian church and edit the *New York Evangelist*. When the Congregation-

Albert Barnes. Courtesy of the Library of Congress

George Duffield. Courtesy of the Library of Congress

alists established a presence in New York City, Cheever became minister for the Church of the Puritans.[34]

Of all the ministers discussed in this book, Cheever was undoubtedly the most personally controversial. He reacted strongly against any opposition to him or to his ideas. His vitriolic writings denounced distillers, Catholics, and slaveholders with equal vehemence. As he turned his invective toward slaveholders, some members of his congregation objected. Cheever responded by using his influence to force these members out without regular letters of dismissal. He then refused the customary Congregational practice of resolving the dispute with a council of ministers. The result was a bitterly divided community.[35]

One of the most universally acclaimed New School ministers was Andover's famous Bible scholar Moses Stuart (1780-1852). He was born in the southern Connecticut township of Wilton and entered Yale in 1797. At first he intended to pursue a career as a lawyer, but the influence of Timothy Dwight led to his conversion. His decision to enter the ministry commenced in a controversial manner. He began as a assistant to the pastor at New Haven's Center Church; but the congregation soon developed a decided preference for Stuart. As a result, they voted to employ Stuart as the permanent pastor, much to the displeasure of the existing pastor. Stuart served Center Church from 1806 to 1810, when he left to accept a teaching position at Andover Seminary.

Stuart rapidly achieved renown for his work in Biblical scholarship. After his appointment as Professor of Sacred Literature at Andover, he became intensely interested in new methods of Biblical scholarship. He produced the first Hebrew grammar text in America and introduced German Biblical scholarship into the United States.[36]

Although his principal interest lay in Biblical scholarship, Stuart also displayed an interest in the theological controversies of his time. During the controversies with the Unitarians, he engaged William Ellery Channing in a pamphlet debate. As the New Haven theology grew, Stuart became an important supporter within Andover.[37]

Certainly other people played important roles in the New School community. The men discussed above, however, were regarded as leaders within their own time, and the controversies that surrounded them indicate their importance to the New School movement. Moreover, these men expressed opinions on a wide variety of social issues, including the reform issues covered in this study through their prolific publications.

Religious periodicals provided a means for clergy to disseminate their views among their fellow ministers. As a general rule, the magazine publishers favored definite views during the theological controversies of the era. The *Christian Spectator* (renamed the *Quarterly Christian Spectator*) was the principal publication representing New Haven theology. During the 1850s, *The New Englander*, also published in New Haven, rose to prominence among the Congregationalists, while the *Presbyterian Quarterly Review* became the leading journal of the New School Presbyterians. Edited by Charles Hodge, *The Princeton Review* expounded Old School ideas, especially those of the Princeton community.[38]

The New York Observer, edited by Sidney E. and Richard C. Morse, was the nation's largest Presbyterian-oriented newspaper. These two sons of Jedidiah Morse were occasionally assisted by their brother, Samuel F. B. Morse, also known for his early American art work, invention of the telegraph, and anti-Catholic literature. The *Observer* publicly maintained a neutral position in the New School/Old School controversies, but the Morse family privately favored New School Calvinism. Lyman Beecher recollected the support of the Morse family during his heresy trial. All three of the Morse brothers attended Yale College. Samuel F. B. Morse later made generous contributions to the Yale theology department and Richard C. Morse also sent his son to Yale. While in New Haven, Samuel and Richard were members of Center Church in New Haven, which had Nathaniel William Taylor and Leonard Bacon for its pastors. Richard later became a member of the Madison Square Presbyterian Church, which sided with the New School after the schism of 1837. Samuel also attended the Madison Square Church when he was in New York.[39]

Within the context of the American religion in general, these two denominations also operated in an environment of dynamic religious growth. At the start of the century a wave of revivals, the Second Great Awakening, swept through the nation. For the remainder of the early national period, a substantial portion of American Protestants remained committed to their religion with an exceptional intensity. The Presbyterian and Congregational Churches, profited from this upsurge in religious interest. Nevertheless, even their remarkable growth seemed less significant when compared to other denominations.

Denominations that stressed an anti-elitist, popular appeal, such as the Methodists and Baptists, were growing at a phenomenal rate. By 1844, the Methodists alone grew from an extremely small denomination at the close of the Revolution to one of the largest Protestant denominations. These churches typically employed either itinerant preachers or men who held ordinary jobs during the week. Especially during their formative years, these denominations openly derided the Presbyterians and Congregationalists for their educated, settled (or hireling) ministry. The Methodists ridiculed Calvinist doctrines. By the 1830s these denominations had moderated some of their anti-intellectual overtones in an effort to achieve respectability.[40]

In a recent study, Curtis Johnson has provided a very useful classification of evangelicals as formalists, antiformalists, and African-American (primarily slaves). He placed the Congregationalists and Prebyterians in the formalist category, with their emphasis on settled, educated clergy and their appeal to middle-class men and women. Antiformalists, such as Methodists and Baptists, relied less on a settled ministry and appealed to men and women at the margins of society. African Americans blended antiformalist preaching with their African heritage.[41]

Outwardly at least, the Presbyterian and Congregationalists accepted the sudden growth of these religions with such popular appeal. They did not denounce Baptists or Methodists with the same vehemence they employed against Unitarians. They worked with other Protestant denominations in Tract and Bible Societies. Yet there was a sense of condescension in their dealings with Methodists. Agents for the Presbyterian-dominated American Home Missionary Society might report that a particular region was destitute of the Gospel, when Baptists or Methodists may have been quite active.[42]

A good example of the sense of superiority by the Congregationalists and Presbyterians comes from a story in *The Autobiography of Lyman Beecher*. The case in which Beecher supposedly outwitted a simple Methodist preacher was provided, in 1863, by a friend of Beecher who made no attempt to conceal his sense of superiority to the Methodists. According to this story, the Methodist preacher was "a pure specimen of the roaring, ranting, shouting class of preachers, whose boast was that they did not premeditate what they should say, but spoke as the Spirit gave them utterance." Beecher invited the Methodist to preach at his East Hampton congregation, leaving the Methodist so disconcerted by this outward display of hospitality that he stumbled through the sermon and left town the next morning.[43]

Of course, any generalizations about Congregationalist or Presbyterian attitudes toward these other denominations are tenuous at best. Robert Baird's comments about Methodists in his survey of American religion were characterized by a more irenic approach and may well have reflected the opinions of a substantial number of ministers. Moreover, the history of these religions during the early national period was characterized by an initial defiance of the older Calvinist denominations, followed by a desire for respectability, so that the Presbyterian and Congregational attitudes might be expected to change over time.[44]

Interdenominational antebellum reform organizations reflected the ambiguous relationships between the two major Calvinist denominations and other Protestants. In theory, many of these organizations were open to all "evangelical" denominations. In practice, however, denominational rivalries remained a formidable barrier to cooperative efforts. National interdenominational societies were governed largely by Presbyterians and Congregationalists. Methodists declined to join other

Protestant organizations through the early 1820s. They established a Methodist Tract Society in 1817 rather than join with the Presbyterians and Congregationalists. The American Bible Society, one of the most ecumenical organizations, counted forty-four of fifty-seven founders from the Presbyterian and Congregational denominations.[45] Even in their temperance efforts, Methodists generally preferred to work within their own community rather than with the Calvinist-dominated American Temperance Society.[46]

At the local level, there may well have been a greater degree of interdenominational cooperation, depending on the circumstances and personalities of each location. In Rochester, Episcopalians and Methodists cooperated with the Presbyterians during the time of Charles Finney's revivals. Prosperous laymen even provided financial assistance to other denominations. After the revivals had concluded, some interdenominational cooperation continued among the city's female benevolent organizations. Although Presbyterian women dominated the Rochester Female Charitable Society, women from other churches also participated in religious benevolent activities.[47]

The response toward religious revivals of the early nineteenth century suggests some of the ambivalent attitudes of the Presbyterians and Congregationalists toward other denominations and toward changes within their own denominations. Revivals, in which large numbers of people might be moved to conversion at the same time, began during the eighteenth century as a trans-Atlantic phenomenon, with a surge in religious interest in England, Scotland, and the colonies. Although revivals in each region had their distinct features, all were characterized by a substantial rise in religious conversions and were connected through a network of like-minded ministers. The theological justification followed the traditional Calvinst emphasis on God's omnipotence. Edwards and other traditional Calvinists held that these conversions were the result of an outpouring of the Holy Spirit according to God's mysterious design. They recognized that a gifted preacher might be the instrument of God's grace but insisted that God alone was the cause of a conversion. The Great Awakening, as the American revivals were termed, has been discussed too frequently to merit an extended discussion here.[48]

The Second Great Awakening, commencing about the beginning of the nineteenth century, demonstrated the greater diversity of American Protestantism. This time most evangelical Protestant denominations participated in the revivals. In spite of the broad appeal, there was such a wide variance in doctrine, conduct of revivals, and class distinction of participants that the phenomenon defies easy categorizations.

Some of the most spectacular revivals came with the camp meetings in the western states. Drawing on their Scottish heritage, with its traditional communion seasons, settlers in Kentucky began to congregate in camps for seasonal revivals, complete with communion rites. In time these events grew into spectacular events, with vast crowds, multiple preachers, and extended activities. The Cane Ridge revival of 1801, and other revivals conducted under the leadership of James McGready, astonished the more conventional easterners and contributed to the eventual withdrawal of the Cumberland Presbyterians into their own organization.[49]

Even within New England and the mid-Atlantic region, revivals provoked a variety of responses. Contemporary observers and subsequent historians have usually associated revivals with the development of New School theology. This generalization is correct if it is not taken too far. New School ministers, such as Beecher, Barnes, and Duffield, were often noted for their skill in conducting revivals. Finney, who used New Haven theology as a basis for his greater departures from orthodoxy, was one of the most conspicuous revivalists of the early nineteenth century. Moreover, the New School emphasis on the importance of means encouraged ministers to work toward producing revivals because they believed that their efforts could make a difference. Individuals were encouraged to believe that they could repent and be converted without passively awaiting the workings of the Holy Spirit.[50]

Old School Calvinists were not opposed to revivals per se. They objected only to what they perceived to be excesses or abuses of revivals. Traditionalists admitted that the minister played an important role in producing conversions, yet they gave absolute primacy to the workings of the Holy Spirit as the sole cause of conversions. They feared that the New School emphasis on means undermined sound theology. Moreover, they felt that New School techniques might produce spurious revivals, in which individuals might undergo false conversion experiences and thus wrongly believe themselves to be regenerate. Finney further complicated the issue through his use of highly emotional techniques, such as the anxious bench or protracted prayer meetings, and through his insistence that revivals depended on the skill of the revivalist.[51]

To be sure, theological ideas were not the only factors affecting revivals. Historians have interpreted the Second Great Awakening either as an expression of faith in the forthcoming millennium or as a means of social control. There is a substantial degree of truth in both interpretations. The revival phenomenon was too varied and too complex to fit into a single interpretation. A revival could easily be an indication of optimism over the future of Christianity. Other historians have argued that revivals resulted from the clergy's desire to preserve order and stability within their districts.[52]

It is also true, however, that revivals could also be disruptive of the social order. Methodist camp meetings were the most obvious examples of disorderly revivals. Finney's attacks on the settled clergy and Presbyterian institutions in general also suggest a disdain for conventional institutions among some revivalists.[53]

This atmosphere provided the background for the growth of New School ideology within the two most important Calvinist denominations. As both denominations professed adherence to the *Westminster Confession*, the two churches were similar enough to allow for interdenominational cooperation. There were also important differences between the two churches. The Presbyterian community was more hierarchical in organization, contained a stronger conservative element, and was ethnically more diverse than the Congregationalists. When the two churches agreed to cooperate under the Plan of Union, these differences created underlying tensions. The tensions were exacerbated by the tendency of New Englanders to be more favorably inclined toward New Haven theology than their Scots-Irish brethren. Throughout the antebellum era, the New Haven theology would grow under these conditions.

5

The Role of Religion in the Republic

As Americans, New School Calvinists believed that a relationship existed between their religion and the future of the nation. Their assumption that a solid religious foundation was essential to the future of the American republic was apparent in their discussions of republican ideology and in their Sabbatarian efforts. They further believed that this nation had a special role in God's work of redemption, which required extraordinary efforts by the American religious community.

In the beginning of the nineteenth century, Americans shared a set of assumptions and values about the nature of government and society that recent historians have labeled "republican ideology," or "republicanism."[1] This system of beliefs, which was inherited from the Revolutionary generation, influenced Americans in different ways. New School Calvinists shared in the prevailing republican ideology; yet their religious outlook gave a special form to their republicanism.

According to this ideology, the best type of government was a republic, in which sovereignty rested with the people at large. Because rulers depended on the public for their authority, they could be trusted to protect the interests of the whole nation. Whereas in a monarchy or an aristocracy the governors might seek to advance their own interests above those of the people, in a republic there should be no conflict between the interests of the rulers and the ruled.

A successful republican government, however, depended on the willingness of the voters to subordinate their own interests to the welfare of the entire community. If individuals pursued their own ambitions, disaster would result. Virtue in a republican society normally indicated a willingness of the citizens to make the necessary sacrifices of their particular interests. In keeping with the republican concept of virtue, the public must elect representatives who would act to secure the interests of the entire population. Ideally, the electorate should select the wisest and best-informed men as their lawmakers. If the voters acted virtuously and pursued the common interests, a republican government might prosper; but if the people succumbed to the influence of corruption, the state would be divided into self-seeking factions and soon the experiment in republican government would collapse.[2]

Although New School Calvinists concurred in the general belief in the superiority of a representative government, their religious outlook shaped their concept of a proper republican system. Political ideology within the Presbyterian and Congregational traditions thus had some distinctive features. Other groups of Americans may have agreed entirely or partially with their variations on republicanism.

In the Congregationalists' and Presbyterians' view, any political system, including republican government, worked only when applied in conjunction with the principles of Christian politics. They argued that the state did not derive its authority from any social compact or consent of the governed. A government's authority rested on Paul's epistle to the Romans (13:1-6), where the apostle enjoined submission to the powers that be for the sake of conscience. God had ordained all civil governments because the nature of man required some institution to preserve order. Lyman Beecher may have overstated the necessity for government with his argument that people needed restraint: "Men are desperately wicked, and must be restrained somehow. Civil rulers are ministers of God, appointed for this very thing." Even a tyrannical or non-Christian government served this function, and thus the Christian had a duty to obey the government. Only in extremely rare cases, where a government was clearly violating God's laws and a revolution was feasible, could the Christian rebel against the government.[3]

In 1838, the *Quarterly Christian Spectator*, New Haven's principal publication, elaborated on the need to obey a government's laws. Men who encouraged the violation of some laws undermined the respect for all law. Even when a law might be unfair, its violation could damage the credibility of government. The writer then presented the question of what prevents the multitudes from burning and killing at their pleasure. "Some are prevented by moral principle, but the greater part are restrained by a reverence for authority, growing out of the custom of submission. . . . Let this restraining power be taken off . . . and there is an end of all order, security, or subordination, in the community."[4]

Although all types of government enjoyed a divine warrant, a republic remained the preferable form of civil authority. Even here, however, the people were not the source of the government's authority. Voters were only the medium of divine sanction. A writer for the *American Biblical Repository* insisted that "the powers that be are ordained of God. . . . By him kings reign, and princes decree justice. The people are the medium—not the source of civil power. God is the fountain of all authority."[5]

After denouncing the false principle that rulers are the servants of the people, the *Quarterly Christian Spectator* explained that "the business of a ruler is not to *serve* but to *govern*. . . . The people may . . . remove him from office; but while he holds it, he is not their *servant* but their *ruler*. . . . In a word, he is not *their* servant—but the servant of *God*, for their benefit. . . . He is or *ought* to be chosen from the people, for his superior wisdom, integrity, and firmness." In this sense, the New School, particularly in New England, retained a largely Puritan attitude toward the purpose of civil government even while they embraced the contemporary republican spirit.[6]

The combination of their Puritan heritage and republican ideology is most apparent in their perceived need for virtue, as defined by religious standards. Ever since the late-eighteenth century, New England Congregationalists equated the political virtue so necessary to a republic with the prevalence of Trinitarian Protestantism. Nineteenth-century clergy continued this line of reasoning. "There is no religion on the face of the earth, consistent with republicanism but the Protestant," William Cogswell asserted. "Rely upon it, then, that if any other religion, but that which the pilgrims brought to this country . . . prevails, utter destruction will befall this fair republic—this land of civil and religious freedom."[7]

New School clergy felt a special distrust toward professional politicians. Office seekers were perceived as unprincipled men who exploited the moral weaknesses of the voters in order to win elections. "There is a set of men in the country who will have power and office, cost what they may," Samuel F. B. Morse complained. "Men who, without a particle of true patriotism, will yet . . . flatter the lowest prejudices and fawn upon the powerful and influential."[8] If the voters were careless about the candidates, the office-seeking politician might be elected. "Little regard is often paid to the moral character of those who are candidates for office. Worth, honesty, capacity, is overlooked; and the fervor of party zeal made to take the place of higher qualifications. And hence, the profane man, the Sabbath breaker, and even the adulterer, are not unfrequently [*sic*] clothed with authority."[9]

The New School community also displayed a distrust of political parties that appeared to hold undue influence with voters and politicians. James McLane, the previously mentioned writer for the *American Biblical Repository* warned that "party is rising superior to patriotism. The bearing of political action is to bring men into bondage; . . . to force men to vote in obedience to orders, issued from some central Court of High Commission, or from some Star Chamber of political dictatorship."[10]

Ever since the American Revolution, clergy, especially in New England, were accustomed to using their professional standing to influence their political issues. With the advent of the first party system, New England Trinitarian Congregationalists generally moved toward the Federalists. As James M. Banner has pointed out, the alliance with the Federalists was not necessarily uniform, nor did it work to the advantage of both the clergy and the Federalists. Nonetheless, the experience left a perception of political involvement by the clergy.[11]

During the antebellum period, New School clergy generally sympathized with the Whig Party, as did many of their Old School brethren. Although Moses Stuart, Andover's renowned Bible scholar, may have been more politically observant than the other ministers, he was probably a good indicator of New School political behavior. Stuart not only was Whig, but he was a friend and supporter of Daniel Webster. In his letters to Webster, Stuart expressed his unqualified admiration for Webster and his hope that his friend would become president. Stuart opposed the Mexican War, with the privately expressed hope that the war would result in the ruin of the Democratic Party.[12]

On the two occasions when Stuart did publish his political opinions, he did so in support of Webster. Stuart's first published political comment came in 1843, after he invited Webster to speak at Andover. The speech prompted some criticism of Webster's service as Secretary of State. Stuart responded with a publication defending Webster. Although it was common knowledge that Stuart wrote the pamphlet, he identified himself only as a person not involved in politics and signed the work "Civis." In defending Webster's conduct as Secretary of State, Stuart displayed an intimate knowledge of British-American relations. (Stuart had submitted a draft of the essay to Webster, and Webster replied with a warm letter of appreciation.)[13]

Stuart's second political publication, *Conscience and the Constitution*, followed Webster's defense of the Compromise of 1850 and the Fugitive Slave Act. Ardent abolitionists had attacked Webster for his support of the Fugitive Slave Law, much to Stuart's dismay. In this controversial book Stuart defended Webster by expressing his own disagreement with ardent abolitionists.[14]

There were, however, limits to Stuart's political activities. He seems

Moses Stuart. Courtesy of Franklin Trask Library, Andover Newton Theological School

to have felt obligated at least to acknowledge an informal rule against preaching politics from the pulpit. In the opening passages of *Conscience and the Constitution*, Stuart denied that he had ever delivered a political sermon or a political lecture. "I never preached a political sermon in my life. Usually I did not go to any meetings for the election of state or town officers. . . . I believe none of all my pupils will charge me with occupying their time in political lectures." He even asserted that he had only voted ten to twelve times during his life, and only during times of peril, such as the "imperial reign of Gen. Jackson."[15]

His explanation for his political restraint is also interesting. He claimed that it would have been inexpedient and divisive for him to engage in politics. "My people were somewhat divided in politics and I did not like unnecessarily to offend those who differed from me, by voting against their wishes." Such an explanation might explain the general lack of public political activity among New School clergy. The possibility of offending Democrats seems to have caused them to exercise a modicum of restraint in using their clerical position to advance their political opinions.[16] Of course, Stuart's disclaimers may be treated with some skepticism. Even if he did not give political sermons or lectures, it is safe to assume that he advanced his views during private conversations.

Other New School clergy seem to have been Whigs, privately if not publicly. George B. Cheever's biographer noted that Cheever supported Henry Clay and the Whigs. In a recent study of American Whiggery, Daniel Walker Howe categorized evangelicals, such as Lyman Beecher, as an important component of the Whig Party.[17]

George Bancroft, a historian who sympathized with the Democrats, could be even more dramatic in pointing to the connection between clergy and Whiggery. He complained of Massachusetts clergymen who instilled a fear of the Democratic Party. "Sermons were preached; and the community was made to believe that there was a danger the bible [sic] would be taken out of their hands. Democracy was said to be a branch of atheism."[18] Bancroft's remarks may also be treated with some skepticism. Despite their Whig sympathies, these clergymen generally did not publish political statements.

There was, however, one dimension of politics that could not escape clerical attention. Occasionally some important New School reform issues were linked to political actions. Although New School clergy were more or less circumspect on purely political questions, they could be quite vocal about laws relating to temperance, slavery, and Sabbath observance. They believed that the moral dimensions of these issues affected the welfare and security of the nation. Indeed, their assertions of human depravity accentuated their perception of the dangers to the republic.

Even with regard to issues that had moral or religious overtones, New School clergy exhibited a desire to compromise between preaching politics from the pulpit and remaining aloof from political questions. Leonard Bacon, a New School minister from New Haven, suggested that "the minister . . . may urge temperance, but not the claims of the Prohibition Party, . . . liberty, but not the claims of the Republican Party." As the antebellum era progressed, the political influence of all evangelical denominations appeared to have increased.[19]

Even if the clergy were restrained in their open advocacy of political issues, they lived during a time when the religious dimension to politics was steadily increasing. Protestants within the so-called evangelical community became more likely to perceive a religious dimension to social and political issues and to vote for the party that best reflected their religious values. Although differences in religious outlook and ethnic background might lead to different political affiliations, antebellum Protestants tended to merge their religious and political values.[20]

New School adherents could justify political involvement by emphasizing a connection between moral and religious values and the survival of the republic. They held that a proper religious orientation was necessary for the continuation of any form of republican government. As Beecher succinctly observed, "Daylight is not more uniformly found in the track of the sun, than civil liberty is found in the track of Christianity and despotism in its absence."[21]

Normally, the churches provided the religious instruction that was considered so essential to the survival of the republic. In this sense, American churches were expected to perform a dual function. Of course, churches continued to serve God by encouraging people to follow Christ's teachings. At the same time, American churches were needed to inculcate those religious and moral values that formed the basis of republican virtue. Although New School Calvinists came to disapprove of a formal alliance between church and state, they believed that the nation's survival depended on proper moral and religious principles.[22]

Yet, as nineteenth-century Americans, New School Calvinists had some difficulty in deciding exactly what was the proper relationship between church and state. In an increasingly pluralistic society, they frequently faced opposition to any government attempt to establish their religious values. They usually resolved this difficulty by asserting that they were merely supporting a universally valid morality that did not depend on any particular religion.

With their Puritan heritage, New Englanders had a stronger tradition of church-state cooperation than did Americans from the mid-Atlantic region. Although nineteenth-century New Englanders may have been less committed to the idea of a covenant than were their forebears, they still believed that they were a special people with a special mission and that God would punish any departure from this errand. An established religion was presumed necessary to complete this mission. Accordingly, New England states continued to support the settled clergy through taxes and assessments. Each community was required to provide for an orthodox minister, which meant Trinitarian Congregationalists until the appearance of the Unitarians. Only recognized Baptists, Episcopalians, and Quakers were excused from church assessments, with the requirement that they would support their own denominations.[23]

This system was acceptable to most New Englanders, as long as the population remained predominantly Trinitarian Congregationalist. As the pressure from the nonconformists increased in the nineteenth century, however, the New England states eventually ceased to maintain an established church. Connecticut maintained its established church until 1818. Massachusetts was the last state to disestablish the Congregational Church in 1833, when the rift between Unitarians and Trinitarians made the system unworkable.

New England clergy such as Beecher and Nathaniel William Taylor initially could not accept this separation of the church and the state. In the bitter struggles that preceded disestablishment, they had fought hard to maintain the familiar system. Once the Congregational Church did lose its privileged status, New England clergy adjusted well to the idea of voluntary support for the church, as Beecher's reminiscences indicate:

> It [disestablishment] was a time of great depression and suffering. . . . For several days I suffered what no tongue can tell *for the best thing that ever happened to the State of Connecticut*. It cut the churches loose from dependence on state support. It threw them wholly on their own resources and on God.
>
> They say ministers have lost their influence, the fact is, they have gained. By voluntary efforts, societies, missions, and revivals they exert a deeper influence then they ever could by queues, and shoe-buckles, and cocked hats, and gold-headed canes.

To Beecher the essential point was that the community should retain its religious orientation.[24]

Although the New England clergy did learn to rely on voluntary support once they lost their state support, some lingering traces of the clergy's antidisestablishmentarian background continued to affect their attitude toward the function of organized religion in the commonwealth. They no longer favored a formal alliance between the church and the state, but they did believe that some form of religious orientation was necessary for the republic.

The desire for a church-state association was less strong among the Presbyterians of the mid-Atlantic region. Presbyterianism had never been the established religion of this area, and the region had always contained a greater religious diversity. Nonetheless, Presbyterians of the mid-Atlantic states, both New School and Old School, developed a remarkably similar position on the importance of religion to the nation's survival. Like their New England counterparts, they believed that any successful government must acknowledge the supremacy of God and provide an extensive system of religious education. Without such a religious orientation, the populace would soon exhibit vices that could destroy the society.[25]

One of the first nationally organized reform efforts, the Sabbatarian movement, demonstrates how the reformers' assumptions about religion and government affected their attitudes toward social and political issues. Because this question also involved questions about government policy on religious matters, it caused early reformers to articulate their views on the importance of religion to the republic.

By tradition, Americans had scrupulously treated Sunday as a holy day. They refrained from such activities as travel and commercial employment in order to devote their time to church attendance. Although New England held a well-deserved reputation for strict Sabbath observance, Americans of other regions had also paid deference to the Lord's day. Even New York City's Presbyterian minister, Gardiner Spring, could recall a time when city officials chained off public streets during hours of worship. In the nineteenth century, however, strict Sabbath observance declined appreciably. Americans became increasingly willing to travel or work on that day, despite the protests of their ministers.[26]

The worst blow to Sabbath observance came in 1810 when Congress passed a law requiring all post offices to remain open seven days a week. Here the national government appeared to require a Sabbath violation. Clergymen complained about the new law at the time of its passage, and they continued to protest against the act during the succeeding years. The most significant protests on that subject began in 1828, when several clergymen, including Beecher, organized the General Union for Promoting the Observance of the Christian Sabbath. This organization, which included both New and Old School Calvinists, coordinated one of the first large-scale petition campaigns of the antebellum era.

Sabbatarians argued that the new law placed an unfair burden on the postmaster who might wish to observe the Sabbath. Moreover, their concerns were amplified by the custom of using the local post office as a congregating place, even on the Sabbath. In spite of these arguments, their efforts failed when the Senate committee argued that Sabbatarians were attempting to impose their own definition of a proper religious observance. "It is not the legitimate province of the Legislature to determine what religion is true or what religion is false," the report declared. "Our government is a civil and not a religious institution."[27]

Along with other Sabbatarian advocates, New School Calvinists continued to argue against Sunday mails, and their arguments display their belief in the universal applicability of moral truths. They responded to the Senate report by asserting that Sabbath observance was not an arbitrary requirement of their religion, but a universal requirement resulting from the nature of man. If humans devoted all of their time to mercenary labor, they might easily lose their sense of religious values. All people must have some regular and systematic religious education, and this instruction could best be accomplished on the Sabbath. Humans might recognize the wisdom of the requirement by observing how all creatures needed some periodic rest or by noting how people required religious instruction. Their cause, therefore, was not based on a religious point of view but on the immutable laws of human nature.[28]

Even though the wisdom of Sabbath observance was evident on consideration, only a divine revelation clarified the issue. In His infinite wisdom, God declared that one day in seven should be set aside for religious purposes because He knew that this ratio was perfectly suited to men's needs. (Lyman Beecher suggested that the wisdom of setting aside one day in seven as the Lord's day was additional evidence of the divine inspiration of the Bible.)[29]

Because the nature of man had created the necessity for regular Sabbath observance, it appeared reasonable to conclude that people who customarily violated the Holy Day must be deficient in morals. An article in the *Quarterly Christian Spectator* demonstrated how New School Calvinists followed this form of reasoning even in the face of contrary evidence. On learning that the United States Military Academy frequently conducted training on Sundays, the magazine's writers concluded that any reports of honorable behavior among the West Point cadets must be erroneous. These young men must be quietly violating God's other commandments.[30]

Other New School writers were even more emphatic in their insistence on the necessity of observing the Lord's day. "If the institution of the Sabbath is abolished, the Christian religion will be abolished with it." Albert Barnes further warned that, "the question of whether this day is to be observed or desecrated is just a question of life or death in regard to Christianity. This is so obvious that it scarcely needs any attempt to prove it."[31]

Sabbatarian reformers used this argument to answer charges that they wished to impose their own religious standards on other Americans. They contended that they were preserving the republic from moral disintegration. "It is impossible in the very nature of things that our civil and political institutions can long survive our public morals," observed George Duffield. "It is just as impossible that our public morals can flourish, or be preserved without religion. And it is further impossible that religion can long exist without a Sabbath."[32] The writers of the *Quarterly Christian Spectator* also protested the importance of the Sabbath with typical vehemence. "Does it need the gift of prophecy to foretell that if the holy Sabbath be not sustained in these united, happy, and exalted States, our free institutions will fall, and our fair and glorious civil fabric, the hope of other nations, will sink into ruin with the republics of ancient days."[33]

In the last lines, the writer for the magazine echoed a common sentiment by suggesting that the United States was destined to serve as the hope of other nations. According to a prevalent assumption, the United States was to play a special role in promoting the triumph of the kingdom of God. Thus, they believed that the destiny of the world was linked to the success of the American nation. The resulting cluster of ideas, commonly termed "millennialism," influenced antebellum reformers to varying degrees, most notably in their anti-Catholic efforts.[34]

In all Christian theology there is a belief that the kingdom of God will triumph on earth and in time. Christ's work of redemption is expected to extend to the process of history, not only to individuals. Although numerous scriptural passages imply the final victory of God's kingdom, the strongest support for this subject comes from the Book of Revelation and the Book of Daniel. The branch of Christian theology that deals with this subject is known as eschatology. It is often popularly known as millennialism because the concluding section of the Book of Revelation (20:1-5) speaks of a one thousand–year period when Christ's church would reign over the earth.

Christians have not agreed about precisely how this triumph of the Kingdom of God is to occur. The Book of Revelation uses a series of remarkably vivid images to convey its message of the struggle between the forces of darkness and the forces of light. These images defy any specific interpretation. Despite some elaborate rules of interpretation, Protestant analysts of the Book of Revelation could only agree on the basic outlines of the book's meaning.

The majority of antebellum Protestant interpreters agreed that the Book of Revelation foretold the trials and tribulations of Christ's Church before its ultimate victory in this world. John, the author of Revelation, first predicted the continued persecution of Christians by the Roman Empire. This affliction would be followed by the rise of the Antichrist, who was believed to be the Papacy or the Church of Rome. The Antichrist would lead an apostasy from the true teachings of Christ. Occasionally interpreters asserted that passages foretold the appearance of Moslems, infidels, or troubles for the church. In spite of these difficulties, God would preserve His true church throughout the centuries, and in the end Christianity would triumph over its opposition. Following its victory, the church would reign gloriously over the earth for one thousand years prior to the last judgement. Beyond this outline, Protestant interpreters could not agree.

In the nineteenth century, two varieties of eschatology, popularly known as "premillennialism" and "postmillennialism" dominated American thought on the subject. The premillennialists received their name because they believed that a second coming of Christ would occur before the advent of the millennium. They viewed the eventual triumph of God as occurring outside the normal historical process, in that God would act directly without the use of human agents. At some time in the future Christ would literally return to earth to bring about His victory over the forces of evil. In 1843 a previously unknown clergyman named William Miller gained national attention for the premillennial position by predicting that the world would end during that year. Despite the temporary publicity that Miller received, premillennialists were a minority in antebellum America.[35]

The more numerous postmillennialists envisioned a second coming of Christ as happening at the conclusion of the millennium. The victory of the kingdom of God would occur within history, without a spectacular return of Christ to earth. Although God would ensure eventual success, He would accomplish His purposes through human agents. Even the millennium itself would not be a cessation of history; it would be the fulfillment of human history as a time when the church would reign over the world. Human institutions would not be changed radically in the millennium; they would simply be infused with Christian principles.

Following the appearance of Jonathan Edwards's work, *The History of the Work of Redemption*, the postmillennialist position became increasingly accepted in America. Samuel Hopkins used postmillennialist assumptions in his calculations that thousands would be saved for every person damned. By the early nineteenth century, both Old School and New School Calvinists generally accepted this interpretation.[36]

Because postmillennialists saw the advent of the millennium as occurring within history, some historians have described them as progressive and optimistic.[37] Instead of passively waiting for God, men might be able to advance the coming of His kingdom through their own acts. It is true that postmillennialism did contain an element of optimism in this sense. Nonetheless, in their eschatology, the coming of the millennium would be a time of fierce struggles between the forces of darkness and of light, with heavy trials for the Christian.

The Book of Revelation itself contains images of dragons, beasts, and the scarlet whore; it tells of battles in heaven and of angels emptying vials that turned water into blood or that produced sores on humans. American postmillennial analysts understood this imagery as foretelling of the troubles that the church of Christ must undergo before its final victory. The advent of the millennium was not to be a time of steady progress toward an easy victory. It was to be an apocalyptic struggle in which the forces of darkness could be expected to fight the progress of Christianity with every means at their disposal. Their major resource was to be the Antichrist, who would pretend to possess the authority of the true church while leading people away from Christ. For reasons that will be discussed in chapter 6, American Protestants, especially New School Calvinists, identified the Antichrist as the Papacy or as the Roman Catholic Church. Anticipation of the millennium was hardly reassuring in the short term.[38]

James W. Davidson's provocative analysis is important to a study of the nineteenth century. Davidson argues that eighteenth-century Puritans commonly accepted the idea of "afflictive progress," in which a situation would appear darkest before a favorable resolution. Just as a sinner's most trying times came before his conversion, so the church would experience its darkest moments just before the dawn of the millennium. The forces of the Antichrist would appear most formidable shortly before their defeat. This paradoxical thinking served to reassure believers that God's work of redemption was still operating according to His plan and to make the victory all the more glorious when it came.[39]

In his *History of the Work of Redemption*, Jonathan Edwards warned of the impending battle. To Edwards, the very nature of Satan made such a struggle appear likely.

> [When] the destruction of Antichrist is ready at hand, and Satan's kingdom begins to totter, and to appear to be eminently threatened, the power of the kingdom of darkness will rise up and mightily exert themselves to prevent their kingdom's being overthrown. . . . Satan has ever had a dread of having his kingdom overthrown and he has been opposing it ever since Christ's ascension, has been doing great works to prevent it, especially since the days of Constantine the Great. To this end he set up those two mighty kingdoms of Antichrist [the Papacy] and

Mohammed, and brought in all the heresies, superstitions, and corrupt opinions in the world. But when he sees all begin to fall, it will rouse him exceedingly.

It seems, in this last great opposition, all the forces of Antichrist, also Mohammedanism and heathenism should be united; . . . there shall be the spirit of Popery, the spirit of Mohammedanism, and the spirit of Heathenism all united.

Lyman Beecher referred to Edwards, as he combined a sense of alarm with an expectation of the millennium, in *A Plea for the West*.[40]

In this all-important struggle between good and evil, God apparently expected the United States to play a vital role in establishing His kingdom on earth. American writers pointed to the advantages that the United States enjoyed as evidence of America's special mission. God had ensured that the settlement of North America was postponed until after the Reformation, when Protestants could colonize the land. One writer even pointed to a plague that struck the Massachusetts Indians just before the arrival of the Puritans as evidence of God's providence. America possessed an abundance of resources that might be combined with advances in communications to propagate the Gospel.[41]

In return for these favors, America was to be the redeemer nation. With its freedom from the corruptions of Europe, the church in America might reach its fullest potential. Then this nation might act as an example to other nations in leading them into a millennium. By this reckoning, missions to foreign nations also helped to advance the kingdom of God.[42]

America's religious messianism also had a political component. During the closing years of the eighteenth century, New England clergy came to associate experiment in republican government with the progress of the kingdom of God. In what Nathan Hatch has labeled "republican millennialism," clergy of the early federalist period expressed the view that the republican form of government was essential to the progress of true Christianity. In contrast to the despotic states of Europe, which used false religion to perpetuate their rule, the freedom offered in America enabled Christ's church to grow and prosper. To be sure, a belief in the special destiny of the colonies had been part of the New England tradition ever since its founding; and the colonial wars against the French, followed by the American Revolution, accentuated the belief in America's providential role. The early stages of the French Revolution convinced many of the clergy that the American example would cause other nations to establish the free institutions that would allow Christianity to flourish.[43]

America's responsibilities as the redeemer nation also presented some special dangers that again demonstrated the postmillennialists' paradoxical combination of optimism and alarm. In their efforts to prevent the millennial dawn, the forces of Antichrist, especially the Catholic states of Europe, could be expected to make every effort to upset the progress of Protestantism and republicanism in America. A writer for the American Education Society portrayed the forthcoming struggle in the strongest terms.

> A conflict is approaching, and it is even now begun. . . . The signs of the times are full of interest, and in some respects of ominous import. They are such as precede a struggle of the prince of darkness to regain his territory lost, and to prevent further inroads upon his usurped dominions. The character of our institutions, and the extent of our country, render it certain that the combat here is to rage with peculiar violence. . . . This great nation is to be Christian or Infidel; virtuous or wicked; free or enslave. . . . Infidelity is sowing its poison; superstition is weaving another winding sheet for the souls of men, and vice is binding in adamantine chains its countless victims. . . . No, it must not be. The agony, and the blood and dying groans of a crucified Savior, exclaim against it. Blessed Jesus, by thy grace and help, it shall not be.

The assertion of this nation's eschatological role displayed the curious combination of an expectation of the triumph of God's kingdom with the fear that the opponents of Christianity would do their utmost to frustrate America's role.[44]

Moreover, if the United States failed in its mission, then God would withdraw His favors and His protection and allow this nation to pass from the scene. Americans were warned that their good fortune also implied an obligation.

> *Our responsibilities and duties correspond with our privileges.* God expects much of us . . . . He has embodied our nation with a moral power, and put into our hands a machinery which, if kept in operation will not fail to make its power felt to the ends of the earth. . . . After all that God has done to make us *such* a nation . . . , if we hold ourselves aloof from His great plans of mercy towards our world, and refuse the honor He would confer upon us, . . . we must expect that He will withdraw from us the light of His countenance and choose others more worthy of His favor.

This writer was, in one sense, continuing the old Puritan Jeremiad that America had a special mission in which it must not fail. The consequences were great.[45]

Even though a postmillennial eschatology amplified the need for a Christian orientation in the United States, New School Calvinists would have still considered a strong religious basis essential for the success of this nation. As two divinely ordained institutions, the church and the state usually incurred a duty to support each other. The American experiment in republican government made this duty even more imperative because of the apparent need for a sense of virtue among the populace. As the New School clergy led their followers to believe that the uplifting influences of Christianity were required to overcome the inherent depravity of human nature, they stressed the need for Christianity in the nation. Furthermore, if the United States were to play its designated role as the redeemer nation, then the church must be influential enough to guide the nation through the difficult times prior to the advent of the millennium.

Even while they asserted the need for a strongly Christian community, New School Calvinists did not perceive any serious conflict about church-state relations caused by their religious activities. Once the Congregational Church was disestablished, New England clergy ceased to request special consideration for their particular denomination. Instead, they insisted that they were merely promoting universal standards of Christian morality that applied to members of all faiths. With their emphasis on fixed, objective standards of morality, however, they were often inclined to assume that their own opinions were always applicable. Throughout the antebellum period they would promote their own beliefs while attacking such perceived evils as Catholicism, liquor, and slavery, all with the expectation that they were providing the necessary religious and moral basis for the republic.

Part Two / Reform

As New School Calvinists embarked on the various reform movements discussed in this part, the assumptions that derived from their religious outlook were expressed throughout their reform rhetoric. Believing that unregenerate humanity was fearfully depraved, they typically credited the most horrifying stories about Catholics, slaveholders, and pagans. With their faith in a fixed, objectively valid truth, they expected all men to accept their religious values and attributed diversity of religious opinions to sinister motives. In short, their rhetoric represented a combination of optimism and fear, which was distinctive to their religious beliefs.

I have based this analysis on the assumption that, in the absence of contradictory evidence, reform rhetoric can be taken as an accurate reflection of an individual's or a group's beliefs. I am not seeking to deny the importance of underlying motivations; rather, I am interested in describing the stated beliefs of these reformers. I am assuming that normally these people meant what they said.

The activities in this study—anti-Catholicism, temperance, antislavery, and the work of major benevolent societies—were selected because they help us to understand the beliefs and attitudes of the preponderance of New School Calvinists. These activities commanded a substantial portion of the resources and energies of the New School community over a sustained period of time. The anti-Catholic impulse pervaded so much of the New School reform efforts that it merits a full discussion. Temperance and antislavery were regarded, then and now, as two crucial issues of antebellum reform. The six benevolent societies that are included in this study were the largest such organizations within the nation, especially in terms of money, personnel, and contemporary publicity. Although the work among New York City's poor did not approach the national scope of the other societies, it was quite important within New York City, and it helps us to understand New School attitudes about poverty.

Other activities have not been included in this study, because the magnitude and duration of these efforts did not approach those mentioned above. Feminism, for example, is not included, because it attracted little serious attention among antebellum New School ministers, and most of that attention was opposition. I have not included reform efforts that were either the work of a comparatively small group of individuals or that existed for a limited period of time. Similarly, I have excluded activities that did not have a suitable connection with the Presbyterian or Congregational communities. In short, I believe that an understanding of New School Calvinism can be best achieved by concentrating on those activities that clearly commanded substantial support within the New School community over a sustained period of time.

❧ 6
The Catholic Church and the Whore of Babylon

An intense hostility to the Roman Catholic religion characterized ante-bellum reform efforts within the Presbyterian and Congregational communities. To twentieth-century observers, the anti-Catholic aspects of antebellum reform do not merit the same admiration as the antislavery or temperance movements. Yet the participants viewed their opposition to the Catholic Church as one of the principal elements of their reform efforts. They worked tirelessly to prevent the spread of what they perceived to be a false religion and to convert laymen away from the Church of Rome. Anti-Catholic militants conceived of their work as an expression of disinterested benevolence. They sincerely believed that they were promoting the glory of God and His church.[1]

In their anti-Catholic rhetoric, New School Calvinists demonstrated the application of their own religious principles. They dismissed Catholicism as a false system of superstition and idolatry. They even claimed that the Church of Rome was the Antichrist foretold in the Book of Revelation. Yet, because they believed it to be a false religion, they needed to explain its continued survival. Their emphasis on human depravity is evident in their assertions that Catholicism attracted sinful men by false promises of salvation without regeneration. Similarly, their belief in the ability of humans to recognize fixed truth is evident in their argument that the Catholic Church must necessarily suppress true religion in order to survive. Their anti-Catholicism shows how their assertions of a millennial role for the United States accentuated their fears of a conspiracy.

It is important to remember that the anti-Catholicism of the nineteenth-century Presbyterians and Congregationalists followed a long and complicated tradition. Colonial Americans, especially in New England, feared and despised the Catholic Church for political and religious reasons. Since the days of Queen Elizabeth I, Catholics had been regarded as disloyal to the English monarchy and the Anglican Church. New England Puritans displayed a particularly strong hostility toward the Catholic Church and still feared the vestiges of the Catholicism within the Anglican Church. They noted with alarm the resemblance between the Roman and Anglican Churches. Any English efforts to promote the Anglican Church in America served to arouse anti-Catholic sentiments in New England. The perceived threat from French Canada increased the hostility toward the Catholic Church.[2]

By the end of the American Revolution, however, anti-Catholicism had declined significantly. The separation from England removed the fears of an established Anglican Church. Accusations that American Catholics were disloyal to the British monarchy became irrelevant after the United States achieved independence. More important, the efforts of American Catholics during the Revolutionary War and the French alliance further softened the hostility toward that religion. In 1791, the Catholic bishop of Baltimore visited Boston and provided a blessing for the city's Ancient and Honourable Artillery Company, marking at least a temporary respite in New England anti-Catholicism.[3]

Nonetheless, by the mid-1820s, an intense anti-Catholicism reappeared in American life. This time the animosities were more noticeably religious, without the political complications of the colonial era. Within the Presbyterian and Congregational communities, anti-Catholicism arose from a refusal to accept the Church of Rome as a legitimate part of the church of Christ. Animosity to the Catholic religion as a religion underlaid nineteenth-century anti-Catholicism.

To be sure, the Catholic community also contributed to the religious tensions. Catholic leaders, especially New York's Bishop John Hughes, were openly hostile to Protestants. Their contemptuous attitude greatly exacerbated the animosities of that era. Hughes seldom missed an opportunity to attack Protestantism or to predict its imminent decline. Moreover, the situation in Europe, where the Catholic hierarchy supported monarchies, was observed with concern by Americans.

One other factor complicated the nature of antebellum anti-Catholicism. This was nativism, or a prejudice against foreigners. A large portion of nineteenth-century immigrants were Catholic. Like many immigrants, they encountered hostility from native-born Americans, which was aggravated by competition for jobs. For these reasons Catholic immigrants were often the subject of nationalists' anger. Nonetheless, anti-Catholicism and nativism were two distinct phenomena. One was a religious prejudice; the other was a prejudice against foreigners in general.[4]

New School reformers were primarily concerned with the religious aspects of anti-Catholicism. They opposed Roman Catholicism as a religion and the Church of Rome as an institution. They believed that they were acting according to the principles of disinterested benevolence by opposing what they considered to be an erroneous faith. Leading ministers such as Lyman Beecher, Edward Beecher, George B. Cheever, Albert Barnes, and others wrote and spoke against the Catholic religion. Religious publications such as the *New York Observer*, the *Quarterly Christian Spectator*, and the *American Biblical Repository* carried articles denouncing the alleged errors of Catholicism. The major benevolent societies, especially the American Home Missionary Society, the American Education Society, and the American Board of Commissioners for Foreign Missions, openly proclaimed that opposition to Catholicism was an important objective. The American Tract Society published a number of works aimed specifically at the Catholic religion.

Furthermore, the movement against the Catholic religion enjoyed widespread support outside the New School community. Members of the other "evangelical Protestant" denominations readily joined the crusade against Rome. Members of other denominations shared many of the presuppositions of New School Calvinism, and these suppositions would have influenced their hostility toward Rome. Old School Calvinists gave greater support to anti-Catholicism than to other reform causes.[5]

Although they were joined by other religious groups in their anti-Catholicism, New School Calvinists were remarkably energetic in their crusade against Rome. Militant New School anti-Catholics insisted that Catholicism was not a Christian religion at all. They considered it a usurpation of Christianity that lured men away from the true faith. The Catholic religion was variously described as the "mystery of iniquity," the "Beast of the Apocalypse," the "mother of abominations," the "Whore of Babylon," and the "masterpiece of Satan." The Pope was referred to as the "man of sin" or the "man of perdition."

The New School religious outlook provided a frame of reference and a pattern in their anti-Catholic activities. Given their belief in the unlimited potential of human depravity, they accepted the most horrifying stories about Catholicism. With their belief in objectively valid moral and religious truths, they could not understand or accept differences in Catholic practices or theology. Instead, they viewed the contest between Protestantism and Catholicism as an apocalyptic struggle preceding the advent of the millennium.

New Haven concepts of a rationally defensible religion exacerbated their inability to comprehend Catholic theology. They defined Christianity as a rationally comprehensible exposition of the moral government of God, which could be fully expressed in human language. They conceived of religious truth as conforming to human standards of reason, morality, and justice. By contrast, the Catholic Church has held that, although faith does not contradict reason, there are aspects of faith that go beyond reason or language. Moreover, the Catholic Church employs symbol and ritual such as candles or relics, and this was especially so in the nineteenth century. New School Calvinists simply could not comprehend these aspects of Catholicism. They dismissed the entire religion as nothing but superstition and idolatry.

In this respect there was a subtle, but significant, difference between New School adherents and the Princeton community. Princeton theologians asserted their unalterable opposition to Catholicism. Nevertheless, these men, especially Charles Hodge, were willing to admit that the Catholic Church was a part of the Church of Christ. (In this respect, the Princeton professors were a small minority, even within the Old School.[6])

In an 1846 issue of the *Princeton Review*, Hodge asserted that the Church of Rome was a part of the visible Church of Christ. He believed that the Catholic Church contained serious errors and corruptions but that these difficulties did not exclude Catholicism from the Church of Christ. All branches of Christ's Church contained errors and corruptions to a greater or lesser degree.[7]

In that article, Hodge revealed a tendency to apply distinctions between the wrongs within an institution and the institution in itself. Although this article was about the Catholic Church, Hodge also applied the same logic to other reform efforts. He compared the extreme anti-Catholic person with the militant temperance or antislavery crusader:

> He [an extreme temperance advocate] takes a common sense view of the case and asserts that a practice which produces all the drunkenness that is in the world, and all the vice and misery which flows from drunkenness, is a sinful practice. He therefore hoots at those who beg to discriminate between what is wrong in itself and universally, and what is wrong only in certain circumstances. . . . The abolitionist is still more summary. Slavery is a heinous crime. . . . It is as much as any man's character . . . is worth to insist that a distinction must here be made; that we must discriminate between slavery and its separable adjuncts; between the relationship itself and the abuse of it; between the possession of power and the unjust exercise of it. . . . It is just so in the present case. Rome is

Charles Hodge. Courtesy of the Library of Congress.

> Antichrist, the mystical Babylon, the scarlet woman, the mother of
> harlots, drunk with the blood of the saints. What room . . . is there for
> argument here? Is Babylon Zion? . . . The case is pronounced too plain
> for argument; . . . and those who do not join in the cry are represented as
> advocates of popery, or at best very doubtful Protestants.

Hodge did not believe that he was defending Catholicism, rather he was
attempting to state the situation accurately.[8]

Hodge's protests notwithstanding, anti-Catholic writers, including New School Calvinists, continued to insist that the Church of Rome was a usurpation of Christianity. They interpreted prophecies in the Book of Revelation as foretelling that the Papacy would be the Antichrist and would take the rightful place of Christianity. (In 1869, Hodge endorsed an analysis of the Book of Revelation that asserted that the prophecies foretold of corruptions that would enter all parts of the church and that the church would triumph in the end.)[9]

From the time of Queen Elizabeth I, a number of English Protestants had held that the Book of Revelation foretold of the Antichrist in the form of the papal apostasy. This Antichrist would usurp the rightful place of Christ's true Church until his downfall just prior to the millennium. The Elizabethan pamphleteer, John Foxe, first associated the Papacy with Antichrist in his *Book of Martyrs*. Later English writers such as Thomas Brightman, in 1616, and Joseph Mede, in 1627, further amplified this theme.[10]

These men developed their arguments by assuming that each symbol in Revelation foretold of a specific event in church history. The task of the interpreter was to discover the connection. Joseph Mede refined this idea with his system of "synchronism," suggesting that the events predicted in Revelation need not be interpreted as occurring sequentially. Mede argued that the book contained two major parts, each predicting the rise and fall of the papal Antichrist. The two prophecies might be paired and synchronized according to a key which Mede had developed. Mede further argued that the one-thousand-year reign of the saints would come after the downfall of the Antichrist, some time in the not too distant future.[11]

New England Puritans maintained this identification of the Papacy with the Antichrist. John Cotton and Cotton Mather both regarded Catholicism as the Antichrist and envisioned the destruction of the Papacy as preceding the approach of the millennium. *The New England Primer* carried a sketch of the Pope as the man of sin, with various parts of his body representing his iniquities. When Harvard inaugurated its annual Dudleian lectures in 1755, one in every four lectures was devoted to demonstrating the errors of "Popery" and identifying Rome as the mystical Babylon. Ministers such as Samuel Cooper approached this task with obvious enthusiasm.[12]

Jonathan Edwards adopted this understanding of the Papacy as Antichrist, and he made it a key part of his postmillennial eschatology. He conceived of the work of redemption as God's glorious triumph over His enemies through the historical process. Edwards saw the Papacy as the greatest of Christ's enemies and believed that the Church of Rome was unalterably opposed to true Christianity. "Though he [the Pope] still acts under the pretense of being Christ's vicar and successor in his kingdom on earth, . . . Popery is the deepest contrivance that ever Satan was the author of to uphold his kingdom."[13]

Subsequent writers continued to associate the Catholic Church with the Antichrist. Samuel Hopkins incorporated Edwards's definition of Antichrist in his own *Treatise on the Millennium*, which asserted that the fall of the papal Antichrist would precede the dawn of the millennium. Nineteenth-century Americans, including George B. Cheever and George Duffield expressed the belief that the Catholic Church was the Antichrist.[14]

Writing his popular series of Biblical commentaries, Albert Barnes also argued that the Book of Revelation predicted the rise of the papal Antichrist. He used the traditional methodology, which presumed that each symbol in Revelation corresponded to a specific event in church history. The commentator's task was to discern the meaning of each symbol. Barnes assumed that prophecy was a literal communication from the mind of God in the form of symbols that might later be deciphered.[15]

Barnes followed the consensus about the overall scheme of the prophecy but had his own interpretation of specific allusions. For example, like most interpreters he assumed that the Beast in chapter 13 was the Catholic Church, but he developed his own explanation. Supposedly, the sign of the Beast was 666 (Revelation 13:18), so Barnes calculated that the Greek word for "Latin" had a value of 666. He assigned to each Greek letter a numerical value. The sum came to 666 in manner as follows:

$$\Lambda \quad A \quad T \quad E \quad I \quad N \quad O \quad \Sigma$$

$$30 + 1 + 300 + 5 + 10 + 50 + 70 + 200 = 666$$

Barnes did not explain how each Greek letter received its value. Other writers used different calculations to arrive at a similar result.[16]

Barnes also used the most vivid image in the book, the "Whore of Babylon" (Revelation 17: 4-5), to establish his point further. This image was of a debauched woman, sitting on a beast. Clothed in purple and scarlet and drunk with the blood of the martyrs, she held a cup in her hands filled of the abominations and filthiness of her fornications. The King James translation emphasized the importance of this figure by showing the name on her forehead as "MYSTERY, BABYLON THE GREAT, THE MOTHER OF HARLOTS AND THE ABOMINATIONS OF THE EARTH" (capitalization in original). Most interpreters assumed that she represented the

Papacy and that her abominations were Rome's idolatry. Barnes asserted that "the meaning here is, that it seemed to be a cup filled with wine, but it was in fact a cup full of all abominable drugs, leading to all kinds of corruption. How much in accordance this is with the fascinations of the Papacy, it is not necessary now to say. . . . The image here is that of papal Rome, represented as an abandoned woman in gorgeous attire, alluring by her arts the nations of the earth and seducing them into all kinds of pollution and abomination." He thus saw a clear condemnation of Catholicism in Scripture.[17]

Barnes agreed with other commentators—including Jonathan Edwards, Samuel Hopkins, Albert Barnes, and George B. Cheever—that the Book of Revelation taught that the downfall of the Antichrist would come in the near future. John stated (Revelation 12:16, 11:2) that the Beast would reign for 1,260 days. Basing their calculations on a common assumption that a day was like a year to the Lord, interpreters explained that these passages meant that the Papacy would exist for 1,260 years. Assuming that the Papacy had arisen sometime in the seventh or eighth century, the time of its collapse could not be far off. One nineteenth-century theory held that the Papacy became the Antichrist in 606, when Boniface III obtained recognition of the Roman Pontiff as head of all churches. Therefore, the fall of the Antichrist should come in 1866. Napoleon's invasion of Italy in 1796 seemed, to some, to confirm this observation by corresponding with the wounding of the beast.[18]

The first important New School scholar to deny that the Book of Revelation referred specifically to the Catholic Church was Moses Stuart in the late 1840s. In his *Commentary on the Apocalypse*, Stuart insisted that the Book of Revelation was intended to reassure Christians of the first century that the church would survive the persecutions of Nero. The images in Revelation referred to imperial Rome and the sufferings of the primitive church. John's only prediction for the future was of a general victory of the church over its enemies. Stuart's interpretation was in keeping with the new presuppositions of German scholarship that a work of the Bible must be interpreted in a manner that could be understood by its immediate audience. Stuart held that early Christians were familiar with the Roman Empire, not the Papacy; therefore, Revelation applied to imperial Rome.[19]

In an 1847 review of Stuart for the *American Biblical Repository*, Edward Beecher insisted that the traditional interpretations of Revelation had comforted Protestant Christians in their struggles against Rome by assuring them that the Papacy was the Antichrist. Beecher complained that Stuart's work denied Protestants the comfort of knowing that their struggles against Rome were predicted in Scripture. He commented that "as this great battle [with Roman Catholicism] is coming to a crisis, . . . a new system of prophetic interpretation arises to strip the people of God of their arms. It [Stuart's work] denies any specific reference to the papal power in the Apocalypse; . . . and leaves us only the general assurance that all the enemies of God shall finally fall." Beecher then objected that Stuart's interpretation neglected the idea that the mind of God might inspire Scripture beyond the capabilities of the writer.[20]

In a comparative review of Stuart and Barnes, the New School publication, the *Presbyterian Quarterly Review*, strongly criticized Stuart. The reviewer could not accept Stuart's methodology of interpreting Scripture in the light of its immediate audience, and he strongly disagreed with Stuart's denial of any predictions about the Papacy. He then warmly endorsed Barnes's analysis, noting that Barnes's efforts to link the Papacy with the Antichrist followed the tradition "in which the great body of the sober, evangelical Protestant commentators of the English school, since the days of Mede, have been of one mind."[21]

If the Roman Catholic Church did exist outside of the true Church of Christ, even to the point of being the Antichrist, New School Calvinists needed to account for its continued success. In explaining the resilience of Catholicism, New School writers once again revealed how their ideology interacted with their reform rhetoric. Their emphasis on human depravity led them to contend that the Catholic Church promised salvation without reform to unregenerate humans. Their belief in the power of truth is evident in their assertion that the Catholic Church must necessarily suppress true religion in order to survive.

New School Calvinists believed that men, in their sinful state, would resist the Gospel with all of their efforts. Even knowing of their transgressions and of the terrible retribution that awaited them in the next world, men would cling to their iniquities until the truth of the Gospel was pressed on them. The Catholic religion allowed the sinner to believe that, by participating in superstitious practices, he could attain salvation without forsaking his transgressions. New Haven's principal publication, the *Quarterly Christian Spectator*, explained:

> We are accustomed to consider the system as a prodigy of error and absurdity, and so it is erroneous and absurd in the extreme; but it has other aspects and attributes, by which its absurdities are veiled, and the whole wonderfully adapted to the depraved heart. It is the most finished product of that wisdom which comes from beneath. . . . It seizes on the deep sentiments of the soul adapted to respond to the claims of religion, throws around them the chains of superstition, confirms the reign of sin,

embodies and baptizes the unchanged depravity of the world, and en–
thrones itself on the earth in the sacred and abused name of Christianity.

Thus, the Catholic Church seemed particularly suited to appeal to depraved humanity.[22]

Precisely because they felt such a firm belief in the potential of human depravity, New School, as well as Old School, Calvinists could credit
virtually every account of superstition and vice among Catholic people
as true. When a traveler, unacquainted with the French language, reported that a French Canadian priest was baptizing a church bell so that
it could ring souls out of purgatory, the news was solemnly received.[23]
Another traveler to Rome reported that Italians prostrated themselves
before a statue of St. Peter and kissed the toe. "To such an extent is this
carried, that the great toe of the image . . . is from time to time worn
away, and the brazier is called in to supply another, that the toe wor-
shippers may not miss the object of their adoration."[24]

Of all the sacramental aspects of Catholicism, penance was the one
least understood and most feared. It seemed to offer the sinner a way to
obtain repeated forgiveness for his or her transgressions without genuine reformation. Because these Protestants thought that Catholics believed that the priest himself had the power to forgive sins, the confessional seemed to give the priests a completely unwarranted power over
the laity. Few people would be willing to disobey their confessor, and
the priest would have access to the secret thoughts and deeds of his
parishioners.[25]

Edward Beecher, like his contemporaries, saw a diabolical clever-
ness in the combination of clerical celibacy with the confessional. It
placed unrequited desires in the breasts of the clergy at the same time
that it gave the priest extraordinary power over his female penitents.
The result was so awful that Beecher insisted that the subject was not fit
for public discussion. "I shall not pollute the public mind by a full dis-
closure of the truth with respect to her abominations. These are things
of which an apostle says it is a shame even to speak." He then devoted
almost fifty pages to speaking of these abominations.[26]

Beecher assumed that for Rome to conduct its system it must rely
on a corrupted clergy. "In short men are needed habituated to speak
lies, in hypocrisy, and having consciences seared as if with a hot iron—
men who are able, with brazen face, to claim all manner of sanctity,
whilst performing all kinds of diabolical deeds. Men are needed fanati-
cal, degraded, cruel, immitigable, [sic] and unprincipled to carry out such
a system." Enforced celibacy was the beginning of the hardening process, for it cut the clergy off from family ties and it denied them a legiti-

mate outlet for their natural desires. The confessional completed the process. Priests were

> constantly thrust into the very centre of the fiery furnace of temptation. This is done by requiring them to hear the confessions of . . . females of all ages, and on all points involved in a thorough confession. Anyone who knows what this implies will not need to hear any thing more. . . . Not one Protestant in a thousand has any idea of what questions are proposed in the schedules of examination set forth in their most authoritative text books. Decency forbids their utterance.
>   Now with regard to this arrangement, it may truly be said that satanic ingenuity could not devise a system better adapted to corrupt and debase the clerical body as a mass. It is no more certain that water will run down hill than it is that they will not resist the temptations to which they are exposed. They will be corrupted and become corrupters.

Beecher simply assumed that immoral behavior could be expected whenever men possessed the opportunity to sin. It is also worth noting that this allegation came from an important minister and president of Illinois College, who was also a member of America's most prominent family of ministers. Stories of Catholic licentiousness were so widely believed that the historian Richard Hofstadter once described anti-Catholicism as "the pornography of Puritans."[27]

New School Calvinists believed not only in the potential of human depravity but also in the ability of men to recognize and accept fundamental truths. They assumed that the Catholic religion could not survive if truth were free to combat error. Therefore, they believed that the Catholic Church would necessarily seek to suppress all forms of learning and true religion. They asserted that the alleged obscurantism of the Catholic Church was not a matter of historical contingency. It was essential to the existence of the religion because an educated or enlightened populace would reject an erroneous faith.

Perhaps the most frequent and severe charge against the Catholic Church was that the Council of Trent had positively forbidden lay Catholics from reading or possessing a Bible without specific permission from their priests. Given the usual Protestant emphasis on the necessity of Scripture as statement of theological truth and as a means to salvation, the accusation was serious. It seemed as if the Catholic Church was condemning its adherents to perdition for the sake of its own survival.[28]

This complaint was not entirely without foundation. The Catholic Church historically has emphasized tradition as well as Scripture. The Council of Trent did place restrictions on the private interpretation of Scripture and on unauthorized translations of the Bible. Because the

Protestant King James version of the Bible was not sanctioned, English-speaking Catholics were required to use the Douai translation. The Catholic Church often opposed efforts of Protestant Bible societies to distribute Protestant translations of Scripture. The Catholic Church, however, had not proscribed Bible reading by Catholic laity.[29]

Militant anti-Catholic writers did not make any distinctions when they charged that the Catholic Church had flatly forbidden lay Catholics from possessing or reading a Bible without permission from their priests. Somehow, an allegation appeared that the Council of Trent had appointed a Congregation of the Index [of Forbidden Books], which supposedly proclaimed that indiscriminate reading of Scripture results in "more harm than good through the rashness of men." The alleged proclamation then announced that anyone reading or possessing a Bible without permission from his priest could not receive forgiveness for sins. Even though Catholics repeatedly denied the authenticity of this spurious proclamation, it was widely quoted and believed.[30]

The proclamation was believable because American Protestants, particularly the New School Calvinists, assumed that the Bible was so antithetical to the Catholic religion that the Church of Rome must be inherently opposed to Scripture. As a singularly forceful expression of the true religion, the Bible was expected to overcome all false religions. "The Bible and the Paganism of India, or of Rome, cannot long live together."[31] The active suppression of the Bible appeared as a necessary part of the overall policy of enslaving the minds of the laity. "If they could read the Bible," Lyman Beecher lamented, "and might and did, their darkened intellect would brighten, and their bowed minds would rise."[32]

Using a similar line of reasoning, anti-Catholic writers held that any form of education and learning was so inherently dangerous to the Catholic religion that the Church of Rome must be opposed to all forms of learning. Travelers' descriptions of foreign lands routinely compared ignorant and superstitious Catholic regions with enlightened Protestant regions. School textbooks discussed the alleged backwardness of Catholic nations. Even the province of Quebec, which had a British government, was described as having a degraded, ignorant population. The *Quarterly Christian Spectator* advised that "We would have them [our readers] understand, that the darkness which covers the hearts of so many in Canada is as gross as that of Spain or Italy. The beast is robbed of his secular arm. . . . But over his own people he reigns as absolutely in Canada as in Rome itself."[33]

To complete its domination over the minds of its members, the

Catholic Church formed, wherever possible, an alliance with despotic or monarchical governments. Just as republican government and Protestantism seemed to go together, so there seemed to be an affinity between Catholicism and despotism. The Catholic Church and monarchies both required a degraded, corrupted populace, and the two systems could offer each other their mutual support. The church could teach obedience to the ruler; the state might use its power to enforce the desires of the church. Lyman Beecher explained how neither system could survive without the other: "If the Catholic religion were simply a system of religious error it might be expected to fade away without a struggle before the augmenting overpowering light of truth; but it has always been, and still is, a political religion . . . [and] the experience of the last thirty years has taught them [the potentates of Europe] that the Catholic Church is as indispensable to the throne as the throne is to the church, and that without her influence over mind they cannot meet and stem the spirit of the age." Here he voiced a frequent complaint.[34] Beecher was not criticizing the well-recognized conservatism of the nineteenth-century popes; nor did he admit that the Catholic Church could be affected by historical contingency. Rather, he was asserting that the Catholic Church was inherently opposed to republican government because it thrived under despotic governments. Similarly, tyrannical governments needed the Catholic religion. George B. Cheever commented that "all tyrants know, with the instinct of despotism, that if Faith instead of superstition gets possession of the people, there is an end to their power of bondage."[35]

If Catholics or their defenders protested that American Catholics were not opposed to republican government, they would be informed that this would not be the case if American Catholics ever gained ascendancy. The Catholic Church was always and everywhere the same. If the Catholic Church did not exhibit its despotic tendencies in the United States, this was only because circumstances restrained its tendencies. In order to gain credibility in the United States, Catholics would appear meek. As Samuel F. B. Morse asserted, "Popery never changes; it is infallibly the same, infallibly intolerant."[36]

One of the most common images of lay Catholics, particularly those of Europe, was that of a slave. The old usage of the word was a person who lacked control over his destiny or the freedom to decide his own fate. The *Westminster Confession* had conveyed that meaning when it described man's natural state as one of bondage to the power of sin. A common description of Catholics was one of mental, as well as spiritual, thralldom. They were denied learning and even the right to think for themselves. The use of superstitious practices not only finished the enslaving process but made the lay Catholic content with his degradation. The *Christian Spectator* described the French Canadians as unaware of their condition:

> Like so many maniacs dancing
>   in their chains
> They shake them with delight
>   and dance again

The article then asserted that, as soon as the minds of these people became educated, lay Catholics would break free of their bondage.[37]

Convents, or "nunneries" as they were called, became an especially powerful symbol of all the alleged evils of the Catholic Church. The seclusion of young women caused anti-Catholic imaginations to envision all forms of immorality, while the persistence of such institutions on American soil seemed to confirm fears that Catholicism survived by enforced ignorance and manipulation of the laity. In 1834, these suspicions of convents led to one of the first serious incidents of anti-Catholic violence and one of the more controversial incidents in the career of Lyman Beecher.

The problem began in late July of that year at the Ursuline Convent at Charlestown, Massachusetts, just outside of Boston. A nun left the convent and then desired to return. Rumors immediately began to circulate that she had been kidnapped and was being held against her will. At the same time, Beecher was in town, delivering a series of anti-Catholic sermons and attempting to raise money for Lane Seminary. Religious tensions rose until the night of August 9, when a group of men marched to the convent and set the building ablaze, causing the sisters and their students to flee. During the days that followed, the threat of further violence remained, as rumors of attack from gangs of Irish workers spread throughout the city. Although many of Boston's leading citizens condemned the violence, the accused rioters were acquitted when tried.[38]

Beecher's significance in the affair became one of the more controversial aspects of his career. Although he delivered some strongly anti-Catholic sermons just prior to the riot, anti-Catholic emotion had been growing before his arrival. Beecher denied having incited the violence, asserting that the mob could not have known about his anti-Catholic sermon that same evening. In his book *A Plea for the West*, which was published the following year, he asserted his support for the basic civil liberties of Catholics. At the same time, he expressed his resentment for the thanks offered to the Catholic Bishop Fenwick for minimizing the Catholic counterviolence following the convent burning. "Has it come to this?—that the capital of New England has been thrown into consternation by the threats of a Catholic mob, and that her temples and mansions stand only through the forbearance of a Catholic bishop?" It seems that Beecher probably did not appreciate the effect of his sermons, nor did he understand why the anti-Catholic violence might provoke a reaction among the Boston Irish.[39]

The most popular piece of anti-Catholic literature of the nineteenth century combined the assertions of Catholic superstition, exploitation of depravity, and suppression of truth to present a story that was widely accepted within the United States. In 1836, a slightly disturbed Canadian refugee named Maria Monk produced a description of life in a convent that seemed to display the unlimited depths of human depravity allowed under the Catholic Church. Her *Awful Disclosures of the Hôtel Dieu Nunnery in Montreal* horrified Americans as few other works had done because it seemed to confirm their worst suspicions about the nature of the Catholic religion. This episode is important to this study because several of the men who assisted in this publication were New School Calvinists.

Maria Monk's story seems patently absurd. She claimed that she came from a nominally Protestant home in Canada. While a young lady, she entered the *Hôtel Dieu* convent in Montreal. Soon after her induction into the order, the Mother Superior explained to her that she must obey the priests "in all things." She discovered what this meant when she learned of the tunnel connecting the convent with a nearby monastery so that priests might pay nocturnal visits to the nuns. But sexual abandon was only the beginning of the horrors. She soon discovered the pit where the babies born of illicit unions were baptized and strangled, with the assurance that the freshly baptized souls would go straight to heaven. "Their little souls would thank those who kill their bodies if they had it in their power." Later, she was compelled to assist in the murder of an adult nun for wishing to escape. When Maria became pregnant, she escaped to New York.[40]

Incredible as Maria Monk's story appeared, it was widely accepted, even in the face of increasing contradictory evidence. The work first appeared in January 1836 and soon became a bestseller. The 300,000 copies it sold made it the second-bestselling book in antebellum America. New York's important publishing company, Harper and Brothers, which had declined to publish the first version, published an enlarged version in July, 1836. For a time, Maria Monk traveled the United States, giving lectures on her alleged experiences and receiving the praise and support of her audiences.[41]

Very soon after the appearance of her book, attacks on her credibility began. A Montreal citizen, J. Jones produced a book entitled the *Awful Exposure of the Atrocious Plot Formed By Certain Individuals against the Clergy and Nuns of Lower Canada through the Intervention of Maria Monk*. Jones's book contained a series of affidavits showing that Maria Monk had a history of broken employment and arrests for prostitution while in Montreal. His evidence also demonstrated that, during the time she claimed to have been a nun, she was either employed as a domestic servant or was an inmate of Montreal's Magdalene Asylum for prostitutes. Jones further intimated that she had received help in fabricating her story. She had traveled to New York in the company of a supposed Methodist minister named William Hoyt. Once in New York, she received help from other Protestant clergy, most notably Reverend John Jay Slocum. Slocum, a New School Presbyterian minister, was appointed Maria Monk's guardian by a chancery court after the publication of her book.[42]

In reply to Jones, Slocum published a defense of Maria Monk's tale. Slocum insisted that the affidavits from Catholics could not be trusted. When Canadians refused to confirm her stories, he charged that priests controlled the lay people. He also produced a letter from an unnamed individual of "undoubted piety" who stated that he had transcribed her account substantially as she had dictated it. Slocum produced testimonials endorsing the character of the transcriber.[43]

Subsequent events, including legal disputes over the profits of the book, suggested that four individuals—Rev. W. K. Hoyt, Rev. J. J. Slocum, Theodore Dwight, and Rev. George Bourne—played crucial roles in preparing Maria Monk's story. All but Hoyt could be identified with the New School; Dwight and Bourne were also active in antislavery campaigns. Theodore Dwight, the most likely author of the book, was a great-grandson of Jonathan Edwards and a nephew of Timothy Dwight. Following his graduation from Yale, he became a notable lawyer and educator and later became editor of the *Protestant Vindicator*. Dwight was a friend of the Morse family, and his offices were located in the same building as the *New York Observer*. George Bourne was another New School Presbyterian minister whose antislavery views had already embroiled him in controversy. It is likely that Dwight wrote the book with suggestions from the other three.[44]

Even in the face of damaging evidence concerning Maria Monk's credibility, she held the support of a very substantial portion of the Protestant community, at least through 1836. Of course, the more vitriolic anti-Catholic publications such as the *Protestant Vindicator* did not hesitate to support Maria Monk and to denounce her critics as tools of the Jesuits. Even the more respectable publications such as the *New York Observer*, one of America's leading religious newspapers, defended the authenticity of her story. The Presbyterian-oriented *Observer* proclaimed that Maria Monk's character and veracity were above reproach. It discounted the affidavits in Jones's book because they came from Catholics. The paper further argued that the crimes described in her book were predictable of life in convents.[45]

In time, other events further diminished the credibility of her story. Her scandalous personal conduct, including an unexplained pregnancy, supported earlier accusations that she had once been a prostitute. More damaging evidence came as prominent Protestants were allowed to examine the *Hôtel Dieu*. They reported that the building bore no resemblance to the one described in the book. A number of anti-Catholic militants still tried to maintain their faith in her account. As late as September 1837, William Stone, one of the Protestants who had inspected the convent, complained that the clergy were afraid to speak out against Maria Monk. By 1837, the *Observer* quietly dropped its support of this book. In June 1837, the *Quarterly Christian Spectator* denounced Maria Monk's book as a fabrication. Thereafter, her credibility continued to diminish.[46]

Even though she eventually lost her credibility, Maria Monk's story had held the attention of hundreds of thousands of Americans, despite serious questions about her truthfulness. In part her tale was accepted because of its tantalizing sexuality. It was sufficiently explicit to appeal to a mass audience in the nineteenth century. David Brion Davis has suggested that her story, and others like it, served as an outlet for the repressed feelings of guilt over their own sexual desires by some readers. It allowed them to project their own unacknowledged desires onto the Catholic community.[47]

Yet there was another reason for the book's success. It fulfilled the readers' expectations of how the unlimited potential of human depravity could combine with the idolatrous practices of the Catholic Church to produce horrifying results. The authors of the work carefully built on the presuppositions of the reader to show the natural progression from idolatry to the most heinous of crimes. The first edition of the book began by quoting Revelation 18:4, "Come out of her, my people, and be not partakers of her sins, and that ye receive not her plagues," thus establishing a connection between the Catholic Church and the mystical Babylon. (Subsequent versions substituted an alleged floor plan of the convent.) In the opening sections, life in Quebec was described as one of ignorance and superstition. People were not literate, and the nuns who conducted schools were themselves so poorly educated that students received almost no genuine education. The population was so superstitious that they collected all manner of relics and prostrated themselves before the communion host. French-Canadian people were taught that a person could go to hell for reading the Bible. Although she came from a nominally Protestant family, Monk resembled her neighbors in that she had little genuine religious education and almost no exposure to the Bible.[48]

When she was inducted into the order and informed of the consequences, the Mother Superior justified the situation by declaring that, "the priests . . . were not situated like other men, being forbidden to marry; while they lived secluded, laborious, and self-denying lives for our salvation. They might indeed be considered our saviors, as without their services we could not obtain pardon of sin, and must go to hell." Later the Mother Superior insisted that priests could not sin. "It was a thing impossible. Everything that they did, and wished was of course right."[49]

Here indeed was an invitation to all the depravities of the human heart. New School Calvinists held that the only reason for the unregenerate person to behave morally at all was the thought of rewards and punishments in this world or the next. Now the priest could offer salvation through superstition or magic. The last restraint on human depravity had been broken. Sexual abandon, lies, even murder and mass infanticide were now acceptable. Maria Monk's *Awful Disclosures* offered a glimpse into the bottomless abyss of human depravity.

For her part, Monk professed to be swayed by the arguments because of her lack of education and because of the pressure of her surroundings. "I had been several years under the tuition of Catholics, and was ignorant of the Scriptures and unaccustomed to the society, example and conversation of Protestants. . . . [I] had not heard any appeal to the Bible as authority, but had been taught by precept and example to receive as truth everything said by the priests."[50]

Even after Maria Monk had been discredited, a belief in the licentiousness of convent life remained. In November 1837 the *New York Observer* published a travel description by George B. Cheever of his journeys in Spain. Cheever had allowed his imagination to operate freely as he watched the devotional exercises of some Spanish sisters. "As we gazed upon the scene, and beheld in these white-robed vestals, the undoubted objects of the lusts of the priesthood, confined as it were, like the inmates of a Turkish seraglio, and constituted in truth a consecrated brothel for the church, we could not but shudder at the spectacle. It reminded us of those orgies of pagan and heathen idolatry in which the most beautiful females, under the pretense of a sacred offering to the deity, were annually prostituted for the passions of the priests." Fears of immorality in convent life later led to demands for state inspections of convents.[51]

Such stories only confirmed the belief that the Church of Rome was the Antichrist, but the Antichrist's years were numbered. Because the prevalent interpretation of the Book of Revelation held that the papal Antichrist would reign for 1,260 years, the time of its final downfall would not be far off. As the redeemer nation, the United States was expected to play a crucial role in the great contest, especially with its example of liberty and Christianity.[52]

Paradoxically, this situation was a cause for alarm and concern. New School Calvinists believed that the Catholic powers of Europe would try to prevent the advent of the millennium by subverting the American nation. Fears of Catholic conspiracies were a standard feature of English and colonial anti-Catholicism. Yet nineteenth-century anti-Catholic writers displayed a special sense of urgency in denunciations of Catholic conspiracies. The intensity is largely attributable to the logic of their postmillennial eschatology, in which America's providential role resulted in accentuated dangers from the opponents of Christianity.[53]

In the battles that would precede the millennium, Americans would need to rise to the challenge or be swept away in the ensuing struggle. If the Americans failed to meet the challenge, they could expect God's anger. "[I]f we do fail in our great experiment in self-government, our destruction will be as signal as the birthright abandoned. . . . The descent of desolation will correspond with past elevation. No punishments of Heaven are so severe as those for mercies abused; and no instrumentality employed is so dreadful as the wrath of man."[54]

In another sense, the prophetic warnings of danger seemed to merge with an American belief in the self-evident appeal of their institutions. Given the prevailing assumption that liberty and Protestantism were so obviously right that no well informed person would refuse to accept them, it seemed reasonable to conclude that as long as the United States offered a shining example of freedom, the Catholic states of Europe could not rest easily. Beecher explained that, "if our light continues, their darkness passes away; and if our prosperity continues, their overturning cannot be stopped till the revolution has traveled round the globe and the earth is free."[55] Austria's Prince Metternich in particular was portrayed as grievously concerned with developments in America. Visitors to Vienna reported that he spent many hours studying maps of the United States in an effort to decide how to handle the threat.

Soon Samuel F. B. Morse and Lyman Beecher were writing that Prince Metternich was directing a grand conspiracy aimed at subverting American liberties through the means of foreign immigrants. They reported that the Austrian Leopold Society was subsidizing immigration in order to support the Catholic Church in America. The conspirators were also developing schools and other institutions that might convert Americans to Catholicism, or else mitigate the hostility to Catholicism.[56]

Once given the right to vote, the Catholic immigrant might also present a serious danger to republican government. Preservation of the republic depended on having a virtuous electorate. Catholics, not being Christian, could not be virtuous. Instead, Catholics were said to be so under the power of their priests that clerics could deliver solid blocks of votes to any politician they desired. Catholics might provide the victory to the candidate who made the most promises to them. An alarmed writer for the *Quarterly Christian Spectator* warned his readers of the impending danger:

> Nor is it wonderful, that the unprincipled politician, who seeks promotion and power, should avail himself of every stepping stone which his keen and scrutinizing eye can discover. The fact that they move in a mass, according to the dictates of a priest, renders them a convenient instrument for the ambitious demagogue. . . . The system is so well arranged in some parts of the country that a bishop or priest can state before the election what numbers of people he can bring to the polls for the person he advocates. *Places can be named where the Roman priests have stated from the pulpit what candidates the people were to support.*

A note in the *Home Missionary* reported how a block of seven or eight hundred Catholics could dominate a community of 1,900 people by voting as a unit. "Of course, where the rest of the community are divided, these hold the balance of power. This was so well understood during a political contest, that both parties made interests with the Catholics."[57]

The *New York Observer*, under the editorship of Sidney Morse, warned its readers that Catholic voters were not merely under the control of their priests, but that the priests were controlled by the Papacy. Therefore, American elections could be endangered through foreign intervention.

And we may not flatter ourselves that any important movement takes place here, without its bearings being considered in the Vatican. Let an emergency arise, in which his Holiness at Rome shall think it worth his while to interfere, and swift as a telegraphic despatch an unseen signal will be made across the ocean, and repeated over our land; all factions and subdivisions among Romanists in America will come to the polls in a solid phalanx. The great party chieftains—whose trade is politics—who live and move and have their being for objects of selfish ambition—will not be slow to perceive and to conciliate this Papal influence. For the sake of its vote *en masse*, they will give it—not at once, but little by little—the stand points it demands; and when it gains these, *then* it will throw off the mask, and hold up its proud front, and ask no favors.

Thus, the *Observer* portrayed a gradual deterioration of American liberties through papal machinations.[58]

Samuel F. B. Morse also marveled at the way in which priests were said to tell their parishioners how to vote. Samuel and Sidney Morse were the sons of the arch-Federalist minister Jedidiah Morse. Their father's involvement in politics did not inhibit them from denouncing clerical involvement in politics by priests because they assumed that Catholics were lacking in virtue and therefore self-serving. Morse portrayed a series of corrupt arrangements between office-hungry politicians and priests. "The bargain with the priest will be easily struck, `Give me office and I will take care of the interests of your church.' The effect of the bargain on the great moral or political interests of the country will not for a moment influence the calculation."[59]

The danger might be turned into an opportunity, however; New School Calvinists believed that, once men understood the principles of Protestantism, they would embrace it as the true religion. New School adherents had assumed that Catholicism relied heavily on ignorance in order to survive. If Catholic immigrants could be converted to American ways of Protestantism and liberty, the advent of the millennium might come that much sooner. The task was great but so was the importance of the mission. "Millions of the Papal world are . . . rolling in upon us, to be enlightened, elevated, Christianized, and taught the privileges and prerogatives of freemen."[60]

Initially, few Americans advocated excluding immigrants or restricting their liberties. They strongly urged the development of secular and religious educational institutions for the preservation of the republic. The perceived Catholic threat caused Protestant writers to insist that it was necessary to strengthen the Protestant foundations of the nation. "And what are the weapons of this warfare? The Bible, the Tract, the

Infant School, the common school for all classes, the college and university, a free press. . .. These, all of these, are the weapons of Protestantism, *weapons unknown to Popery.*"[61]

To counter the growth of Catholicism, anti-Catholic reformers enlisted the aid of the benevolent associations. The major benevolent associations expected to combat Catholicism by strengthening American Protestantism in general. Benevolent societies devoted a substantial portion of their efforts to pointing to the "errors" of the Church of Rome. The American Tract Society printed tracts about the Catholic religion. Both the American Home Missionary Society and the American Education Society openly proclaimed opposition to Catholicism as one of their major objectives. Other societies were devoted to combating Catholicism directly. The vituperative Protestant Reformation Society and the slightly more respectable American Protestant Association were attempts to organize national anti-Catholic societies similar in structure to other benevolent organizations.[62]

The common school was a major focus of the hopes for converting the Catholic. With their assumption that Catholicism could not withstand the light of genuine learning and education, Protestants believed that the common school would turn Catholic children into Protestants. To further this end, American schools developed an anti-Roman bias. Textbooks routinely associated Christianity with Protestantism. Catholicism was described as either a non-Christian religion, or at best a highly corrupt form of Christianity. The alleged backwardness of Catholic nations was usually contrasted unfavorably with the progressiveness of Protestant nations. Students used the Protestant King James Bible to the exclusion of the Catholic Douai version, despite Catholic protests that their church only approved of Catholic translations of Scripture.[63]

In their haste to convert the Catholics, Protestant educators did not understand why Catholics should have a grievance against public schools. Indeed, they conceived of themselves as perpetuating the truth in opposition to Roman error. Catholics had no right to insist that erroneous ideas be introduced into public schools. When Catholics protested against the exclusive use of the King James Bible, insisting that either Catholic students should use the Douai version or that no Bible should be used, Protestants interpreted this action as an attempt to remove the Bible from the public school entirely. Responding to the Bible question, George B. Cheever insisted that the inherent correctness of the Protestant position allowed them to deny the validity of Catholic complaints. "We affirm that their superstitions are not to be treated with the same respect as the word of God, and that they have not the same claim to a conscientious regard."[64]

In 1852, the Catholic bishops, led by Bishop John Hughes of New York, renewed a decade-old demand for their own school system, with public funding if possible. His demands were accompanied by his customary denuciation of Protestantism. The issue became explosive. Public schools were perceived as a means of liberating lay Catholics from the control of their clergy. Without such education Catholic voters might undermine the republican government. Now the Catholic withdrawal from public schools seemed to endanger the future of the republic. Consequently, the education issue became one of the bitterest points of Catholic-Protestant relations in the antebellum era. Americans reacted to the Catholic demand for separate schools with riots, new organizations, and heightened anti-Catholic activity.[65]

Fears of Catholic domination of the United States received new confirmation from the visit of a papal representative, Monsignor Gaetano Bedini, in 1853. Sent to resolve some internal disputes within the Catholic community and to bestow a papal blessing on American Catholics, Bedini's visit aroused a storm of opposition. Americans who regarded him as an agent of the papal conspiracy vehemently protested this visit. Soon riots and violence followed Bedini as he toured the United States.[66]

The public school issue and the Bedini visit highlighted an overall difficulty for New School Calvinists in accepting the Catholic immigrant. Catholics perplexed reformers by not discarding their old religion upon entering the United States. New School Calvinists in particular were not prepared to comprehend the failure of what they had accepted as a self-evident truth. With the increasing numbers of Catholic immigrants, moreover, the Catholic community was well on its way to becoming the largest single denomination in the United States. Consequently, New School Calvinists' fear of the Catholic Church grew more acute with time. The years just prior to the Civil War marked some of the strongest anti-Catholic outbursts.

As a vital dimension of the New School Calvinists' reform activities, anti-Catholicism received widespread support from the New School community. Their anti-Catholicism is noteworthy because their rhetoric conformed so closely to the logic of their theology and philosophy. Not comprehending the sacramental and symbolic aspects of the Catholic religion, they dismissed it as nothing but superstition and idolatry. Once they rejected its validity, they could not understand why any knowledgeable person would willingly remain a Catholic. Believing in the unlimited potential of human depravity, they assumed that the Catholic

Church attracted sinful men with false promises of salvation. They also credited the most heinous offenses to Catholics. Yet, with their fixed idea of truth, they assumed that the Church of Rome must suppress the truth in order to survive. They even assumed that the Catholic nations of Europe would predictably seek to prevent the United States from fulfilling its millennial role. In all their anti-Catholic efforts, they believed that they were promoting the interests of God and His true church.

Indeed, the patterns displayed within the anti-Catholic rhetoric would be repeated throughout the New School reform efforts. The temperance crusade, for example, reflected the same logic. In the case of the temperance crusade, the emphasis on fixed, immutable truths turned the movement toward the condemnation of all forms of alcohol.

7

The Temperance Crusade

Perhaps the most popular issue of antebellum reform, the temperance crusade also exhibited the extremist tendencies of antebellum reform. Unquestionably, the movement began as a well-needed effort to correct a serious social problem. Temperance advocates, however, went beyond correcting the abuse of alcohol to asserting that the mere use of intoxicants was sinful in itself. This shift to a condemnation of all alcohol was called "ultraism" in its own time, a term that has remained with us.

This uncompromising outlook among New School temperance reformers is not surprising, given the frame of reference provided by the New Haven theology. Believing that moral truths were fixed and immutable, New Haven adherents were unwilling to accept the idea that alcohol could be acceptable under some circumstances and unacceptable under others. Thus, they asserted that alcohol in itself, not merely the abuse of alcohol, was sinful. With their assertions of the inherently iniquitous nature of alcohol came allegations that liquor could be associated with all the depravities of human nature. Later, their emphasis on fixed and immutable truths appeared in their condemnation of fermented beverages, including wine. They even accepted dramatic reinterpretations of Scripture to establish the inherently sinful nature of wine.

Within the last thirty years, historians have produced a more sympathetic understanding of temperance reformers. Instead of being viewed as merely a "rural-evangelical" issue or a "symbolic crusade" by a declining middle class, the temperance cause has been treated as a serious effort to alleviate a genuine social problem. Moreover, historians have questioned the assumption that temperance reformers were fearful of a declining social status. The strongest temperance advocates frequently were upwardly mobile men who were innovators in industry and technology.[1]

It is necessary to realize that excessive alcohol consumption created serious social problems in the antebellum era. Americans consumed an incredible amount of liquor. Distilled beverages were especially popular, with whiskey being the most common drink. The human costs of the drinking problem were enormous. Families, lives, and jobs were all seriously harmed by the consumption of liquor.

Alcohol consumption had always been sanctioned in early America. Because Americans incorrectly believed that alcohol was a stimulant, they thought that it could provide valuable assistance to workers engaged in arduous occupations. Farm workers and mechanics typically expected a ration of whiskey to fortify them against the physical demands of their jobs. On social occasions liquor provided a basis for friendly gatherings. Special events such as births, weddings, and even the ordination of ministers were customarily celebrated with the copious consumption of liquor. Of course, inns and taverns prospered through the sale of alcohol.[2]

The unsettled social conditions of nineteenth-century America amplified the consumption of liquor. W. J. Rorabaugh has argued that, as the United States was transformed from an agricultural to a semi-industrial society, the changes in the old social order resulted in new anxieties among the younger generation. Rorabaugh has suggested that the rising generations of the nineteenth century had been led to expect significant achievements during their lives, yet their rural backgrounds had left them poorly prepared to accomplish these goals. As a result, their failure to achieve their expectations caused Americans to drink alcohol in massive quantities. Moreover, the highly transient lives of many Americans, particularly young men, encouraged the development of drinking as a means of social intercourse.[3]

At the same time Americans were turning to strong drink in increasing quantities, the traditional social mechanisms that had restrained excessive drinking were breaking down during the process of industrialization. In the eighteenth century, as well as the earliest years of the nineteenth century, workers and their employers lived in small units that resembled an extended family. Farm laborers might live with the farm owner, and they would share in both the extra efforts of harvest time and the relaxation that followed. Similarly, in urban areas apprentices and masters lived in the same quarters as part of a small unit. Under such circumstances, the distinction between work and recreation was vague. Employers and their workers might share a drink as a ges-

ture of unity. By the nineteenth century, however, larger factories replaced the small shops. Such fraternal drinking could no longer exist.
Workers, who were now separated from their employers by substantial
social barriers, drank in saloons, among their fellow laborers. Here they
could become intoxicated away from the supervision of their employers. Instead of serving as a bond between employers and employees,
alcohol now accentuated the independence of the workers.[4]

Certainly there were laws to curb the excessive use of liquor. Inns
and taverns were required to have licenses in order to sell intoxicants.
Normally, the town selectmen recommended individuals of good reputation and standing for the privilege of liquor licenses. Grocers, who
sold alcohol for off-premise consumption, were also licensed by the local government. Ever since colonial days, public intoxication was a mis-
demeanor.[5]

Nonetheless, existing laws did little to alleviate the growing abuse
of alcoholic beverages. Liquor consumption had become too embedded
in American culture to be changed easily. Nineteenth-century Americans consumed an estimated average of four gallons of alcohol each year.
"Americans drank at home, and abroad, alone and together, at work and
at play, in fun and in earnest. They drank from the crack of dawn to the
crack of dawn. . . . Americans drank before meals, with meals and after
meals." Given the extent of the alcohol problem, it was clear that some-
thing needed to be done.[6]

The first organization intended to curb alcohol consumption was
the Massachusetts Society for the Suppression of Intemperance, which
was created in 1813. Its members, who consisted of conservative Federalist leaders, attempted to solve the problem through stricter enforcement of existing regulations. They wanted to restrict liquor licenses to
reputable members of the community so that dealers would police themselves. These early reformers aimed at minimizing the abuse of intoxicants while accepting the temperate use of both distilled and fermented
beverages.[7]

By the mid-1820s, however, temperance advocates ceased to tolerate even the moderate use of distilled beverages. In 1826, several prominent Massachusetts clergy and laymen created the American Society for
the Promotion of Temperance, more commonly called the American
Temperance Society. This society served as the major temperance organization until it was superseded by the American Temperance Union in
1835. Like most benevolent organizations the American Temperance
Society worked through a national headquarters and local auxiliaries.
The national organization published material, employed agents and

speakers, and provided guidance to local temperance groups. These local organizations raised money and supported temperance efforts within their communities.[8]

Under the leadership of Justin Edwards, the American Temperance Society promoted the idea that the only solution to the alcohol problem was entire abstinence by the whole community.[9] The movement no longer concentrated on reforming the drunkard. Rather its members desired to terminate moderate drinking among respectable members of the community.

At approximately the same time that the American Temperance Society was being created, Lyman Beecher delivered his famous *Six Sermons on the Nature, Occasions, Signs, Evils, and Remedy of Intemperance.* When published, this work proved to be one of the major statements of the temperance movement. With greater detail and force than previous writers, he portrayed the inevitable downward course of the intemperate drinker to his ruin. Beecher then catalogued the evils inflicted on the entire community by intemperance. The most important part of his sermons came when he proposed complete abstinence from distilled beverages by the entire community as the only solution for intemperance. He reasoned that it was futile to expect the alcoholic to reform himself when hard liquor was common in most households. In proposing this remedy, Beecher joined with the American Temperance Society in turning the attention of the temperance cause against even the moderate use of alcohol.[10]

With the widespread alcohol problems in nineteenth-century America, some action was necessary. Entire abstinence by the whole community may well have been the best solution to America's drinking problems. In advocating total abstinence, the temperance movement received widespread support from the American religious community.

By the early 1830s, however, a subtle change developed within the temperance movement that would alter the nature of the campaign. At first, temperance leaders criticized any use of distilled beverages as inexpedient because it encouraged excessive drinking. Later, they condemned even modest drinking as inherently wrong and as a violation of fixed moral law. This alteration in attitudes toward liquor, which developed gradually between 1828 and 1833, produced a strident tone in the temperance movement and led to accusations of extremism, even from people who previously were sympathetic to the temperance efforts.

As in other reform movements, New School Presbyterians and Congregationalists provided most of the leadership and direction for the militant temperance crusade. As a general rule, New School Calvinists were more likely to condemn moderate drinking as inherently sinful, rather than inexpedient. Old School Calvinists frequently affirmed their commitment to total abstinence, yet usually they were more hesitant to insist that alcohol was intrinsically sinful.

Other evangelical denominations supported the temperance movement but were less visible than the Presbyterians and Congregationalists. In theory, the temperance cause was a multidenominational effort. In practice, the leadership of the American Temperance Society was dominated by Presbyterians and Congregationalists. Members of other religious denominations, such as Baptists and Methodists, did serve in temperance organizations. Certainly members of all religious persuasions abhorred the excessive consumption of alcohol, yet the most prominent leaders of the American Temperance Society belonged to the two major Calvinist denominations, including Justin Edwards of Andover Seminary, the Congregationalist minister John Marsh, and Eliphalet Nott of Union College. Other Presbyterian and Congregationalist leaders such as Lyman Beecher, Albert Barnes, George B. Cheever, and George Duffield gave their unstinting support to the militant temperance cause.[11]

Methodist ministers, for example, gained a reputation for their opposition to alcohol, and the Methodists employed similar concepts of fixed truths. Methodist conferences frequently formed their own temperance societies. Even so, the American Temperance Society itself found little support from the Methodists. In fact, only one of the founders of the Temperance Society was a Methodist minister. When the second *Annual Report* listed thirty-four ecclesiastical bodies that supported their organization, only one Methodist conference was included.[12]

New School Calvinists conceived of right and wrong as based on truths that did not vary with time or circumstances. They had great difficulty in accepting the idea that the moderate use of hard liquor could be acceptable under certain circumstances and unacceptable under others. It was difficult for them to understand how a substance that caused so much harm could have legitimate uses. They reasoned that a substance that was evil in its effects must be evil in its nature, or *malum in se*.[13] Commenting on the sale of hard liquor, Barnes noted that "there is somewhere a correct standard of morals—a standard by which a man's whole conduct and course of life is to be traced; and that this business cannot be vindicated by reference to that standard."[14]

A writer for the *Quarterly Christian Spectator* suggested that the law of habit produced a highly probable downward progression from occasional use to frequent intoxication. A portion of the New School Calvinists saw an infant's habits of self-gratification as the beginning of human depravity. Once developed, these impulses were so strong that humans would not free themselves from the slavery of habit. A similar situation existed with regard to alcohol. An individual might begin drinking with friends at enjoyable social occasions. Thereafter, the association between liquor and good times would remain firmly fixed in his mind. In an effort to recreate the mirth surrounding his first use of alcohol, he would turn to drink in increasing quantities until he became confirmed in his intemperance.[15]

Temperance writers, such as Justin Edwards, assumed that the human body would become accustomed to the effects of alcohol. Soon the user would need greater amounts of liquor to produce the same effects that a smaller quantity had once produced. The steady deterioration from temperate use of alcohol to intemperance seemed almost inevitable. Men who continued to use alcohol in moderation were degenerating at a slower pace than other men. An 1831 report of the American Temperance Society noted that "most persons given to intemperance, proceed from one degree of wickedness to another, till, having been often reproved, . . . they bring sudden and remediless destruction upon themselves. And they destroy not only themselves, but a multitude of others."[16]

An 1833 report of the American Temperance Society further elaborated on the Society's opposition to moderate drinking. "We consider moderate drinkers as the main, if not the only cause of the continued use of distilled liquors; but for them, the manufacturer and vendor would soon disannul their covenant with hell, and abandon their traffic in death. What has already been said of one regular temperate drinker, is applicable to all. Their moral sense is debased; they are enslaved to appetite; they are in league against truth, reason, and revelation, with the enemy of their race." In this passage the writer demonstrated the rigid tone of these reformers. Anything less than total abstinence was in opposition to truth, reason, and God.[17]

The images of chains and slavery appeared appropriate to describe the habitual user. He was enslaved to the power of drink in much the same way that the unregenerate was under the dominion of sin. The force of habit was so strong that the drinker would continue on the path to his inevitable ruin unless his intemperance was arrested. The drinker might cry out and wish to escape his fate, but the power of the alcohol was too strong.[18]

Their belief that the moral law must agree with the laws of nature encouraged temperance writers to demonstrate how intoxicants violated some set rules of nature. Alcohol, they contended, did not exist naturally. It came only from dead or decaying vegetable matter. Hence, it must be "wrested" from nature by violence. Intoxicating beverages were not gifts from nature's bounty, but the by-product of decaying matter. To their authors these arguments were significant. Advocates of temperance assumed that the moral law must be consistent with nature. Otherwise God, who had created both nature and the moral law, would be contradicting Himself.[19]

Having declared that hard liquor was inherently immoral, militant temperance advocates then asserted that the drinker was so far beyond the means of grace that most of the crimes and social ills in the United States could be attributed to hard liquor. Stories and statistics purporting to prove the disastrous consequences of distilled beverages were routinely circulated, with little dissent. Contemporary observers estimated that anywhere from three-quarters to nine-tenths of the nation's prison inmates committed their crimes because of alcohol. Similarly, insane asylums were populated largely by intemperate men. Most of the poverty in America was attributed to the influence of alcohol, not to the social conditions of the poor. Temperance reformers saw total abstinence as a panacea for all problems. The *New York Observer* noted with satisfaction that the temperance movement had left the Dedham, Massachusetts, jail without a single inmate. "This pleasing fact, we suppose, may be set down as one of the happy results of the Temperance Reform. When the Reform shall have done its perfect work, we may hope to see not only prisons, but almshouses and even hospitals become vacant."[20]

A substantial portion of the temperance literature repeated that a seemingly innocent first experience with alcohol could prove to be the beginning of many a young man's ruin. Even the slightest use of intoxicants was to be avoided because of its potential consequences. Much of the temperance literature came in the form of stories that often followed the same pattern. A young man has excellent prospects for a successful career, plus a virtuous young wife or sweetheart. He meets with false friends who introduce him to hard liquor. Soon he becomes a habitual drinker. He loses his job and begins to abuse his family or sweetheart. He continues this downward course until he finally realizes that liquor is the cause of his troubles. He takes the pledge never to drink again, whereupon happiness is restored.[21]

Justin Edwards could be even more dramatic about how alcohol released the depravities inherent in human nature. He cited cases where whiskey contributed directly to murder:

In 1833 a young man committed a murder. He was tried and pronounced guilty. 'Yes,' said he, 'I am guilty,' and pointing to his mother, who stood by him said 'She was the cause of it.' She had become incensed against a man and resolved to take his life. She agreed with her son that he should shoot him. . . . but she was afraid that her son, . . . would shrink back. So she got a bottle of whiskey and went with him to the spot. . . . The son relented and said that he could not shoot him. The mother produced the whiskey and said 'Drink that.' He drank it, shot the man, and was hanged. She was the cause, whiskey the means, the death of the neighbor and son the result.

It [alcohol] renders the soul reckless, and leads it to rush headlong upon its ruin. Under its influence, a husband killed his wife while [she was] nursing her babe. . . . A father took a little child by his legs and dashed his head against the house, and then, with a bootjack, beat out his brains. Once that man was a respectable merchant in good standing, but he drank alcohol; his wife was drivin [sic] from her home, and his little child murdered.

As president of the American Temperance Society, Edwards acted as an important spokesman for the movement. His social position meant that when he insisted that alcohol was a cause of the most heinous of crimes, his opinions received widespread attention.[22]

If alcohol was intrinsically sinful, merchants and distillers who profited from other men's ruin should cease producing and selling intoxicants. At first temperance advocates refrained from denouncing the character of liquor merchants. They suggested that, in previous years, men did not realize the dangerous potential of their trade. Consequently God had "winked at" their indiscretions. With the modern knowledge of the nature of liquor, men should stop selling it, but without recriminations for past acts. When certain distillers remained unmoved by their pleas, however, reformers looked on these merchants as deliberately trafficking in death and damnation.[23]

George B. Cheever, Salem's outspoken Congregationalist minister, earned both fame and notoriety through his attack on one such distiller in 1835. In his piece, *The Dream, or Deacon Giles' Distillery*, Cheever created a character who bore a striking resemblance to a local Unitarian Deacon, John Stone. In brief, the story told of a Deacon Amos Giles who operated a local distillery. Having labor difficulties, Deacon Giles was forced to hire some strange-looking fellows who were in fact demons in disguise. Although singularly efficient, his assistants resented the manner in which they were exploited. Determined to obtain satisfaction, they secretly marked each barrel of liquor with such labels as

George B. Cheever. Courtesy of the Library of Congress

distilled death and liquid damnation. When the merchandise was sold, the labels suddenly appeared, thus ruining Deacon Giles's business.[24]

Deacon John Stone resented the resemblance between his business and the story, with the implication that he was marketing death and damnation. Stone brought a charge of libel against Cheever and obtained a conviction. Cheever then enjoyed thirty days of martyrdom in the Essex County jail.[25] He did not seem to feel that he had done any wrong to Deacon Stone. From Cheever's perspective, Stone was at fault for his persistent refusal to recognize the iniquity of liquor.

Through their tactics of persuasion and denunciation, temperance reformers succeeded in substantially reducing the quantity of alcohol consumed in the United States. As distilled beverages lost their respectability, fewer people purchased or sold liquor. An unexpected boost for the temperance cause came in 1840 with the creation of the Washingtonians. This society of workingmen, organized to provide mutual support for each other's abstinence, existed apart from the clerically oriented American Temperance Society. Although the Washingtonians resisted the clerical domination of the American Temperance Society, they did extend temperance activity into the working classes.[26]

Nonetheless, by the mid-1830s, temperance reformers were not happy with the progress of their cause. Too many distillers and consumers still resisted the pleadings and denunciations of the temperance movement. In response temperance reformers began to campaign for the legal prohibition of alcohol.

Temperance reformers first attacked the licensing of taverns and inns. Since colonial times innkeepers were required to possess licenses to sell alcoholic beverages. By limiting the number of people who could sell liquor, these laws protected the innkeepers' businesses, and thus ensured the availability of inns for travelers. The other purpose of these laws was to restrict the licenses to respectable members of the community who could maintain control over their customers. These laws were intended to prevent excesses and were based on the assumption that the moderate consumption of alcohol was legitimate.

These laws were considered unacceptable because any license to sell alcohol was a license to sin. Governments, as ordinances of God, were expected to uphold His decrees, not encourage disobedience. A report for the American Temperance Society explained that "the licensing of sin is not the way to prevent or restrain it, but is the way to sanction and perpetuate it; by declaring . . . that if practised [sic] legally, it is right; and thus preventing the efficacy of truth and facts in producing the conviction that it is wrong."[27]

In Massachusetts and elsewhere, temperance reformers succeeded in capturing control over local governments. Once in power, these men denied liquor licenses to all applicants. The effect of their actions was to make the sale of alcohol illegal, even though there were no new laws prohibiting alcohol.

Drinking, however, continued despite the removal of licenses. Existing laws contained too many loopholes and too few punitive sanctions. Therefore, temperance forces began to press for more stringent laws against alcohol. In 1851 the state of Maine passed a prohibitory law that would become the model for state prohibition in the 1850s. This law provided for the effective enforcement of laws against drinking by closing the loopholes of previous legislation. The new law provided for search and seizure of dealers' stocks, thus eliminating the need for testimony from customers. The Maine law also gave liquor cases priority for trial and specified more stringent punishments. By 1855, Massachusetts, Rhode Island, Vermont, Michigan, Connecticut, New York, Indiana, Delaware, Iowa, Nebraska, and New Hampshire all enacted versions of the Maine law. Temperance crusaders had succeeded in bringing the power of the government to their cause.[28]

John Marsh defended the shift toward coercive measures by emphasizing the relationship between God and civil governments.

> Civil government is an ordinance of God, established for His glory and the good of men. Rulers stand in the place of God. . . . And in all acts of legislation they must be on the Lord's side—resisting all evil, protecting the people from evil doers, and sustaining the principles of God's moral government. In all his conflicts with evil, the Governor of the Universe never gives license; no, not for an hour. It is always PROHIBITION PROHIBITION. . . . The licensed vender selling poison to his weak brother and bringing him to the drunkard's grave is the criminal protected by the State; and the cries of the broken-hearted victim and his beggared family will go up, and not in vain, into the ears of the Lord of Sabaoth.

This statement demonstrates Marsh's firm belief in both a fixed moral law and the government's obligation to uphold that law.[29]

Even these political victories were in themselves an admission of failure. Antebellum reformers had traditionally relied on moral suasion as the means to obtain the desired results. They expected that the power of a self-evident truth ought to move all but the most obstinate sinner. In one of their most important causes, moral suasion achieved only partial success. In their efforts to eradicate what they considered an obvious evil, they were compelled to rely on the power of the government rather than the power of persuasion.

At approximately the same time that they first entered the political arena, temperance forces also became involved in disputes over fermented beverages. This controversy primarily centered on the use of wine, with beer and cider receiving less attention. (As will be discussed below, the use of wine involved Scriptural arguments.) Although historians have concentrated their attention on legal battles, the disputes over fermented beverages were equally important and divisive in the nineteenth-century religious community.

Temperance advocates had initially restricted their demands for total abstinence to distilled beverages. In fact, very early in the temperance movement, some people even thought that wine might be used to wean men from the use of whiskey. Other reformers did not encourage the use of wine, but they generally refrained from attacking fermented beverages.

In spite of the sacramental and curative uses of wine, the similarities between distilled and fermented beverages caused difficulties for these reformers. Both wine and whiskey contained the same basic ingredient, alcohol. Both drinks produced the same intoxicating effects. Even if fermented beverages were less potent than distilled drinks, they were still intoxicants. One observer commented that, "if these principles [sinfulness of alcohol] apply with equal force and truth, both physically and morally to every form of strong liquor in proportion to their intoxicating power and quantity consumed, why make a distinction?" If distilled beverages violated a fixed moral law, fermented beverages must, logically, also be illicit.[30]

The difficulty was that the Bible seemed to sanction the use of wine. Wine had appeared in the Old Testament with both favorable and unfavorable mentions. In the New Testament, Paul had recommended wine to Timothy. Jesus Christ Himself made wine in His first miracle at Cana. At the Last Supper, He elevated the use of wine to a sacramental level for communion services. In the nineteenth-century culture, Scripture was considered a direct revelation from God, which was literally correct in all aspects, historically and morally. To go against Scripture by condemning wine was unthinkable.

In 1830, Moses Stuart first approached this problem. He admitted that the Old Testament tolerated the use of pure wine, which he described as a mildly fermented beverage. Nonetheless, he argued that the Bible strongly condemned drinking to intoxication, the use of strong wines, or any wines mixed with drugs. Nineteenth-century wines, he argued, contained more alcohol than did Biblical wine. Therefore, they would not meet with scriptural approval. He concluded that the Bible allowed a demand for total abstinence, but he admitted that this demand was justified by expediency.[31]

Stuart's efforts did not resolve the wine problem. By admitting that Biblical wines were mildly intoxicating, he implicitly conceded that the Bible might sanction what appeared to be violations of a fixed and immutable moral law. Other militant temperance advocates soon embraced the so-called two-wine theory, because it offered a rationale for condemning all intoxicating beverages.

Essentially, the two-wine theory was an argument that Biblical wines might be either intoxicating or nonintoxicating, with only the nonintoxicating wines being acceptable. Some speculation about the possibility of a nonintoxicating wine began as early as 1835.[32] In 1837 and 1838, Dr. Eliphalet Nott, president of Union College in Schenectady, New York, gave one of the first full expression of the two-wine theory in his *Lectures on Temperance*. According to this theory, the Bible mentioned both fermented and unfermented wines, with the unfermented beverages being preferred. There were at least nine Hebrew words that translated into wine. The two most common words were *tirosh* and *yayin*. *Tirosh* was the unfermented juice of the grape, a nonintoxicating beverage. Wherever the word *tirosh* appeared in the Bible, it was always used with approbation. *Yayin* was a generic name for all types of wine. In cases where it was used to mean an unfermented beverage, the intent was clear and the beverage was mentioned with approval. On other occasions *yayin* was used to indicate fermented wines, and in these cases the word was clearly used with disapproval.[33]

As the theory developed, it appeared that the ancients had a method of preventing the fermentation of grapes. They boiled the grape juice down into a thick syrupy substance and then stored it inside a goat's stomach. At a later date the syrup could be mixed with water and consumed. Allegedly the syrupy nature of the substance plus its insulation from the air prevented its fermentation. The ancient people supposedly preferred the unfermented wine as being of a higher quality than fermented wine. (Proponents of the two-wine theory did not explain why later generations could not prevent the fermentation of grape juice at normal temperatures.)[34]

Once introduced, the two-wine theory proved to be the most internally divisive aspect of the temperance program. These disputes, with the concurrent arguments about communion wine, aroused as much controversy within the evangelical community as had the prohibition battles. It was the wine issue, not prohibition, that resulted in accusations of ultraism.

Even men who agreed that wine was inexpedient would not accept this reinterpretation of Scripture. The most serious opposition to the two-wine theory came from faculty members of Princeton Seminary and the College of New Jersey. These Old School Calvinists had supported the attacks on the consumption of distilled beverages and had even approved the expediency of abstaining from wine. Samuel Miller, a professor at Princeton, explained that he personally had profited by avoiding wine, despite his disagreements with the two-wine theory.[35] Yet these men believe that this theory was a novel reinterpretation of Scripture.

Writing a lengthy article in the *Princeton Review*, which was later republished separately, John MacLean, a professor at the College of New Jersey, complained that believers in the two-wine theory placed their own judgment above God's revealed desires. Their Biblical research appeared so weak to him that they were merely grasping for justifications for their opinions. He went to considerable effort to establish that there was no knowledge of any practice of boiling grape juice within the Middle East.[36]

The bulk of the article was devoted to insisting that this method was the opposite of the orthodox approach. "We are not at liberty first to decide whether a thing is right or wrong, and then, in accordance with that decision, determine what Christ did or did not do. . . . First [they] trust to their own unaided reason, to ascertain what is right and wrong, and [they] then go to Scripture to have their opinions confirmed."[37]

MacLean did not disagree with the idea of entire abstinence in itself, if Biblical arguments were not used. "Had those who favor [temperance] contented themselves with urging *the expediency* of total abstinence from all intoxicating drinks they would have met no opposition from us."[38] He certainly contended that excessive use of alcohol was wrong. Moreover, MacLean understood how the situation in nineteenth-century America might require men to forgo wine for the sake of their fellow men. "Whether there is anything in the present condition of our own country . . . that calls at this time for entire abstinence from every species of intoxicating drink, is a question for serious and prayerful inquiry."[39] His objection was that temperance militants distorted the word of God to achieve their own ends.

Undeterred by the criticism, Edward Delavan, the president of the New York Temperance Society, proceeded to carry the crusade against wine to its next logical step, denial of fermented wine at communion. From 1834 through to the early 1840s, Delavan campaigned tirelessly against communion wine, insisting that the drunkard could not be reformed if he tasted wine at communion. In 1841, he even started his own magazine, *The Enquirer*, to oppose the use of communion wine. Delavan and other militants succeeded in making the use of communion wine into a serious issue. Ministers who used fermented wine might find their authority questioned.[40]

Not surprisingly, conservatives reacted against any alteration in the celebration of the Lord's Supper. James W. Alexander, of the College of New Jersey, complained that the wine question "tends . . . to divide Christians at the very spot where they should unite, namely at the Lord's table. It is a firebrand cast into our churches, and I am unable to see how it can fail to rend into two bodies every religious community which does not promptly extinguish it."[41] The *New York Observer*, which strongly supported both the temperance cause and the Maine law, questioned the militants' stand on the wine question. Its editors derided Delavan for pursuing a "hobby" that other men considered an absurdity.[42]

In an effort to find an acceptable solution to the wine question, the editors of the *New York Observer* suggested that Americans should abstain from wine because of expediency, even if pure wine was not innately sinful. They further argued that Americans should refrain from beverages that were sold as wine because it was a "notorious fact" that nine-tenths of all products that were bottled and labeled as wine were not the true fruit of the vine. Instead of using fermented grapes, wine merchants used distilled alcohol or drugs to create an intoxicating effect. The allegedly spurious wine was flavored through a combination of unspeakably vile adulterants. Madeira, for example, was said to derive its nutty flavor through the addition of ground cockroaches. Other wines were similarly flavored.[43]

Nonetheless, the two-wine theory achieved a sizable popularity that lasted until well after the Civil War. By 1848, even the cautious Moses Stuart accepted the two-wine theory. It allowed the militant temperance crusaders to reconcile their unalterable opposition to all intoxicants with their faith in the Bible. Having argued that intoxicants violated fixed moral laws as well as laws of nature, they could rest assured that Scripture supported their view. Most important, they could feel confident that Jesus Christ did not produce intoxicating beverages at Cana.[44]

The more militant attitude gained support in the newly organized American Temperance Union, which was created as a successor to the American Temperance Society. In its second convention, at Saratoga Springs, New York, in 1836, the Temperance Union adopted a pledge of total abstinence "from all that can intoxicate" (meaning wine). Even so, the members of the convention conciliated conservatives by adopting a statement that the members of the convention made no judgment on whether wine was inexpedient or sinful. By 1840, the annual report of the American Temperance Union endorsed the two-wine theory. The authors condemned the use of fermented wine as immoral and insisted that the only legitimate "wine" was an unfermented grape juice. The opponents of wine gradually obtained control over local societies and gained further support for the condemnation of all fermented wine.[45]

Although precise statistics are not available, it appears that by the late 1830s the portion of the temperance community that considered wine to be intrinsically sinful was substantial, but far from unanimous. With the growing militancy of temperance organizations came a serious decline in membership. For example, as the New York state society adopted a more radical position between 1836 and 1839, its membership declined from 229,000 to 131,000.[46]

With some notable and important exceptions, the most visible supporters of the two-wine theory within the Calvinist community came from the New School. This militant temperance issue received its greatest support from the New York State Temperance Society, which was located in upstate New York, an area well known for its New School sympathies. This particular organization continued to place Edward Delavan into leadership positions, despite his well-known opposition to communion wine. Men such as George Duffield, Albert Barnes, and Moses Stuart also supported the two-wine theory.[47] Not all New School Calvinists favored the two-wine theory, but a disproportionate share of its supporters did come from the New School.

Furthermore, the most vocal opponents of this idea came from the Old School institutions, Princeton Seminary and the College of New Jersey. Of course, some prominent adherents of the two-wine theory were Old School Calvinists. Eliphalet Nott, for example, was an Old School Presbyterian. Yet, on balance, the Old School members were far less committed to the two-wine theory than were New School Calvinists. For example, in 1842 the Old School General Assembly pointedly refused to make abstinence from intoxicating drink a condition for communion.[48]

Despite some of the extremist positions of militant temperance advocates, it must be remembered that the temperance crusade was one of the most popular of all antebellum reform movements. In large part, this popularity resulted from its value to the community. Between 1825 and 1850, the temperance movement helped to reduce alcohol consumption in America significantly, thereby performing a notable service to the nation. Even if their rhetoric reflected the uncompromising nature of their ideology, these reformers were seeking to correct a genuine social problem.

New School temperance activities are noteworthy because they conform so closely with New School ideology. More than in other reform efforts, temperance efforts reflected a commitment to a fixed, immutable truth. (Of course, other themes, such as depravity, are also apparent in their temperance rhetoric.) Having witnessed the harmful effects of liquor, temperance militants concluded that all alcoholic beverages must be intrinsically sinful, without regard to circumstances. In order to defend their assertion that alcohol violated unchangeable laws of morality, temperance militants proposed dramatic and controversial reinterpretations of Scripture. To its adherents the scriptural argument against wine was the predictable product of a belief in fixed, immutable truths. The rhetorical patterns demonstrated in their anti-Catholic activities held through the temperance movement. In the crusade against slavery, New School Calvinists would again act within the same pattern of perceptions. Indeed, the antislavery campaign included debates over the scriptural justifications for slavery, or questions of whether slavery was inherently sinful, that bore a striking resemblance to temperance rhetoric.

❧ 8
Chattel Slavery

Of all the programs of antebellum reform, the crusade against slavery involved the greatest diversity of opinions, motives, and characters. Unlike other reforms, where the Congregationalists and Presbyterians exerted a preponderant influence, the antislavery movement included atheists, Unitarians, Transcendentalists, anarchists, freethinkers, and various nonconformists. People such as William Lloyd Garrison, Abby Kelley, and Theodore Parker often overshadowed the more conventional Congregational and Presbyterian reformers. Members of each persuasion entered the cause for their own reasons, and at times they devoted a disproportionate amount of their energy to battling one another.

Although they were only one of many groups involved, numerous New School Calvinists played a crucial role in the antislavery movement. These men and women combined an abhorrence of slavery with a belief in the basic soundness of American institutions. Their antislavery activities were less radical than those of the Garrisonians and were therefore acceptable to a larger audience.

As in New School anti-Catholic and temperance activities, their antislavery rhetoric demonstrates the nature of their ideology. Given their strong sense of human depravity, they were initially reluctant to condemn coercive institutions such as slavery. Indeed, many New School Calvinists never became militant abolitionists. In time, however, New School principles undermined the traditional justifications for slavery, thus allowing increasing numbers of its members to perceive slavery as intrinsically sinful. As these men and women became convinced of the inherent sinfulness of slavery, they crusaded against it with uncompromising vigor. With their belief in human depravity, they argued that slaveholders could perpetrate the most savage cruelties. They interpreted

Scripture in a way that demonstrated the eternal iniquity of slavery. Believing that a system of iniquity could not withstand the light of truth, they asserted that a slave power conspiracy would seek to suppress all liberty in the United States.

In order to understand the New School attitudes toward slavery, it is necessary to appreciate the fact that antislavery was a novel and controversial reform movement. To twentieth-century observers, the crusades against liquor or Catholicism have diminished respectability, whereas abolitionism appears so self-evidently right that it is difficult to understand why anyone could not be opposed to slavery. To the nineteenth-century mind, however, temperance and anti-Catholicism were considered respectable reforms, and abolitionism was radical. Slavery, which had existed for eighteen hundred years after the birth of Christ, was widely accepted within the United States. Men who deplored the existence of the institution did not challenge the essential rectitude of slaveholders. Nineteenth-century abolitionists challenged a long-standing institution and braved the wrath of fierce opposition.

For all of its offensive features, slavery had been justified since antiquity by the necessity of preserving the social order in the face of human iniquity. The classical defense of slavery rested on the presumption of original sin and received the endorsement of such notable theologians as Thomas Aquinas. In this sinful world, God had ordained certain systems of subordination as a means of preserving order. These included governments, families, private property, and the various forms of servitude that have existed throughout history. Although these systems of subordination were subject to abuse, it did not follow that the systems themselves should be abolished. If men might throw off one system of subordination, then all such coercive institutions might be endangered, and the entire arrangement of social order, necessitated by man's original sin, might be open to question.[1]

Conservative nineteenth-century Americans—including Old School Calvinists such as Charles Hodge, George Junkin, and Nathan L. Rice—also accepted this justification of slavery, at least in part. They thought that some coercive institutions were necessary for the sake of social order in a sinful world. The fact that slaveholders might abuse their relationships to their bondsmen did not imply that the relationships were inherently sinful any more than the fact that rulers might abuse their powers implied that governments were illicit.[2]

A number of the best-known abolitionists followed the argument that an attack on slavery was an attack on all coercive institutions to its logical conclusion and became anarchists. If slavery could not be challenged without calling civil governments into question, then perhaps civil governments also might be illicit. Abolitionists such as William Lloyd Garrison, Adin Ballou, Henry Wright, and Maria Chapman concluded that any institution that interfered with a person's moral choice must be sinful. Garrison used his newspaper *The Liberator* to articulate his philosophy of anarchy and nonresistance. He later created new controversies within the abolitionist movement over such questions as the sinfulness of voting. Adin Ballou attempted to organize the Hopedale community on the principles of Christian anarchy.[3]

These radicals played a significant role in antislavery agitation by focusing public attention on the wrongs of slavery. Their contributions were especially important in the early phases of the movement, before the cause had achieved respectability. Nonetheless, their disapproval of American institutions limited their influence among more conventional Americans. In order to reach a larger constituency, antislavery activists needed to develop a less radical justification for their position. In attacking slavery without attacking all institutions, New School Calvinists, among others, played a vital role in the abolitionist movement.

Those New School adherents who became abolitionists condemned the institution of chattel slavery as inherently sinful, while refusing to condemn all coercive relationships. The disagreements over the legitimacy of government helped to distinguish the Garrisonian radicals from the more conventional abolitionists. People such as Albert Barnes, George B. Cheever, or the children of Lyman Beecher were decidedly not anti-institutional. All of them favored government sanctions to support prohibition. Cheever publicly defended the death penalty. Henry Ward Beecher later would be caricatured as a spokesman for capitalist management. Even Theodore Weld, who was a student of Charles Finney and was thus theologically more radical than the others, did not support the anarchist position of the Garrisonians. By attacking only the institution of slavery as intrinsically sinful, these men and women were able to influence a larger portion of the population than the Garrisonians.[4]

Significantly, virtually all antislavery Presbyterians and Congregationalists came from the New School. New Haven theology may not have caused its adherents to become abolitionists, but it did prove to be more conducive to antislavery than Old School Calvinism. Once these men and women did become abolitionists, their religious beliefs helped them to comprehend their activities, and their religion is reflected in their rhetoric. Given their belief in the fearsome extent of human depravity, they initially upheld the necessity for coercive institutions; however, once they became abolitionists, they propagated the most frightful stories of atrocities by slaveholders. Their belief in universally valid moral truths led them to assert that slavery was inherently sinful, even to the point of offering new interpretations of Scripture. As in their anti-Catholic activities, they attributed the survival of slavery to conspiratorial forces.

Because the theoretical justification for slavery relied on the concept of original sin, New School changes to the doctrine of original sin subtly undermined the justification for slavery.[5] The contradictions and injustices of the slave system now appeared less acceptable. The shift in theology was comparatively minor. It did not produce an immediate rejection of chattel slavery. Instead, it facilitated the later adoption of an antislavery position by New School adherents. Few of the original New Haven theologians considered slavery to be intrinsically sinful. It was not Lyman Beecher, but his children, who crusaded for the African Americans' freedom.

In another sense, the New School's partial rejection of man's bondage to sin also encouraged its members to turn against chattel slavery. Having rejected the belief that men are enslaved to the power of sin, New School Calvinists were reluctant to accept the idea of men's slavery to other men. In a letter to Garrison, Theodore Weld once succinctly summarized how the New School concept of free moral agency could affect their attitudes toward slavery. Weld had insisted that "no condition of birth, no shade of color . . . can annul the birth-right charter which God has bequeathed to every being upon whom he has stamped his own image by making him a *free moral agent.*"[6]

The benevolent principle provided another reason for New School Calvinists to condemn slavery. Following the lead of Samuel Hopkins, New School Calvinists believed that true virtue consisted of a calculated regard for the greatest possible good of all beings. Slavery appeared to violate this standard because masters could make an unfair profit by exploiting their slaves. Samuel Hopkins was one of the first Congregationalist ministers to oppose slavery.[7]

Three aspects of the slave codes in particular made slavery appear especially offensive in light of the benevolent principle. First, the law forbade slaves from learning to read and thus made them dependent on their masters for religious instruction. Second, the law neither recognized nor protected slave marriages. Third, the law allegedly allowed a master almost unlimited authority to control his bondsmen. New School belief in the extent of human depravity heightened the impact of these features.

New School adherents held that all persons would inexcusably persist in sinful lives until they received the Gospel and embraced true

Christianity. Slaves were no exception. Despite their unfortunate condition, they were still capable of obeying God's law of benevolence and therefore would be judged according to His exacting standards of justice. Antislavery writers held that Southern laws effectively prevented masters from teaching their slaves to read and write. Without the ability to read, slaves could not receive God's scriptural revelation by themselves and depended on their masters for religious instruction. Men such as Charles Beecher complained that this practice resembled the "Papist" customs. Thus, the law even allowed a master to deny salvation to his bondsmen by refusing religious instruction.[8]

Antislavery writers argued that even a master who provided religious instruction to his servants might distort the teachings of Christ for his own purposes. Whenever slaves were instructed in religion, they were told of their duties to their masters. Harriet Beecher Stowe asserted that the slaves were taught

> that his master's authority over him, and property in him . . . is recognised [*sic*] and sustained by the tremendous authority of God himself. He [the slave] is told that his master is God's overseer; that he owes him a blind, unconditional, unlimited submission. He is taught that it is God's will that he should have nothing but labor and poverty in this world; and that, if he frets and grumbles at this, he will get nothing by it in this life, and be sent to hell forever in the next.
>
> Furthermore, the slave is taught that to endeavour to evade his master by running away, or to shelter or harbour a slave who has run away, are sins which will expose him to the wrath of that omniscient Being whose eyes are in every place.

She claimed that under these circumstances blacks not only received a distorted version of Christianity but that many slaves angrily rejected religion altogether.[9]

The nonrecognition of slave marriages provided further evidence of slavery's allegedly immoral effects. The law allowed slaveholders to break apart marriages for their own convenience, and abolitionists assumed that this was a frequent occurrence. Certainly the prospects of separating husbands from their wives seemed cruel enough. Antislavery writers suggested that the practice had even worse effects by encouraging licentious behavior among the blacks and by weakening family ties. Henry Ward Beecher assumed that without the ability to form lasting relationships slaves would be unfaithful to their spouses. "At the South adultery among slaves is not held to be reason for church discipline. . . . Do you know that at the South in marrying slaves the minister leaves out the words, 'What God has joined together let no man put asunder?'

It must be left out, for perhaps in a few weeks the husband will be separated from the wife, and sent to another wife, and if he is a member of the church it does not hurt his standing; and then another and another, till perhaps he may have twenty wives, and still his letter of recommendation from one church to another is as good as ever." His sister, Harriet Beecher Stowe, also reported that a slave marriage was merely a "temporary union of interest, profit, or pleasure, formed without reflection, and dissolved without the slightest idea of guilt."[10]

To the New School Calvinists, chattel slavery exhibited its most offensive features by interfering with the religious development of the slaves. Because New School adherents believed that without Christian education all humans would remain sinful, the slave system appeared to condemn slaves to lives of sin. Failure to recognize slave marriages further contributed to the moral depravation of the slaves. The most important manifestation of benevolence was in the salvation of souls, for God's glory and man's happiness. These New School Calvinists believed that the slave system allowed an owner to frustrate God's plan of salvation for the sake of his own material gain. Charles Beecher complained of the enormous iniquity of this system with his remark that "if the slaves have souls; if they are in danger of eternal destruction; . . . how great the guilt of that system which thus imperils their salvation—a system which, not content with stripping them of all their rights here, tends directly to defeat their last hope of happiness hereafter."[11]

Abolitionists argued that laws giving the masters tyrannical power over their bondsmen were necessary to maintain control over the slaves. Because this system deprived blacks of their liberties, it became necessary to deprive the slave of any means of redress for unjust treatment. As one Northern minister, E. P. Barrows, commented, "Slaves being in the most absolute sense the property of their masters, it is necessary that the latter should have unlimited control over them; otherwise they would cease to be slaves. It would be an insufferable annoyance that these 'personal chattels' should speak, and complain of the hard treatment to which they might happen to be subjected. . . . Resistance to their owners, on the part of these 'personal Chattels' must by no means be tolerated." Barrows believed that cruelty and oppressive measures were the natural and predictable results of slavery, not unfortunate accidents. The system itself created new injustices in order to maintain control over the slave population.[12]

Conservative Northern clergy, Old School and many New School, also condemned any practice that might prejudice the slaves' spiritual welfare or cruelty by the masters. Furthermore, they considered it to be an undesirable institution, which all good Christians ought to strive to remove. In spite of these sentiments, they considered injustices to be abuses of the system, which did not mean that slavery, considered in itself, was sinful. They believed a distinction existed between the evil effects of slavery and the institution itself. Where slavery existed without these injustices, no sin occurred.[13]

To a greater extent than Old School Calvinists, New School Calvinists denied the distinctions between the effects of slavery and slavery in itself. As with alcohol, they reasoned that what produced evil consequences must be evil in its nature, or *malum in se*.[14] The natural and foreseeable effects of the slave system would be injustice, cruelty, and irreparable damage to the slaves' temporal and spiritual welfare. Any benevolent action toward the slave occurred in spite of the system. As Barrows commented, "The system of slavery, then, being evil in all its tendencies, is SINFUL." Later he argued that "the system of slavery is directly opposed to the fundamental law of love . . . and that it is evil in all its tendencies. For each and all of these reasons it is SINFUL."[15]

To be sure, New School Calvinists reached this position slowly and hesitantly, and the idea of slavery as *malum in se* did not receive unanimous acceptance. They retained a sufficient emphasis on sin and depravity to cause them to accept the necessity of coercive institutions. Lyman Beecher's well-known vacillations at Lane Seminary led to the withdrawal of Theodore Weld and other students. The American Home Missionary Society endeavored to avoid open conflict by discretely declining to appoint slaveholders as missionaries but without establishing an official policy. Until 1857, the New School Presbyterian General Assembly carefully qualified its condemnations of slavery to avoid accusations of personal guilt. Their reluctance to condemn slavery as inherently sinful caused James G. Birney to include New School Presbyterians in his complaint that American churches were a "bulwark of slavery."[16]

As numbers of New School Calvinists concluded that slavery was intrinsically sinful, they demanded its immediate abolition. If slavery was a misfortune, then it might be eliminated gradually. As a sin, however, it ought to be abandoned without delay. The transgressor should recognize his offenses and desist immediately.

Most antislavery writers were sufficiently realistic to understand that slavery would not be abandoned quickly. This seeming discrepancy between their demands and expectations caused some confusion about the meaning of "immediatism." It can be understood best as a statement of principles rather than as a plan of action. Even though slavery would not disappear suddenly, immediatists held that it was a sin, which ought to be renounced without delay. The duty of the Christian was to give witness against the sin.[17]

At the same time, New School abolitionists began to describe slavery as uniformly oppressive. Their assumption that the system of slavery was as cruel as it could be demonstrates how the New School believed that unregenerate humanity was depraved in the most frightful sense of the word. Certainly the evils of slavery were real enough. Even under the best conditions, slaves led a difficult life, and a harsh master could make life quite miserable for his bondsmen. Nonetheless, some antislavery writers employed the same strident rhetoric that appeared in anti-Catholic and temperance literature. Because the slave system was cruel, abolitionists assumed that it was as cruel as it could be. Because masters exploited their bondsmen, these writers assumed that planters extracted the last ounce of toil the workers could produce. They portrayed life on the plantation as one of unremitting drudgery, privation, and beatings.[18]

This horrid picture of slavery was consistent with the New School's concept of human depravity. According to their theories, the unregenerate person adhered to the selfish principle at the expense of every other good. Any seemingly moral behavior was motivated entirely by the expectation of rewards and punishments. Furthermore, people could accustom themselves to cruelties habitually practiced, as custom seared the conscience and made people insensible to their brutality. Not all antislavery writers held that slavery was uniformly brutal, but some used the most extravagant rhetoric. Soon the distinction between slavery considered in itself and its abuses became irrelevant. "The system cannot be abused. Its very fundamental principle includes every infamy which can insult manhood or degrade a man!" Henry Ward Beecher complained. "Why to talk of the *abuse* of a system which has this for its elementary principle, is as wild as it would be to talk of the abuse of robbery, the abuse of murder, the abuse of adultery!"[19]

Theodore Weld demonstrated his conviction that the greatest cruelties could be expected from slaveholders because of human nature. His two major works, *American Slavery as It Is* and *Slavery and the Internal Slave Trade*, catalogued incessant barbarities as typical of the slave system. With his wife's assistance, Weld combed through thousands of publications in an enormous search for evidence to support his charges of beatings and mutilations. Normally, he used advertisements for runaways that described injured or disfigured slaves. He insisted that these wounds were not accidents, but the product of deliberate acts by the masters.[20]

He supported this assertion by referring to the laws of human nature, particularly with regard to men's lust for power. He explained why planters routinely treated their slaves worse than beasts:

> We repeat it, SLAVEHOLDERS TREAT THEIR SLAVES WORSE THAN THEY DO THEIR BRUTES. Whoever heard of cows or sheep being deliberately tied up and beaten and lacerated till they died? or horses coolly tortured by the hour, till mangled flesh, . . . or of hounds stretched and made fast at full length, flayed with whips, red pepper rubbed into their bleeding gashes, and hot brine dashed on to aggravate the torture? Yet just such forms and degrees of torture are *daily* perpetrated upon the slaves. Now no man that knows human nature will marvel at this. Though great cruelties have always been inflicted by men upon brutes, yet incomparably the most horrid ever perpetrated, have been those of men upon *their own species*. . . . Every reflecting mind perceives that when men hold *human beings* as *property*, they must, from the nature of the case, treat them worse than they treat their horses and oxen. It is impossible for *cattle* to excite in men such tempests of fury as men excite in each other. . . .
>
> The greatest provocation to human nature is *opposition to its will*. If a man's will be resisted by one far *below* him, the provocation is vastly greater, than when it is resisted by an acknowledged superior. . . . The idea of *property* having a will, and that too in opposition to the will of its *owner*, and counteracting it, is a stimulant of terrible power to the most relentless human passions, and from the nature of slavery, and the constitution of the human mind, this fierce stimulant must, with various degrees of strength, act upon slave holders almost without ceasing.

Thus, Weld reasoned that barbarities and nothing else could be expected from the slave system.[21]

Weld also insisted that blacks faced the greed of a master determined to make the greatest possible profit at the expense of his bondsmen.

> To increase the master's wealth, the slave is driven night and day; and since his necessary supplies of food, clothing, and shelter are to be subtracted from the master's gains, they are dispensed with the most niggardly hand. Every thread that can be spared from his back, every grain of corn from his mouth, and every item of convenience from his miserable hut, are rigorously withheld. In short there is not a jot or tittle of the slave's comforts which can escape the all-grasping clutch of avarice. To describe plantation slavery in a single sentence, it is that system which degrades man not into property merely, but into an inferior species of property, whose worth consists in its fitness to procure that which is esteemed a far higher species of property—MONEY.

To extract the utmost labor from the slaves under these conditions, planters relied on the brutal exertions of the overseer, whom Weld described in the most explicit terms:

> An overseer must be the lowest of all abjects [*sic*], consenting to be loathed and detested by the master who employs him; and at the same time he must be the most callous of all reprobates, in order to inflict tortures, from the sight of which the planter himself sometimes recoils with horror. He must find his supreme delight in human torture; groans must be his music, and the writhings of agony his realization of bliss. He must be that unspeakably vile thing, a scullion of avarice, wielding the clotted lash for another's wealth . . . Such is the monster to whose unlimited control the planter commits his hundreds of slaves. One injunction only is laid upon him, and that is, to make the largest crops possible.

Once again, Weld held that there was no limit to human iniquity.[22]

In another example, he provided an account of slaves in Albemarle and Fauquier counties of Virginia. According to his impeccable sources, slaves' huts were drafty structures, without floors, heated only by small fireplaces. The inhabitants spent the winters under these conditions with only one or two cotton blankets each and poor, if any, bedding. Even worse, they were compelled to go without footwear through the Virginia winters or at best had only cheap shoes and no stockings. Weld did not explain how the slaves avoided frostbite in the Virginia winter.[23]

Accusations of rampant sexual abuse of female slaves were another common feature of antislavery literature. Writers asserted that illicit sexual relations between masters and female slaves were a common occurrence, often with the woman being coerced into the relationship.[24]

George Bourne told a dubious story about lust and rapacity in the old South. Near Charlottesville, Virginia, a "whitewashing" scheme had been developed to "diabolical perfection." A man began his business by acquiring female slaves of mixed or nearly white ancestry. Then he, his sons, or his overseer would force themselves on the women in order to produce even whiter children. The process continued until the owner had almost pure white slaves, who could be sold into Southern brothels. According to Bourne this entire enterprise operated as a respectable business, in full public view, without the least censure.[25]

Bourne's acknowledged role in the fabrication of Maria Monk's *Awful Disclosures* did not appear to diminish his credibility as an abolitionist. In 1841, four years after Maria Monk had sued Bourne for her share of the profits from the sale of her *Awful Disclosures*, Weld cited Bourne as a reliable witness on the condition of slaves, quoting from Bourne's publications. Weld even used Bourne's position as editor of the scurrilously anti-Catholic *Protestant Vindicator* as evidence of his veracity.[26]

Uncle Tom's Cabin, the most powerful and most popular antislavery work of that era, also reflected the religious assumptions of the New School. Harriet Beecher Stowe was far more observant and sophisticated than Weld or Bourne. She understood that the conditions of slaves varied throughout the South. Compared to Weld's, most of her characters appear believable. Still, the work shows the influence of Lyman Beecher on his daughter.

Prior to the publication of *Uncle Tom's Cabin*, Harriet Beecher Stowe had already achieved a respectable standing for her contributions to periodical literature, especially *Godey's Magazine and Ladies Book*. As she developed a stronger religious interest during the 1840s, she also contributed articles to the *New York Evangelist*. Indeed, the years leading to the production of her most famous novel were characterized by a steadily increasing commitment to New England Calvinism. Her status as the daughter and wife of two leading New School ministers assured that religion would be a critical factor in her life. Then, during the mid-1840s, she experienced a second conversion, as she came to feel her full dependence on God. She would later assert that many of the inspirations for the novel came to her while attending church.[27]

The principal white characters of the novel can be divided into Christians and non-Christians. Christians detest slavery, and non-Christians cannot be trusted to hold human property. The slaveholders of her book vary in their outward appearance and in the treatment of their bondsmen. The one consistency is that all the non-Christian slaveholders display the sense of selfishness that dominates the unregenerate heart.

Stowe did not believe that merely owning a slave excluded a person from the Christian community. Nevertheless, a genuine Christian must make every effort to bring about the end of Southern servitude. Of the characters in her book, Mrs. Shelby, little George Shelby, and Eva St. Clare all exemplify the Christian virtues. They are unabashedly pious, honest, and benevolent. All express their detestation of slavery and do their best either to assist or else free as many slaves as they can. Stowe later described Augustine St. Clare as the type of person who might someday provide the leadership within the South to end slavery. Although he is not at first an avowed Christian, he does express a greater concern for his fellow men than nominal Christians do. He is a naturally indulgent and democratic person who understands the injustice of the slave system. At the end of his life, he openly embraces Christianity.[28]

Among the non-Christian characters, George Shelby appears to be

Harriet Beecher Stowe. Courtesy of the Library of Congress

a humane and gentle slaveholder. He provides for the physical welfare of his bondsmen and grants them a reasonable degree of freedom. Yet that appearance is deceptive. George Shelby's humanity is motivated by a desire to secure the approbation of his wife and other people. When his virtue is tested, he fails. He indulges in speculation. After losing his money, he resists his wife's entreaties to part with his physical possessions in order to pay his creditors. Instead he sells Tom, his most faithful servant, down the river. He thinks that he is being humane merely because he did not sell Eliza for presumably immoral uses. Later in the story, he still refuses to make the sacrifices necessary to redeem Tom. When Mrs. Shelby says that she can raise some money by teaching music, he will not allow her to work. His vanity proves to be stronger than his concern for his faithful servant. He even suggests that Aunt Chloe, Tom's wife, should find another husband, thus encouraging adultery among his servants. He is willing to place his wealth and pride above the spiritual welfare of his servants.[29]

Presumably, Marie St. Clare is a more typical example of a self-indulgent slaveholder. She is a chronic hypochondriac who is so obsessed with her own concerns that she is blind to the needs and feelings of other people. Because of her inexhaustible self-pity, she cannot understand how she abuses her servants. She even allows one child to die because of her refusal to purchase milk, and she does not understand why it is wrong to beat slaves or to break up families. She simply cannot recognize the humanity of her bondsmen. Only her natural indolence restrains her despotism toward her servants.[30]

Whereas Marie St. Clare's laziness tempers her treatment of her servants, nothing restrains the rapacity of Simon Legree. Stowe used him to represent the epitome of human depravity. Early in life, Legree had rejected the pious influences of his family. As a plantation owner he is motivated solely by greed and passion. He values his slaves as nothing more than a means to make money and works them to death for the sake of his own profit. Yet even his greed cannot restrain his passion for power. When Tom defies his will, Legree savagely beats the old man to death. Like the *Hôtel Dieu* convent, Simon Legree's plantation represents the bottomless abyss of human depravity.[31]

Unlike Weld, Stowe did not contend that Legree was a typical slaveholder. Instead, she argued that the system was horrid because it allowed people like Marie St. Clare or Simon Legree to claim title to other human beings. Selfish people like these existed in all parts of the nation. In the South, however, these unregenerates were allowed to control the lives of other people. Stowe defended the realism of her portraits by pointing to Northern examples of such people.[32]

Although the white characters of the novel can be divided into Christians and non-Christians, the blacks are more complicated. Most of them contain the potential for becoming exemplary Christians, but their spiritual development is stifled by the institution of slavery. Either they are left in ignorance of the Gospel or they have become so embittered by their experiences that they reject religion. Although Stowe describes their plight with evident sympathy, she cannot exclude the possibility that these men and women are damnable sinners who will go to hell.

Like her readers, Stowe had been raised to believe that God would judge all people according to His exacting standards of justice. All humans, including slaves, were expected to adhere to God's rule of benevolence, and God would treat them accordingly. Moreover, Nathaniel William Taylor had taught that God could not make exceptions to His law without destroying His moral government. Early in their lives, the Beecher children had learned the fearful consequences of this doctrine when Catherine Beecher's much-beloved fiancé drowned while in an unconverted state. Despite a universal fondness for the young man, the family assumed that he would probably be condemned to perdition. Within a few years after publication of the novel, Harriet Beecher Stowe would be forced to confront the same agony following the drowning of her own son before an unmistakable conversion experience.[33] If God could be so severe with Catherine's fiancé or Harriet's son, then Harriet could not assume that He would forgive the transgressions of her black characters.

With the benefit of hindsight, the historian can see traces of Stowe's ambivalence toward her father's religion that eventually led her to the Episcopal Church. During the 1850s, she was a Congregationalist in good standing, and her husband was a leading New School minister and professor at Andover. Ten years later, following the Civil War and the death of her son Henry, Stowe entered the Episcopal Church, in part because of her doubts about the exacting standards of God's justice.

According to God's law, these slaves were sinners, but their circumstances made them objects of pity rather than condemnation. Topsy is the most obvious victim of moral neglect. She has been raised without any affection or any religious instruction. Consequently, she turns to theft and other sins. In time, little Eva's love and purity redeem Topsy from a life of iniquity. There are other examples of spiritual desolation. George Harris, Eliza's husband, angrily rejects Christianity because of the wrongs practiced on him. The attitude is understandable but fatal to his soul. Dinah turns to drink after slavery causes the death of her baby. She is surprised to learn about the Gospel. Quimbo and Sambo represent the potential of all slaves to change their lives. Although their behavior is deplorable throughout most of the book, they are converted after the inspiring sacrifice of Uncle Tom.

Stowe's depiction of Tom reflects her regard for Samuel Hopkins's concept of disinterested benevolence, or a willingness to sacrifice one's own welfare for a greater good. Her appreciation of this aspect of Hopkins would later be incorporated into her highly fictionalized account of his life, *The Minister's Wooing*. In this later novel, the principal characters at some time renounce some personal desires for the sake of a greater benevolence. Yet even her fictionalized Samuel Hopkins did not approach the level of self-sacrifice displayed by Uncle Tom.[34]

Of all the characters, Tom embodies the virtues of Christianity to the greatest extent imaginable. In recent years, the term "Uncle Tom" has acquired a derisive connotation because of his forbearance under continued injustice, but that was not Stowe's intention in creating him. On two separate occasions Tom refuses opportunities to escape, because of the greater good of the community. He literally allows himself to be sold down the river because he realizes that only his sale can prevent the break up of the Shelby plantation. (Stowe calls this a "manly disinterestedness.")[35] Later, he declines a chance to escape from Simon Legree, because he believes that he can lead other souls to salvation. Although he is willing to sacrifice his own welfare, he will not surrender his principles to the slave system. He courageously refuses to obey Legree's orders to abuse other servants, and he dies rather than reveal the secret of the runaways. Throughout the novel, he adheres to his principles with an absolute consistency.

Northern non-abolitionists were distressed by the disparaging characterizations of slavery by people such as Weld or Stowe, because the conservatives believed that abolitionist literature was unjust to Southerners and because they feared that harsh denunciations of slaveholders only delayed emancipation of African Americans. Conservative Northerners, who included many New School and virtually all Old School Calvinists, did not approve of slavery, but they considered the immediatists to be extremists. Nathan L. Rice and the editors of the *New York Observer* argued that stories of cruelty were atypical and that many Southerners were genuinely concerned with the welfare for their bondsmen. Rice cited the laws of Southern states that provided for removing a slave from a master convicted of cruelty. The *Observer* repeatedly carried accounts of Southerners who desired to see an end to slavery and who made a sincere effort to take care of their bondsmen. They believed that the way to eliminate slavery was to promote the Gospel among Southerners so that masters would emancipate their slaves without coercion. They believed that harsh rhetoric only delayed emancipation because slaveholders would refuse to listen to any antislavery pleadings.[36]

Conservative Northerners also rejected the description of slavery as *malum in se* because the Bible suggested that slavery was a legitimate relationship if masters and servants remembered that all were brothers in Christ, despite differences in earthly callings. Slavery had existed among the ancient Israelites, without God's disapproval. Leviticus 25:39-46 had advised Israelites to make heathens into slaves. Commenting on slavery in the Roman Empire, Paul had emphasized mutual obligations for the servants and masters. Servants were to obey their masters, and masters were advised to "give unto your servants that which is just and equal; knowing that ye also have a Master in heaven." (Colossians 4: 1). Conservatives were reluctant to depart from Scripture or to become wise above what is written.[37]

Antislavery writers, therefore, developed a biblical argument against slavery. Like the biblical temperance argument, these arguments demonstrated a commitment to fixed and immutable moral truths, which existed independently of circumstances. Because of the nineteenth-century attitudes toward the Bible, the scriptural slavery arguments were among the most important parts of the slavery debates within the Protestant community.

Antislavery writers had another reason for insisting that Scripture offered no support for involuntary servitude. Having concluded that slaveholding was a violation of God's law, they could not allow the Word of God to sanction the practice without questioning Scripture. Any biblical apologies for slavery would furnish new arguments to Deists, atheists, and other skeptics. George B. Cheever explained:

> It is impossible to believe an institution that grows out of theft, cruelty, and murder, and perpetuates all those iniquities, . . . to have come down from God. . . . If the moral delinquencies of the Koran and the book of the Mormons are admitted to be insuperable objections against any supposition of those books being from God, so as to take away all obligation upon any person even to examine their claims, would not the sanction of human slavery, . . . much rather release a man from any such obligation? Let a man know what slavery is . . . and then tell him that *such as it is*, it is supported and commanded in this book, and would he not have reason to say, "This being the case, I am not bound to examine any farther. I know that this book can not be from God?"

Conservative ministers complained that Cheever, and those like him, were reaching their conclusions before they began to study Scripture, thus placing their own judgment above revelation.[38]

Beginning with Samuel Hopkins, the earliest efforts to demonstrate the incompatibility of slavery with Scripture were based on the law of love. The Bible taught the principles of benevolence throughout its contents. Jesus enjoined His disciples to "love thy neighbor as thyself." Slavery as a system of exploitation contradicted this rule of love, and hence benevolence.

Although these assertions were plausible, they did not refute specific scriptural references to slavery, such as Leviticus 25 or Paul's epistles. Abolitionists responded to these passages with a series of arguments designed to show that the Bible was a decidedly antislavery work. Theodore Weld, Angela Grimké, Albert Barnes, George Bourne, and Cheever insisted that a careful reading of Scripture would support the abolitionists' position. They claimed that Moses decided that he could not abolish slavery outright, so he instituted restrictions that would make the institution impractical. Terms of servitude for Jews and gentiles were allegedly restricted to seven years. All bondsmen were to be freed every fifty years, in the year of the Jubilee. Christian abolitionists insisted that these and other restrictions had effectively eliminated slavery in Palestine by the first-century A.D. Christ did not speak against slavery because it did not exist in His community. Abolitionists dismissed the argument of Moses Stuart and other scholars that these restrictions applied only to Hebrew bondsmen, not to heathen captives, and that the purpose of the passages in Leviticus was to protect the Israelites by encouraging them to exploit gentile tribes.[39]

Paul's letters presented a more difficult problem. His epistles to the Ephesians and Colossians contained specific instructions to bondsmen to obey their masters, thus appearing to condone the master-slave relationship. Paul even had persuaded the errant servant, Onesimus, to return to his master, Philemon. Albert Barnes argued that merely prescribing duties of master and slave did not imply an approval of the relationship itself. The apostles had merely instructed people on how to behave until that relationship could be dissolved. Barnes conceded that amid their denunciations of other practices, Paul and the other disciples had not condemned slavery. He suggested that, while the apostles recognized the iniquity of slavery, they worked to abolish it by inculcating general principles of morality. To preach directly against slavery would have only created hostility against Christianity.[40]

Cheever was not satisfied with Barnes's scriptural analysis. He conducted his own biblical research and concluded that the key passages in the New Testament were translated incorrectly. The Biblical writers translated the Hebrew word for a hired servant into the Greek word *doulous*, which meant a bound servant. Cheever argued that the original intention of the writers was to refer to a hired servant. Therefore, any New Testament discussions of servitude applied only to a voluntary relationship between two parties. He thus asserted that the New Testament provided no justification for slavery.[41]

One more Scripture passage contributed to the debate on slavery. Deuteronomy 23:15-16 stated: "Thou shalt not deliver unto his master the servant which is escaped from his master unto thee; He shall dwell with thee, even among you, in that place which he shall choose in one of thy gates, where it liketh him best: thou shalt not oppress him." Conservatives, including Moses Stuart, interpreted this passage to mean that slaves escaping to Israel from heathen lands would not be returned to their masters. Antislavery writers insisted that this passage forbade the return of any fugitive slave for any reason.[42]

In arguing that Scripture did not sanction slavery, these abolitionists alienated possible supporters. Conservatives believed that the use of scriptural antislavery arguments resembled the biblical temperance arguments in misinterpreting Scripture. Like many other New School Calvinists, Leonard Bacon wished to see an end to slavery, but he could not accept scriptural arguments that slavery was intrinsically sinful. He complained that the "violence put upon the sacred records by High Churchmen, or by Universalists, does not exceed the violence with which these men . . . torture the Scriptures into saying that which the antislavery theory requires them to say." Yet for those men who considered slavery to be intrinsically sinful, the logic of their beliefs left them little choice but to employ the Bible against slavery. If slavery violated fixed and immutable moral principles, then the Bible could not appear to sanction the institution.[43]

Because these men and women considered slavery to be sinful, they could not accept slaveholders as fellow Christians. Therefore, abolitionists struggled to terminate any pretense of Christian fellowship with slaveholders. Within both the New School Presbyterian and the Congregational Churches, abolitionists endeavored to pass resolutions declaring slavery a sin. To the participants, these ecclesiastical battles against slavery rivaled the political battles against slavery in importance. By giving witness against the sin of slavery, militant antislavery activists expected to perform their duty as Christians.[44]

Yet, for all of their efforts, abolitionists failed to make any progress among Southerners. After 1835, every effort to promote their doctrines in the South met the most violent opposition, both legal and extralegal. Southerners burned abolitionist literature, and mobs attacked men for mere possession of antislavery material. State legislatures enacted laws that prohibited antislavery agitation. These repressive measures were justified as necessary to prevent slaves from revolting.[45] Abolitionists also faced mob violence in the North, often from leading members of the community or "gentlemen of property and standing."[46] Eventually, this violence subsided in the North, while Southerners tightened their restrictions on freedom of discussion.

To the New School Calvinists, it appeared that the Southerners feared the truthfulness of their arguments. Such a perception fit into their belief that error or iniquity could not survive the light of truth. "Based on injustice and oppression, it [slavery] 'hates the light, neither comes to the light, lest its deeds should be reproved.' . . . Hence, every attempt in the slave-holding states to expose, with manly plainness, the wickedness of the whole system of slavery is perilous in the extreme."[47] By developing the issue of civil liberties, antislavery writers were able to appeal to those Americans who did not necessarily sympathize with blacks. They could tell Northern whites that their own liberties were threatened by Southern slavery.[48]

Despite the abolitionists' efforts, the institution of slavery continued to expand. Their impatience with the South increased accordingly. In time they began to see the growth of slavery as the result of a concerted effort by the Southern planters and their Northern sympathizers to perpetuate or extend this system of iniquity. Abolitionists labeled their opposition the "slave power," and called their efforts the "slave power conspiracy." Not only Congregationalists and Presbyterians, but even men such as the Unitarian Theodore Parker, adopted this terminology.[49]

New School Calvinists believed that a system of iniquity would desire to extend its dominion. Once again, Southerners acted in a way that seemed to confirm the warnings that a slave power conspiracy existed. From the annexation of Texas to the Dred Scott decision, Southern actions could be interpreted as part of a design to enhance the power of slavery at the expense of northern freedom. The annexation of Texas, the Mexican War, the Fugitive Slave Act, the Kansas-Nebraska Act, and the Dred Scott decision all seemed to provide evidence of the dangerous influence of the "slave power." Each of these issues had a separate history, yet men who accepted the idea of a slave power conspiracy perceived a pattern of Southern machinations.

The Fugitive Slave Act of 1850 appeared as a singularly onerous demand of the slave power, for it required Northerners to participate in the iniquity of slavery. This law apparently contradicted the injunctions of Deuteronomy 23:15-16, which was interpreted as forbidding the return of any fugitive slave for any reason whatsoever. The actual number of fugitive slaves was less important than the fact that abolitionists perceived that a federal law required the violation of God's law. Charles Beecher expressed the opinion that a law that contradicted values of right and wrong nullified the Christian's duty to submit to the powers that be. "A law which does me some injury is one thing. A law which makes me do wrong is another. The first I may submit to while seeking its repeal. To the latter I must not give place by subjection, no, not for an hour. I must resist unto blood, striving against sin." When combined with the dramatic instances of escaped slaves being returned to servitude, the act aroused Northern emotions as few other issues had done.[50]

Moses Stuart voiced a plea for submission to the law. Writing in defense of his friend Daniel Webster, Stuart expressed his long held views regarding Scripture and slavery. He argued that as slavery was not explicitly condemned in the Bible, men were not justified in placing their own judgment above the law. Moreover, he insisted that Deuteronomy 23 was intended to apply to slaves of heathens escaping into ancient Israel only. Governments were ordained by God and men had a duty to obey the rightful authority. For his efforts he received a torrent of abuse, with people questioning his intelligence, piety, and scholarship.[51]

After the passage of the Fugitive Slave Act, additional Southern political victories seemed only to confirm the threat of the slave power conspiracy. The passage of the Kansas-Nebraska Act, the subsequent violence in Kansas, and the Dred Scott decision all contributed to the strident anti-Southern rhetoric of the 1850s. Discussing the feuding in Kansas, Henry Ward Beecher explained how all attempts at compromise with iniquity only encouraged aggression. "The Compromise of 1820—. . . and like all compromises since the world began, between unscrupulous Power and timid Liberty—was but a device of Knavery for taking a breath. The peace always promised for such concession is a peace for repairing damages, for forging arms, and for arraying new influences and implements." Once he had framed the issue in terms of right versus wrong, Beecher removed all basis for compromise and accommodation.[52] William Goodell echoed Beecher's sentiments on the Kansas-Nebraska Act with a comment that the new law meant that "there is to be no toleration of freedom, if slavery prevails; and no toleration of slavery if freedom prevails."[53]

As in other reform activities, the New School antislavery efforts illuminate the nature of their ideology. Even though not all New School adherents were militant abolitionists, their theology proved to be more conducive to abolitionism than did Old School Calvinism. Once New School Calvinists embraced militant abolitionism, they applied their religious principles with their usual vigor. Fully believing in the depravity of unregenerate humanity, they credited the most heinous offenses to slaveholders. Because they argued that slavery violated unchangeable moral laws, they proposed scriptural antislavery arguments that resembled the scriptural temperance arguments. Their demands for immediate abolition demonstrates their attitude that there could be no compromise between righteousness and iniquity. Moreover, their belief in men's ability to recognize truths is evident in their assertions that the slave system must necessarily suppress free inquiry in order to survive. Thus, the crusade against slavery became an uncompromising struggle between good and evil.

Because the New School abolitionists campaigned courageously against an entrenched social injustice, it is easy to perceive within them twentieth-century ideas of social reform. Nevertheless, an examination of their benevolent organizations demonstrates the limitations of this approach. Although laboring to improve the lives of other humans, they operated within a framework that was derived from their religion, not twentieth-century ideas of reform.

9

Benevolence, the Social Order, and the Kingdom of God

New School Calvinists were reformers in a limited sense of the word. They wished to remove perceived evils and to promote their religious values, but they did not advocate a fundamental restructuring of Northern society for social or economic objectives. To the extent that they expressed any vision of an ideal society, they looked forward to the triumph of God's church during the millennium. Otherwise, they were satisfied with American society and its capitalist economy.

To be sure, New School adherents were sympathetic to their less-fortunate brethren, both in the United States and abroad. Many New School adherents worked tirelessly and generously in their benevolent organizations. Nevertheless, they believed that true charity was a moral force rather than material assistance. They exhibited an attitude that Henry May has described as one of complacency, especially in perceiving poverty as a result of attitudes by the poor.[1]

The voluntary benevolent associations help us to understand New School attitudes toward charity and benevolence. These were societies organized outside of the formal church structure for specific purposes. They were governed by boards of directors, who could fill vacancies within their own ranks. Routine business was managed by one or more permanent employees. Local auxiliaries and branch societies provided money and carried the societies' business to large portions of the population. Although they remained outside of the churches, these societies maintained friendly relations with the Presbyterian and Congregational communities.

During the antebellum, era six organizations dominated the benevolent activities within the Presbyterian and Congregational communities. These were the American Bible Society (ABS, founded in 1816),

Table 1. Monetary Receipts of the Major Benevolent Organizations

	Benevolent Organization						
Year	ABCFM	AHMS	AES	ATS	ASSU	ABS	NYAICP
1815	24,860	...	...	...	...	...	...
1820	90,670	...	13,490	...	...	41,361	...
1825	55,744	...	19,389[a]	...	9,853	44,833	...
1830	87,019	48,124	41,200	60,210	70,521	143,449	...
1835	163,340	101,565	90,141	92,307	92,347	98,306	...
1840	241,691	85,413	74,620	117,596	85,249	94,880	...
1845	255,112	125,124	37,529	152,376	70,713[a]	159,738	27,779
1850	251,862	150,940	21,624	308,266	207,764	284,459	25,807
1855	310,427	193,548	24,952	413,173	184,277[a]	346,767	95,018
1860	429,799	185,216	23,738	344,602	234,436	435,956	40,565

Note: This table illustrates the relative size and importance of the various benevolent societies. Gross receipts provide one measure of the level of activity of each society. The size of their revenues indicates that, by nineteenth-century standards, these were truly large-scale operations. Receipts for the ABCFM, the AHMS, and the AES consisted almost entirely of donations, while the receipts for the ATS, the ASSU, and the ABS reflected both donations and sales. Except for the ABS, the figures are derived from the organizations' annual reports (the AHMS and the ATS contained summary charts; figures for other societies were extracted from each year's reports.) The figures for the ABS came from William Strickland's *History of the American Bible Society*, p. 358. Ellipses points (...) indicate that data are not available because the date is prior to the formation of that society. Abbreviations are defined in the text.

[a]Figures for year not available, so figures for the following year are substituted.

the American Sunday School Union (ASSU, 1824), the American Tract Society (ATS, 1825), the American Education Society (AES, 1815), the American Home Missionary Society (AHMS, 1826), and the American Board of Commissioners for Foreign Missions (ABCFM, 1809).[2] Another benevolent organization, the New York Association for Improving the Condition of the Poor (NYAICP, 1843) is also included in this chapter because it was one of the few organizations that dealt directly with the problems of urban poverty. One measure of their level of activity, the total monetary receipts, is shown in Table 1. The table demonstrates that, by contemporary standards, these were substantial organizations.

One of the most truly ecumenical organizations, the American Bible Society, operated for the single purpose of distributing Scripture as widely as possible. Local societies disseminated Bibles and raised money for the national organization. Because virtually all Protestants agreed with these goals, the society received widespread support, and its achievements were impressive. In time, the Bible Society began distributing the Bible in foreign lands and producing its own translations. By 1854, the Bible Society had assisted in the production of the Bible in approximately one hundred thirty eight different languages.[3]

While the Bible Society concentrated on distributing copies of Scripture, the American Tract Society produced its own body of evangelical literature. The tracts published by this society were intended to be easily readable discussions of evangelical truths. The society's directors enthusiastically expressed the hope that the "silent unseen influence of tracts" would reach and convert thousands of men and women who might otherwise remain beyond the reach of the Gospel. To ensure that its publications were acceptable to all Protestants, the Tract Society employed a committee with representatives from different Protestant denominations, but predominately Presbyterians and Congregationalists. In fact, an 1826 issue of the *Methodist Magazine* complained that the Methodists representatives were selected for the Tract Society without their knowledge or consent. The literature emphasized themes common to Protestants and avoided controversial issues, such as slavery. In 1858 the Tract Society withdrew publication of a tract on the duties of a master because of Southern objections that the work's silence on biblical sanctions for slavery implicitly condemned the institution.[4]

Another benevolent organization, the American Sunday School Union, also employed the printed word as a means of propagating evangelical truth. Its creators wanted to use Sunday schools to inculcate moral and religious truths in young people. To accomplish this objective, they encouraged the formation of Sunday schools by publishing advice to Sunday school teachers and by employing traveling agents. A more substantial portion of the Sunday School Union's efforts were devoted to producing a body of children's literature. These works were frequently combined into collections that would form a Sunday school library.[5]

The American Education Society existed to help pay for the education of potential ministers. A pious young man who wanted to enter the ministry could apply to the Education Society for assistance if he required money. The society provided a stipend, either as a loan or a grant. Although it concentrated on Presbyterian and Congregational candidates, the society did assist members of other denominations. Despite its comparatively small size, the Education Society played a substantial role in educating future clergy. The Education Society's 1846 annual report estimated that approximately one-third of the graduates of theological seminaries had received some aid from the organization or its affiliates.[6]

The American Home Missionary Society was the product of an agreement between Congregationalists and Presbyterians. Until 1826, the Presbyterians of northern New York had supported their home missions through the United Domestic Missionary Society. In that year, the Presbyterian organization joined with Congregationalist supporters to create the American Home Missionary Society. This organization supported clergy in sparsely populated western areas as well as in some eastern parishes. In keeping with the Congregationalist and Presbyterian tradition of maintaining a settled ministry, the Home Missionary Society provided a portion of a minister's salary, and the congregation provided the remainder.[7]

Like the other benevolent organizations, the Home Missionary Society tried to emphasize common themes and avoid controversial issues. In the case of chattel slavery, however, abolitionist members of the society wanted to pursue a more aggressive policy against slaveholders. Through the 1830s and early 1840s, the society's officers tried a variety of techniques to evade the issue. They would decline to appoint known slaveholders as missionaries but avoided asking whether prospective missionaries held slaves. As antislavery sentiment grew in the 1850s, however, the society adopted new rules against slavery and closed its missions in the Southern states.[8]

The grandest benevolent organization of all, the American Board of Commissioners for Foreign Missions, endeavored to hasten the advent of the millennium by promoting the conversion of the world. The foreign missionary organization was both the oldest and the largest of the six major benevolent organizations. In time, the organization supported missionaries in virtually all parts of the world, most notably Polynesia, China, India, and the Middle East. The board also supported missions to the North American Indians.[9]

In theory, the ABCFM sought to create a native ministry that could multiply the efforts of the few Americans. Rufus Anderson, who became secretary for the board in 1832, articulated a position that called for missionaries to focus their efforts on teaching a core of disciples the Gospel and then allowing these disciples to assume responsibility for the nascent churches. Missionaries were to move on once the native churches became self-sustaining. In practice, however, missionaries found themselves involved with the affairs of local churches. They asserted that instruction in English was essential to training of an educated native ministry. Even as the local churches grew in size, Americans assumed a greater supervisory role.[10]

Of all the benevolent efforts, foreign missions involved the greatest sacrifice, with little expectation of material rewards. Young men and women traveled to strange lands with foreign cultures to propagate the Gospel among non-Christians, usually leaving behind both the comforts of Western civilization and the support of their families. Historians who would attribute antebellum reform solely to a desire for social control underestimate the altruistic nature of missionary efforts.[11] Often their exertions reached truly heroic proportions as they faced disease and death in primitive cultures.

The New York Association for Improving the Condition of the Poor was a local organization, with a far more limited purpose than the other organizations. It aimed specifically at removing the conditions causing poverty within New York City, specifically the moral deficiencies of the poor.

Although the NYAICP exhibited less clerical involvement than did other benevolent organizations, its most important member can clearly be identified with the New School. Robert M. Hartley, the secretary and general agent of the association, exerted such a powerful influence on the organization that one historian has described the NYAICP as the "lengthened shadow of one man [Hartley]."[12] Hartley was a warm friend of Albert Barnes and had sided with the New School during the Presbyterian Schism.[13]

The NYAICP aimed to reduce poverty by a system of moral improvement for the impoverished. To this end, it attempted to link material assistance with moral reformation and to terminate any assistance to undeserving recipients. It tried to establish a system of home visitation to ensure that all it beneficiaries were adhering to its prescribe moral standards. In its annual reports, the NYAICP denounced indiscriminate alms giving for encouraging indolence among the poor.[14]

Within these benevolent societies, religious values might be propagated either through support of clergy or through other means, most notably the printed medium. This distinction created a clear division among the organizations discussed in this chapter. Foreign and home missionary societies and the Education Society existed to support clergy, while the other organizations existed to promote religious values in general. The former organizations were a controversial innovation, in that they performed work previously managed exclusively by the churches. Conservative Presbyterians complained that the lack of doctrinal standards or church discipline within a voluntary society enabled New School adherents to introduce erroneous theologies into the church. Consequently, the ABCFM, the Home Missionary Society, and the Education Society became another grievance of Old School Presbyterians.[15]

Moreover, the three organizations that supported clergy were exclusively Presbyterian and Congregationalist, while the others were interdenominational, at least in name. The extent of the interdenominational cooperation for the latter four societies could vary, depending on the preferences of the other denominations. Episcopalians, for example, were divided into high church and evangelical factions during the antebellum period. The evangelical Episcopalians embraced tract, Bible, and Sunday school organizations but not organizations that contributed directly to the support of clergy. The high-church proponents were decidedly less enthusiastic about interdenominational cooperation.[16]

The beliefs and attitudes of the New School Calvinists can be better understood by examining their actions within these societies. Although modern historians may include these organizations within the broad category of antebellum reform, these men and women did not conform to twentieth-century concepts of reform. They did not attempt to alter the essential fabric of Northern society. Rather, they emphasized the correction of individual failings through the propagation of religious values. With their adherence to objectively valid truths, they applied the same religious principles to both American and foreign cultures. Their fear of the potential depravity of the unregenerate remained strong, but they also believed that, once their religious values triumphed, the Kingdom of God would reign over the earth for the next millennium.

In light of their belief in the self-evident and objectively valid nature of truth, members of these benevolent societies initially expected that the mere presentation of this truth would move all but the most obstinate sinner. The Tract Society, in particular, frequently reported that its publications had changed the lives of readers. The society considered religious literature to be "amazing instruments of light."[17]

Their belief in self-evident truth is also apparent in their attitudes toward non-Western religions. Since these reformers considered the essential truths of religion to be discernible without divine revelation, they believed that even the heathen ought to be able to comprehend the basic principles of religion and morality. For this reason, advocates of foreign missions insisted that God would hold all non-Christians accountable for their failure to obey His law. A writer for the *Christian Spectator* explained: "We believe that the heathen, if they were so disposed, are perfectly able to discover the character of God from his works. . . . But this they do not; and, therefore, we believe that God accounts them guilty and deserving of everlasting punishment. They have so blinded their own minds to *sin*, that *they never will* obey the law of nature, . . . until they shall receive the clearer light of revelation. . . . Believing these things we cannot refuse to communicate to them the light which we possess, without incurring great guilt." Once again, New School adherents demonstrated their commitment to a rationally defensible religion.[18]

If heathens had freely and culpably rejected the essential truths of religion, it followed that they would exhibit all the depravities of unregenerate human nature. The secretary of the ABCFM, Samuel Worcester, warned that "it is a delirious dream of infidelity, that the various systems of paganism are only so many diversified forms of the true religion. . . . You will find the dream as false as it is delirious." Missionary advocates simply dismissed all pagan religions as efforts to placate an offended deity with superstitious and idolatrous practices. They further attributed every form of immorality to non-Christians, including sexual abandon, infanticide, human sacrifice, and other abominations. The Gospel was necessary for the happiness of the pagan in this world as well as his salvation in the next.[19]

A short children's book by the Sunday School Union described the most barbarous practices among Polynesian natives before the arrival of Christian missionaries. The writers considered atrocities to be a frequent occurrence in Tahiti and provided a vivid account of a supposedly commonplace massacre. The victorious warriors had entered a village where they murdered the noncombatants. "No age or sex was spared. The aged were at once despatched, through embowelling and every horrid torture was practised [sic]. The tenderest infants were perhaps transfixed to the mother's heart by a ruthless weapon—caught up by a ruffian hands, and dashed against the rocks or the trees, or wantonly thrown up in the air, and caught on the point of the warrior's spear, where it withered in agony and died. . . . and when the horrid carnage has been over . . . [the warriors retired] some having two or three infants hanging on a spear they bore across their shoulders." These stories came from a children's book! The authors of the work used these awful accounts to teach their young readers that "wherever idolatry exists, brutality and cruelty of every form prevails to a large extent. There is nothing good, except where the Gospel has carried its light and blessings."[20]

The major benevolent organizations also considered the Roman Catholic Church to be a major obstacle to their concept of Christianity. With the partial exception of the American Bible Society, these benevolent organizations considered the demise of the Catholic Church to be one of their most important objectives. The Tract Society published a number of anti-Catholic works, including one of the more popular nineteenth-century anti-Catholic books, *Thoughts On Popery*, by William

Nevin. Its directors also boasted of the number of Catholics converted by their tracts. The *Home Missionary*, a publication of the Home Missionary Society, warned of the Catholic menace with great regularity.[21]

The directors of the ABCFM viewed Catholicism as an especially dangerous enemy of truth, and they happily predicted its downfall. An annual report described the Church of Rome as directed by "the very spirit of the great enemy of God and man [i.e., Satan]. This great body, thus wonderfully constructed and held together, seems to be the masterpiece of all his works."[22]

In the late-1830s, American and French missionaries clashed in Hawaii, in a manner that demonstrates how anti-Catholicism might combine with a belief in the self-evident nature of truth. The mission to Hawaii had been singularly successful in converting natives to Protestant Christianity. Then French Catholic missionaries arrived and undermined the success of the Americans by converting natives to Catholicism. Much to the Americans' relief, the Hawaiian government expelled the Catholic missionaries for violating the government's decrees against idolatry. The French complained that the American missionaries had persuaded the native rulers to expel the Catholics. In 1839 a French frigate arrived in Honolulu to demand that the French missionaries be readmitted to the islands. Faced with the threat of French cannon, the government agreed.

In the United States, the American Board reacted to these developments with a mixture of indignation about the French and defensiveness about their own actions. Initially, they expressed outrage at the interference of the French with the sovereignty of the Hawaiian government. Later, as reports that the Americans had initiated the expulsion of the French reached the United States, the board became more defensive. American Protestants had always insisted that they would not need to repress Catholicism through government action. The truth of their arguments was supposed to be a sufficient weapon. Now their agents were accused of causing the Hawaiian government to expel Catholic missionaries.

After reviewing the reports, the board concluded that the Americans were not at fault. It asserted that the Hawaiian government had forbidden idolatry in order to prevent a return to pagan practices. Allegedly, the native rulers saw the Catholic religion as so obviously idolatrous that it violated these laws. Therefore, it seemed natural that the Hawaiian government would ban Catholicism without requiring the instigation of the American missionaries.[23]

All of these organizations shared the same restricted view of their roles as reformers. They believed that, by removing obstacles to the progress of Christianity, they could serve both the spiritual and temporal welfare of their beneficiaries. They perceived little reason to address wider issues of social and economic policy within American society, except for their antislavery efforts. They sympathized with the poor and underprivileged, but they firmly believed that the most effective assistance was propagation of the Gospel.

The case of ABCFM missionaries in Hawaii provides an interesting example of the New School vision of an ideal society. After obtaining the conversion of the islands' leading chiefs, the missionaries were able to exert a substantial influence on the development of the society. The sacrifices endured by these men and women in Hawaii were genuine; they faced isolation, disease, and life without the comforts of New England society. There is no reason to doubt that the missionaries sincerely sought the material and spiritual welfare of the islanders.[24]

The instructions to the first missionaries advised them to "aim at nothing short of covering the Sandwich Islands with fruitful fields, and pleasant dwellings, and schools and churches, and of raising the whole people to an elevated state of Christian civilization." To accomplish this end, the missionaries introduced both the Gospel and American concepts about law and private property. Under the influence of Rufus Anderson, however, the focus of the missionary work changed to creation of a native church and eventual closure of the Hawaiian mission. By 1863 the Hawaiian Islands mission officially closed and transferred its functions to the Hawaiian Evangelical Association.[25]

Nevertheless, the appearance was deceptive. By 1863 the Hawaiian Evangelical Association was dominated by former missionaries and the children of missionaries. In order to circumvent restrictions regarding political participation, many missionaries had severed their connections with the ABCFM while remaining in the islands as influential political and religious leaders. Even without the official sanction of the ABCFM, missionaries and their families had become a dominating force in the islands.[26]

Although transplanted New Englanders overshadowed the natives in church and government, the missionaries considered Hawaii to be one of their greatest successes. Moreover, they were pleased with their roles in the introduction of Western ideas of law and civilization. In 1864, Rufus Anderson, perhaps the person most tolerant of native cultures within the missionary endeavor, provided an account of missionary work in Hawaii. He pointed to the progress of the natives under the missionaries tutelage. "The Hawaiian people have been *humanized* by the gospel. When traveling among them it was hard to conceive . . . how they could have become so obedient to written laws, so observant of the rights of property."[27]

In time, these missionaries became more active in promoting the transformation of the islands to a capitalist economy. Many of the men and women engaged in commercial or agricultural pursuits, with the approval of the ABCFM. Anderson noted with pride the sugar mills and plantations developed by missionaries and former missionaries, with the conviction that these activities were elevating the material conditions of the natives.[28]

The missionaries' efforts to bring what they believed to be the benefits of Western legal systems to the natives led to one of the most unfortunate events in the history of native Hawaiians. Believing that private ownership of land would promote industry and economic growth among the natives, missionaries and their friends persuaded the Hawaiian monarchy to introduce Western concepts of land tenure to the islands. In 1848, the best farming land was divided among the people and the chiefs in what was known as the "Great Mahele." To their credit, the missionaries ensured that the common people would receive land suitable for farming and tried to prevent the government from granting land titles to foreigners. Soon after the Great Mahele, however, the government authorized foreigners to purchase land from the natives, and, predictably, the natives soon sold their land for far less than its value. An effort to elevate the natives became a first step toward a plantation system with the land owned by Western investors.[29]

Among the leaders of the ABCFM, Rufus Anderson was perhaps most noted for his desire to limit the missionary functions to the preaching of the Gospel while minimizing other forms of Western influence. He discouraged the creation of high schools, believing that such institutions would merely create a native elite, without advancing the Gospel. He also advocated transferring church authority to a native ministry as soon as practicable, even with the recognition that native churches might not meet New England standards.[30] Yet it would be a mistake to characterize Anderson as sympathetic to non-Western cultures. He believed the best way to use the limited resources of the ABCFM was to teach the Gospel and trust its influence on native cultures. When he argued for tolerance of the alleged faults of a native ministry, he merely argued that the "civilizing" influences of the missionaries required more time than originally anticipated. He applauded the importation of American ideas of law, including land-ownership law, into Hawaii.[31]

The missions to the Cherokees marked one of the few times when a benevolent organization publicly took a stand on a controversial issue. With the support of President Jackson, the Georgia government pressured the Cherokees to leave their land, and the state government forbade missionaries from living among the Indians without permission from the state government. The ABCFM publicly protested these actions, and its missionaries faced imprisonment to assert their right to minister to the Cherokee. The protests proved to be of limited duration, however, as the missionaries gradually decided that the best course of action was to acquiesce in Andrew Jackson's policy of moving the Indians west of the Mississippi.[32]

The New School adherents' limited concept of reform is most apparent in the efforts of the New York Association for Improving the Condition of the Poor to assist the city's impoverished citizens. Members of the NYAICP firmly believed that the causes of poverty were moral and that moral reformation of the poor was the only permanent solution to the problem of poverty. In time, the association did promote reforms aimed at improving the environment within New York slums. Throughout the antebellum era, however, the association's emphasis clearly remained on the alleged vices of the poor.

In its annual reports the NYAICP described the most important causes of poverty as intemperance, indolence, other vices of the poor, and indiscriminate relief. Its members recognized that some people might be reduced to poverty by unavoidable misfortune and thus were entitled to charitable assistance. The vast majority of the city's poor, however, were said to be responsible for their own indigence. The 1849 *Annual Report* described the character of what it termed "voluntary pauperism": "In prosecuting this work, a large amount of *voluntary destitution* has been discovered, chiefly among persons of foreign birth, who appear to regard labor as the greatest of evils, and exemption therefrom as their peculiar privilege. They live in indolence, intemperance, and filth. . . . If once aided they will certainly apply again; and if helped through a winter, will not only look for it as long as they live, but probably so train their children as to expect it after them." The association proposed to resolve the problem of these unworthy recipients by denying them aid, thus forcing them to work for a living.[33]

In order to prevent the undeserving poor, or paupers, from receiving assistance, the NYAICP maintained an elaborate system of visitors and record keeping. If a beggar or other alms seeker requested help from a member of the association, he would be directed to the visitor for his district. The visitor would then determine what, if any, assistance would be appropriate. Transactions were recorded to prevent duplicate grants of assistance. Visitors were instructed to give only the minimum amount necessary. Later, Robert Hartley's son stated that the NYAICP "was primarily and directly to discountenance indiscriminate alms giving.[34]

The association justified its policy by arguing that alms given indiscriminately were worse than wasted, because these gifts paid a bounty for indolence and vice. Thus, any effort to eradicate poverty that did not create a change of character "would be to lop off the branches of the Upas, and leave the poisonous root to shoot out with more baneful luxuriance." The annual reports repeatedly reminded their readers of the passage in Genesis 3:19 "In the sweat of thy face shalt thou eat bread," and 2 Thessalonians 3:10 "if any would not work, neither should he eat."[35]

The desire to prevent abuse of their charity is understandable. Under some circumstances, this refusal to aid people capable of self-support may even have been commendable. Yet members of the NYAICP demonstrated a remarkable determination to prevent the least amount of assistance for reaching the "undeserving poor." Virtually every annual report carried some comment about the dangers of indiscriminate almsgiving as rewarding the alleged vices of the poor. One passage described why indiscriminate charity was not true benevolence, but rather selfishness. "Impulsive benevolence is selfish, indolent, indiscriminate, and generally produces evil. Not so true charity. It is governed by principle. It is intelligent and judicious. It ascertains the character and condition of the needy, and graduates relief in amount and extent, according to their necessities. It seeks, in a word, the highest good of its object, and is satisfied with nothing less." A later annual report criticized any giving that "gives merely or mainly to be relieved from importunity, or to avoid the pain, denial would inflict on themselves. Such inconsiderate impulsiveness is not charity, but selfishness; and those who yield to it, may prove themselves the foes rather than the friends of humanity."[36]

When a drought combined with a financial panic to produce a local depression in 1854, the NYAICP again demonstrated its unwavering commitment to scrupulous discrimination in the dispensation of charity. During the height of the depression, many New Yorkers decided to take emergency measures, consisting largely of ward committees and soup kitchens, to dispense aid to the unemployed. The NYAICP vehemently denounced these measures as a dangerous inducement to profligacy among the poor. Discussing soup kitchens the 1855 *Annual Report* commented that "soup kitchens are not a new form of relief. . . . They have been tried over and over again, until their mischiefs have been so fully ascertained, that they now find favor nowhere. It is now a recognized principle among sound social economists and philanthropists, that the poor should not be aided in promiscuous masses at soup kitchens, but by personal visits at their homes." After the recovery, the NYAICP complained that these indiscriminate methods of relief had increased the level of poverty.[37]

This belief that the profligacy of the indigent was the primary cause of poverty explains the NYAICP's reluctance to sympathize with labor reforms that would directly improve the material condition of the working classes. Undoubtedly, Hartley and his fellow members of the NYAICP believed that the honest, sober workman was capable of supporting a family and advancing economically. Their advocacy of moral instruction as the solution to poverty was a predictable result of their perception of reform as applied toward individuals, not society.

One annual report reminded its readers that laborers might take advantage of their employers.

> Capital has rights, as well as labor. Such rights being reciprocal, they can never on sound economical or ethical principles, be antagonistic. If capital is sometimes oppressive, labor is as frequently unreasonable. . . . How often are prejudices created by sensational writers and by other well-meaning but misinformed persons against the so-called "hard-hearted employers who cheapen labor, and wrong the poor out of their just earnings." . . . Facts show that employers are as often victimized by the workers as the workers by the employers, with this difference—in the case of the poor the courts are open for legal redress, but the employers have no indemnity for spoiled or unexecuted work, for the poverty of the poor is their protection.

Of course, such remarks did not have the same insensitivity as Henry Ward Beecher's notorious remarks that a man ought to be willing to live on bread and water. The NYAICP clearly was not noted for its sympathy toward labor movements.[38]

Robert Hartley later expressed disapproval of shorter working hours because workers would waste their free time.

> Much has been spoken and written of what would be the elevating effects on the character and condition of the working-man, by giving him four hours a day for self-improvement and the benefit of his family. But, unfortunately for this pleasant theory, when he had twelve hours at command instead of four, as during the recent strikes, the advantages of leisure were not verified by the results. It was found here as elsewhere, that idleness and profligacy too often go hand in hand together. Lounging about street corners, gossiping and drinking at liquor-shops, neither tends to his own elevation nor to the happiness of his household, but rather to thriftless, dissipated habits and domestic wretchedness. . . . As

labor is the poor man's wealth, less than this [a full day's work] is a wanton waste of that wealth.

Hartley did not consider himself to be unsympathetic to labor, even in his advocacy of the twelve-hour day. Hartley and his fellow volunteers devoted long hours of their personal time in an effort to alleviate poverty. He was simply applying the logic of his beliefs.[39]

In time, the work of the NYAICP members would cause them to become more sympathetic to the circumstances of poverty. Realizing that physical incapacity might prevent even the most upright worker from rising above poverty, the NYAICP instituted programs for medical assistance during the 1850s. Concurrent with the interest in health, the organization also became interested in the housing situation within New York. The NYAICP constructed a model tenement to show landlords how to build satisfactory housing, and it supported legislation forbidding cellar apartments.[40]

Nevertheless, these efforts were not intended to supplant the strict discrimination between the deserving and the undeserving poor. It would be entirely inappropriate to view the NYAICP as an antebellum expression of the Social Gospel of the later nineteenth century.[41] The New School convictions about the nature of humanity was apparent in their emphasis on correction of individual vices as the solution to poverty within New York City.

The ultimate aim for all these benevolent societies was the triumph of the Kingdom of God. The millennium would come as men and women learned of true Christianity. The Church of Christ would reach enormous proportions, overcome its enemies, and dominate the world for one thousand years. Neither the church nor the world would change radically; rather, they would be infused with Christian principles.

Because of their importance in advancing the millennium, the efforts of the benevolent societies could be expected to arouse the hostility of the enemies of God. Participants in benevolent organizations asserted that their opponents might unite in order to hinder God's work. An 1830 *Annual Report* of the American Board of Commissioners for Foreign Missions expressed the peculiar combination of optimism with a concern about their enemies.

> A most marvellous [*sic*] tendency has been observed in all sorts of evil to coalesce, for the purpose or resisting truth. . . . Among the more remarkable sights that the men of this generation have beheld, there is nothing more wonderful, than the ease and rapidity with which those forms of wickedness, which have been usually found discordant, have lately been

associated together, ... thus Popery and infidelity,—the most abject
superstition and the most undisguised blasphemy, stand ready to aid each
other, and to engage openly and violently, in the contest with true
religion. . . . No sooner does an enemy of the truth hoist his colors, than
all other enemies of the truth, . . . cheer him, as if by a sympathy not less
quick and unerring than a natural instinct.

In this passage, the directors saw the same alliances of the forces of
darkness that Jonathan Edwards had predicted would occur before the
final battle between good and evil. Just as Edwards had predicted that
infidelity and Catholicism would unite, the missionary directors perceived such an unholy alliance as a sign of the times.[42]

Whether seeking to secure the millennium through foreign missionary endeavors or to reduce poverty through moral elevation of the
indigent, members of these benevolent organizations shared a religious
framework for their activities. Believing in the viciousness of the non-
Christian population, they focused their energies on bringing the Gospel to the unenlightened. Their assurance of an objectively valid truth
inspired them to apply their own religious principles universally. These
efforts focused on the spread of religious doctrine to the intended beneficiaries. However, they did not perceive a need to restructure the economic or social organization of Northern society, for they believed that
society could be improved through the promotion of true religion.

As the United States progress through the nineteenth century, however, the seemingly straightforward mission of promoting the true religion became more complicated. The New School community faced
questions about doctrinal orthodoxy or denominational disagreements
during the final years of the antebellum era.

❧ 10
The Closing Years of Antebellum Reform

Through the mid-1830s, New School adherents could claim that they were working as part of a unified Protestant reform effort. Beginning with the Presbyterian schism in 1837 however, the appearance of solidarity began to disappear. The loss of unity was accompanied by a change in the style and tone of New School reformers. To be sure, they continued to promote their reform crusades, and generally they adhered to the basic tenets of New School Calvinism; but these years were characterized by increasing denominational consciousness, diverging trends in theology, and an increasing reliance on political action for their reform efforts. At the same time, denunciations of the "Papal conspiracy" and the "slave power conspiracy" became increasingly shrill.

The Presbyterian schism of 1837 was disturbing to New School adherents because it seriously undermined their concept of a unified Calvinist community. Ministers such as Lyman Beecher and Albert Barnes had always declared their orthodoxy in the strongest terms. They could not understand Old School accusations of heresy because they did not realize how they had compromised the Calvinist emphasis on God's sovereignty even while they preserved the traditional vocabulary.

An understanding of the schism rests on the distinction between moderate conservatives and ultraconservatives. The moderates, led by the Princeton theologians, were personally inclined toward a strict Calvinism but were also willing to tolerate a modicum of variations in the interpretation of the Westminster standards. Although their toleration did not extend to New Haven theology, they generally discounted the extent of New Haven ideas within the Presbyterian community, and they were unwilling to use extreme measures against alleged heresies. In contrast, the ultraconservatives, consisting of such men as Ashbel Green, George

Junkin, Joshua Wilson, and Robert Breckinridge, demanded complete uniformity in interpretation of Presbyterian doctrine, and they were willing to use extreme measures to combat alleged heresies.[1]

Until 1837, the New School adherents prevented ultraconservative attacks, largely because of the mediation of the moderates. By that year, however, the moderates became frustrated by the perceived growth of New Haven theology within the Presbyterian Church, as evidenced by the failure to convict Barnes or Beecher of heresy. Convinced that the danger to the Westminster standards was real, the moderates joined with the ultraconservatives to remove the New School. At approximately the same time, Southern Presbyterians became alarmed by the antislavery propensities of the New School and joined with the ultraconservatives.

During the 1837 Assembly, the ultraconservatives obtained a declaration that the 1801 Plan of Union had been unconstitutional and irregular. They then removed three synods in western New York, plus Ohio's Western Reserve Synod, that had been created under the Plan of Union. Because these four synods were strongly New School, this action reduced New School adherents to a permanent minority, should they decide to remain within the church. The Assembly then terminated relations with the American Education Society and the Home Missionary Society and created its own board for foreign missions. The session concluded with a condemnation of sixteen alleged doctrinal errors of the New School.[2]

New School forces retreated to Auburn, New York, to plan their next move. There they decided to deny that they favored any doctrinal errors, that the conservatives had acted constitutionally in excluding the four synods, and that the conservatives constituted the true Presbyterian Church. They passed a point-by-point refutation of the Old School's allegations of unorthodoxy, adopting a comparatively conservative explanation. The members of the Auburn meeting further decided that representatives from the four excluded synods should present themselves at the next General Assembly meeting and demand their seats.[3]

When representatives from the four excluded synods attempted to gain admission to the 1838 General Assembly, all the discords of the previous years culminated in one rancorous session. After the moderator of the Assembly refused to recognize the contested delegates, the rebellious representatives proceeded to conduct business on the floor of the Assembly, claiming that they were the rightful assembly. After electing their own moderator, the New School party voted to adjourn to a more tranquil location. Now two separate organizations existed, both claiming to be the rightful Presbyterian Church. Approximately four-ninths of the Presbyterian Church joined the New School and remained with it until the reunion in 1869.[4]

In the years following the schism, New School Presbyterians developed their distinctive style. The Auburn response to Old School charges of heresy remained an unofficial standard of orthodoxy for the New School. It served to guard against further doctrinal innovations, especially any hints of perfectionism. The New School, however, maintained its association with Congregationalists through the Plan of Union, and voluntary societies received the support of the New School.

The passage of time, however, made relations between the Presbyterians and Congregationalists more difficult. The Plan of Union continued to result in a disproportionate share of Presbyterian churches in the northwest, even in regions populated by New England emigrants. By the 1850s, the two denominations were moving is separate directions. In 1852, a convention of Congregationalist ministers met at Albany to terminate the alliance. Members of the convention desired to establish Congregational churches west of New England, but the Plan of Union had worked in favor of Presbyterians in frontier areas. "They have milked our Congregational cows, but they have made nothing but Presbyterian butter and cheese," declared one delegate. In the years after 1852, Congregationalists established their own churches in the Midwestern regions of the United States.[5]

With the establishment of Congregational churches in what had been Presbyterian territory came new competition for financial support. Now the American Home Missionary Society became unable to satisfy all parties. Almost inevitably, there would be friction about the distribution of a limited amount of funds. New School Presbyterians complained that the Home Missionary Society's policy of supporting only one minister in a given area limited the ability of New School Presbyterians to create churches in areas that possessed a Congregational minister. The Presbyterians attempted to resolve this difficulty in 1853 by creating a church extension committee while maintaining their affiliation with the Home Missionary Society. Nonetheless, Presbyterians continued to believe that the Congregationalist-dominated board unfairly distributed its funds. In 1860, the New School Presbyterians dissolved all their ties with the Home Missionary Society, amid mutual recriminations.[6]

As the rift developed, New School Presbyterians became increasingly bitter toward their Congregationalist brethren. They conceived of themselves as having suffered through the turmoil of the schism for the principle of interdenominational cooperation, only to find the Congregationalists promoting sectarianism. The *Presbyterian Quarterly Review* expressed a sense of bewilderment and betrayal at the abrogation of the Plan of Union. "Generous people themselves, they [New School Presbyterians] cannot understand narrowness in others. Full of the spirit of an enlarged and cooperative Christianity, they cannot think of charging an aggressive and pertinacious sectarianism on those whom they have been accustomed to see in the van of their brethren."[7]

As a result of the rising sense of denominationalism, New School Presbyterians moved to define their own identity as a distinctly Presbyterian body. One product of their denominational self-consciousness was a new publication, the *Presbyterian Quarterly Review*, created in 1852. In two series of articles, it asserted that the New School was the genuine Presbyterian organization. In a series entitled "Old and New Theology," the *Review* insisted that New School doctrines were consistent with Calvinist principles and the *Westminster Confession*. The only difference between the New School and Old School lay in the method of explaining the Westminster standards. Another series, on "The Spirit of American Presbyterianism," was designed to show that Presbyterians had usually allowed a wide latitude in explaining the *Westminster Confession* and that the Old School had departed from tradition with the expulsion of the New School synods. The *Review* even rejected the name "New School Presbyterians" in favor of the term "Constitutional Presbyterians," and it described the Old School as the "Exscinding Presbyterians."[8]

In their efforts to affirm their own orthodoxy, however, they revealed how greatly they had been influenced by the New Haven assumptions that reformed theology must be compatible with human standards of reason, morality, and justice. They asserted that men neither share in the guilt of Adam's sin nor receive the imputed righteousness of Christ's Atonement. Rather, ever since Adam, men have become sinners through their own acts. Christ's Atonement served the public justice of God so that all men may be justified through the acceptance of it. The only inability that men possessed was moral, which the *Review* called an indisposition.[9] When Albert Barnes published a New Haven–oriented treatise on the Atonement, the *Presbyterian Quarterly Review* staunchly defended Barnes against the accusations of rationalism and unorthodoxy made by the *Princeton Review*.[10]

Having asserted their own orthodoxy, New School Presbyterians proscribed any further doctrinal innovations. In particular, they rejected any suggestion of perfectionism, or Oberlin theology, in their community. Shortly after the appearance of Finney's *Systematic Theology*, George Duffield published a series of highly critical reviews in the New School–

oriented *American Biblical Repository*. Duffield, who had once been charged with heresy himself, castigated Finney for his denial of man's dependence on God. When the Congregationalists at the Albany convention refused to condemn "Oberlinism," or when the *New Englander* stated that the terrors of Oberlin had been exaggerated, the *Presbyterian Quarterly Review* reacted with shocked indignation. Its editors accused the Congregationalists of protecting the Oberlin heresies in order to establish their own churches in the Midwest.[11]

At the same time that Presbyterians and Congregationalists were separating ecclesiastically, the two denominations were moving in different directions theologically. The conservative tendencies in New School Presbyterian theology grew stronger with the passage of time, until the New School became sufficiently orthodox to reunite with the Old School in 1869. Meanwhile, Horace Bushnell was laying the foundations for liberal Congregationalism.

Henry Boynton Smith's appointment to Union Theological Seminary in 1850 further accelerated the development of a more conservative theology. Smith centered his theology on a deep sense of awe at the Incarnation of God and man in the person of Jesus Christ. Even though he was raised in a Unitarian family, Smith underwent a profound conversion experience while a college student. Later, he traveled to Germany, where he studied under some of the most important German Protestant scholars of the time. Throughout his career he continued to stress the importance of Christ's mediatorship in all Christian theology.[12]

Unlike Taylor, Smith did not see Christianity as an entirely rational system. To be sure, he believed that his faith was reasonable and that faith without reason was blind. Yet he also believed that unaided reason (or philosophy) was insufficient. Faith and philosophy must complement each other. Faith and philosophy converged at the one central principle of Christianity, the role of Jesus Christ. "For the highest idea which men can frame is that of a union of divinity with humanity. . . . Through Jesus Christ and Him alone, does finite man come to the Infinite I am."[13]

Smith further differed from Taylor in rejecting an ethical system as the basis of Christianity. While he did not deny the importance of ethics, he believed that an ethical, or moral, system was an insufficient description of Christianity. "Nor can such an ethical system satisfy man's profoundest wants, or solve the real problems of his destiny. . . . It is mute before our deepest experiences of conscious guilt for our radical sinfulness, and of joyful freedom in a holiness which our wills did not and could not originate."[14]

With his return to a Christologically centered theology, Smith also found value in systematic theology and traditional confessions of faith. He praised the *Westminster Confession* as one of the best expressions of scriptural truth. This return to confessionalism, when accompanied by a renewed emphasis of the importance of Jesus, served to bring the New School closer to the traditional Calvinist theology. As Smith, and others like him, grew in importance, the eventual reconciliation with the Old School Presbyterians became more feasible.

In contrast to the New School Presbyterians' movement toward a more conservative theology, as exemplified by Henry B. Smith, the Congregationalists were moving toward a more liberal theology. Slowly, the rising influence of Horace Bushnell was leading New Englanders beyond the theology of Taylor and the other New Haven divines. Although he was a student of Taylor, Bushnell relied more on the metaphysical speculations of Samuel Taylor Coleridge than Common Sense realism.[15]

Bushnell was troubled by the ambiguities of human language. Words were either symbols of physical items (such as a "pen") or representations of ideas (such as "spirit"). In the latter case especially, there was no precision in the usage of language. Theologians may debate the doctrine of sin without the same understanding of the word "sin." For these reasons, Bushnell was skeptical of creeds and confessions. Instead of an overreliance on a single creed, he recommended that theologians attempt to find different modes of expressing the same truth.[16]

Bushnell's discussions of the Trinity, the Incarnation, and the Atonement reflect the extent of his departures from traditional Calvinism. Rather than contemplating the mysteries of the Trinity, he suggested that the Father, the Son, and the Holy Spirit were three different expressions of the same truth of God's love. The importance of the Incarnation was its manifestation of God's love to man and of His desire to bridge the gap between humans and God. To reveal Himself to men, God must assume a finite, or human, form. Christ's assumption of a human form manifested God's desire to reunite mankind with Himself. Regarding the Atonement, Bushnell did not ask whether it was an act of retribution or a governmental action. Rather, he asserted that the importance of the Atonement rested in its effect on humanity. In one sense, Christ's suffering attested to the love of God for humans. In another sense, the Atonement was a reenactment of the ritual sacrifices of the Judaic tradition, thus encouraging men to believe that their sins would be forgiven. He believed that a dogmatic statement could not express the meaning of the Atonement any more than a dogmatic statement about the theater could express the meaning of a tragedy.[17]

Thus, both Smith and Bushnell were moving beyond the New Haven theology, but in different directions. Smith, and most New School Presbyterians, were discovering new value in the Westminster standards. Bushnell, with a substantial number of Congregationalists, was pointing to the limitations of language to undermine the utility of all creeds. Nevertheless, both men also demonstrated a desire to replace the ethical emphasis of New Haven with a Christological emphasis. Through their actions these men were further defining the differences between Presbyterians and Congregationalists at the same time that they were challenging the supremacy of New Haven theology. (Of course, New Haven theology remained a vibrant theology in antebellum America. Bushnell's work was quite controversial during the antebellum era. Smith and Bushnell did not supplant New Haven theology during the 1850s; rather, they laid the foundation for its decline.)

Even at Yale, Taylor's theology was subtly being undermined. New scholars were being trained in the assumptions of German philosophy and theology, not the Scottish realism of Taylor's generation. Although equally committed to evangelical religion, new scholars were less committed to the antebellum emphasis on fixed, immutable truths and more willing to accept the subjectivity of truth. Like Smith or Bushnell, the importance of these changes would become more apparent in the postwar era than in the prewar period.[18]

With the changes in theology, there was also a decline in emphasis on revivals, at least within the Presbyterian and Congregational communities. Bushnell's first major work, *Christian Nurture*, argued that a proper Christian education would make a revival unnecessary. Calvin Stowe, the son-in-law of Lyman Beecher, expressed his disgust with excesses that resulted from highly emotional techniques. "A system producing great revivals which sweeps two or three hundred into the church . . . of whom in less than a year there are scarcely twenty or thirty remaining, all the rest returning like dogs to their vomit, being tenfold more the children of hell than before . . . [is] radically defective."[19]

New School reform activities also reflected a growing conservatism within the movement. As a general rule, New School Calvinists did not embrace new reform movements. They turned away from voluntary action and toward ecclesiastical and government action.

Both the changes in New School religious outlook and the difficulties in their reform efforts occurred independently of each other. The appearance of new theologians, such as Bushnell, reflected a predictable progression in theology, especially in view of new metaphysics coming from Germany. The rift between the Congregationalists and Presbyterians resulted from desires of each denomination for its own autonomy. The New School reform efforts fell short of their goals for reasons not related to New School religious beliefs. Despite some notable achievements, New School reformers discovered that many of the people targeted by their activities, such as Catholics and slaveholders, remained beyond the reach of their arguments. Nevertheless, perhaps there was a mutually reenforcing effect between the changes in religion and the frustrations of the reformers. The loss of evangelical unity may have accentuated doubts about the self-evident nature of truth, which would make New School adherents more likely to use political action. Concurrently, the inability to achieve complete success with their reforms may have created further doubts about the self-evident nature of their religious ideas.

New School attitudes toward the antebellum feminist movement, for example, displayed the limits of their reform tendencies. To the extent that members did express any opinions on women's status, they opposed any departure from a woman's "natural sphere." Like most nineteenth-century Americans, New School Calvinists conceived of a divinely ordained order between the sexes. They found support for this position in scriptural passages, including 1 Corinthians 11:8-9: "For the man is not of the woman; but the woman of the man. Neither was the man created for the woman, but the woman for the man." Discussing this passage in his series of Biblical commentaries, Albert Barnes stated that

> The woman was made for the comfort and happiness of man. Not to be a slave, but a help-meet; not to be the minister of his pleasures, but to be his aid and comforter in life; not to be regarded as of inferior nature and rank, but to be his friend, to divide his sorrows, and to multiply and extend his joys; yet still to be in a station subordinate to him. He is to be the head; the ruler; the presider in the family circle; and she was created to aid him in his duties, to comfort him in his afflictions, to partake with him of his pleasures. Her rank is therefore honourable, though it is subordinate. It is, in some respects, the more honourable because it is subordinate; and as her happiness is dependent on him, she has the higher claim to his protection and his tender care.

Undoubtedly Barnes, and other New School Calvinists, did not conceive of this attitude as antagonistic to women. Rather, the greatest happiness of both sexes would come from men and women fulfilling what he believed to be their divinely ordained roles.[20]

Thus, it is not surprising that, with exception of a few ministers such as Henry Ward Beecher or Theodore Weld, New School adherents expressed little sympathy for the incipient women's movement of the antebellum era. Congregationalist clergy denounced any attempts by female abolitionists to speak to mixed audiences. A study of New England ministers' sermons to women's organizations noted that during the 1830s ministers became increasingly insistent on the importance of women remaining within their own sphere, often using Paul's epistles for their texts. Another study of early feminist leaders noted that one of the most striking characteristics of these women was their rejection of evangelical religion in favor of Unitarianism or Universalism.[21]

Another New School minister, Milo J. Hickok of Rochester, elaborated on the role of women. Believing that women in Christian lands enjoyed a better status than women in other areas, he also believed that women's proper happiness depended on their remaining within their divinely ordained roles. "Let it be left to those females who have *rejected* the gospel of Christ, or embraced destructive errors, to clamor for '*woman's rights*,' and to plan to overleap the barriers which God's providence and human propriety have erected about them," wrote Hickok. "They have thrown away the scepter of their power, and it is not strange that they chafe under a divinely appointed *subjection* which they cannot cast off. Let them embrace the true religion, and they will cease to obtrude themselves into positions for which the God of nature never designed them." Hickok concluded his sermon by exhorting women to employ their gifts by advancing the cause of religion.[22]

To a surprising extent, however, New School adherents simply remained silent about the women's movement. Although feminist activities were covered in the secular press, in general the religious periodicals surveyed in this study did not discuss the feminist movement. Ministers in the antebellum era did denounce feminist activities, but the extent of their publications was markedly less than in the postwar period. For example, a study of nineteenth-century religion and feminism cites three pages of articles in religious periodicals, but not one is from the prewar period. Although it is difficult to make inferences from this silence, quite probably most New School Calvinists considered feminism to be a transient issue. During the prewar period, the women's rights movements remained the domain of a small minority of women. When the movement grew in size and importance after the Civil War, ministers became more active in their complaints that feminism was a "reform against nature."[23]

During the latter phases of antebellum reform, voluntary societies also lost some of their popularity, as the Presbyterians began to favor church-affiliated organizations. As noted above, the New School Presbyterians withdrew from the Home Missionary Society in 1860. In 1854, they also created their own board of education, which replaced the American Education Society.[24]

Even though the American Tract Society did not involve itself with clerical affairs, it also came under criticism from New School Presbyterians. In an 1844 article for the *American Biblical Repository*, Julian Sturtevant complained that the Tract Society was deprecating the importance of regular clergy by suggesting that written material might do the work of the church in converting souls. In 1854, the New School General Assembly voted to supplement the work of the American Tract Society by producing its own denominational tracts.[25]

At the same time that New School Calvinists were becoming more denominationally conscious in their reform activities, they were also becoming more politically active. This shift toward political action marked a further departure from their belief in the power of moral suasion. As reformers discovered the limited efficacy of the presentation of religious truths, they became increasingly willing to rely on the power of the state to enforce their moral standards.

Their most notable political successes came with the prohibition of alcoholic beverages. Voluntary temperance pledges had substantially reduced the consumption of alcohol, but temperance advocates soon wanted complete abstinence. Beginning with the Maine law of 1851, they won enactment of laws against liquor. By the time of the Civil War, eleven states made the sale of alcoholic beverages illegal.[26]

The Catholic Church also came under political attack during the 1850s. Political anti-Catholicism achieved a remarkable surge with the sudden appearance of the Order of the Star Spangled Banner, or Know Nothings (later the American Party), in 1854. The organization was created as a secret society to protect Americans from foreign, especially Catholic, influences. It quickly achieved national importance by combining anti-Catholic with antislavery programs. At its height, the organization placed eight governors and about one hundred congressmen into office. After 1855, however, the organization declined almost as quickly as it appeared.[27]

Even after the decline of the Know Nothings, political anti-Catholicism remained a potent force. The Republican Party combined anti-Catholicism with antislavery to rise to prominence. Republican candidates portrayed their Democratic opposition as beholden to the Catholic interests. A common form of anti-Catholic political activity was the lay trustee legislation, which restricted the Catholic practice of giving clergy ownership of church property. By 1855, Michigan, Connecticut, Maryland, Massachusetts, Indiana, Pennsylvania, Arkansas, New Jersey, and New York had all restricted clerical ownership of church property. In Michigan and elsewhere, Bible reading in public schools, using the King James version, became a disputed issue. These efforts, however, did not stop the growth of the Catholic Church in the United States, which added to the frustration of reformers.[28]

Certainly the political battles against chattel slavery were among the most important issues of the 1850s. These contests have been chronicled too often to require a full discussion here. It is worth noting that political abolitionism marked another departure from moral suasion to political action. More important, from the abolitionist viewpoint, the "slave power" was growing in strength even as abolitionist sentiment grew in the North. The Mexican War, the annexation of Mexican territory, the Compromise of 1850, the Kansas-Nebraska Act, the continued feuding in Kansas, and the Dred Scott decision all appeared to be victories for slavery.[29]

The perceived failure to halt the growth of Catholicism or slavery led to a heightened fear of conspiracies. Throughout the 1850s, denunciations of these two alleged conspiracies became increasingly shrill in response to the growth of these two institutions. Events seemed to confirm the suspicion that a system of sin or falsehood would always seek to suppress truth or freedom.

The political events surrounding the slavery controversy could be made to fit into the preestablished pattern of a system of iniquity attempting to expand its power. The complicated series of quarrels in Kansas were portrayed in the familiar terms of a conclusive contest between righteousness and iniquity. When Preston Brooks beat Charles Sumner senseless on the Senate floor, it only appeared to confirm accusations that slaveholders were accustomed to imposing their will through violence.

As the Civil War approached, warnings that either slavery or freedom must perish appeared more threatening. It is true that many of the grievances against the South represented a genuine concern over the plight of slaves. Moreover, the desire of Republican politicians to find an issue to differentiate themselves from the Democrats added to the denunciations of the slave power. Yet, for many of the Presbyterian and Congregationalist communities of the North, the issues fitted perfectly into their pattern of viewing all moral issues as a contest between good and evil, in which only one side would survive.

When the Civil War did break out in 1861, a substantial portion of Northern clergy perceived the hostilities as a part of an apocalyptic battle preceding the millennium and as a result of America's millennial role. Of course, not all Americans shared such an apocalyptical attitude toward the war. For this portion of Americans, however, the war could be made to fit into a millennialist pattern. The war, with its demands on the attention of the people, also marked the end of antebellum reform.[30]

❧ In Retrospect

In the years following the Civil War, the innovations of Taylor, Beecher, and other New Haven theologians were eclipsed by subsequent developments in theology. Within the Presbyterian community, the Old School and New School moved closer together, until the two sides were reunited in 1869. The Congregationalists generally moved toward a more liberal theology, following the lead of Andover Seminary. By the 1880s, Andover theologians had promulgated their concept of "progressive orthodoxy," which emphasized figurative interpretation of the Bible and such new ideas as future probation of souls. Later, the Social Gospel of Washington Gladden and Walter Rauschenbusch achieved its own prominence. As Taylor and the other New Haven theologians passed from the scene, the issues that dominated theological debates in New England no longer seemed important.[1] Yet, for the modern historian, it is essential to understand the New School movement on its own terms. New School Calvinism had a significant impact on two of the most important Protestant denominations.

New School Calvinists conceived of themselves as defending Calvinist orthodoxy by making minor modifications in terminology in order to accommodate rationalist criticisms. They still clung to the name of Calvinism and used such terms as "human depravity," "slavery to the dominion of sin," and "redemption through Christ." Despite these vestiges of orthodoxy, they believed that this system could be justified according to human standards of reason and justice if it was explained correctly. They believed that, in theory, all people could know and obey God's law, but that humans freely and culpably rejected God's law. People would continue to sin until they confronted the truth of God's word. With their belief in fixed, objective truths, New School Calvinists could not readily accept compromises or disagreements. They also believed that a system of sin or error would make every effort to suppress true religion.

One of the principal tenets of New School ideology, the emphasis on human depravity, is readily evident in their reform literature. Stories of Catholic licentiousness were credible to audiences who already believed that unregenerate humans were totally depraved. Similarly, allegations of atrocities by slaveholders rested on the assumption of human depravity. Supposed barbarities by heathens, or the schemes of alcohol vendors, were plausible to people who believed in the fearful extent of human wickedness. Even the NYAICP's efforts reflected their belief in human immorality, with its assertions that indolence was the cause of most poverty.

This emphasis on depravity was tempered, however, by the New School belief in the ability of all people to recognize and obey God's law, which provided a theoretical basis for all of their efforts. Indeed, their concept of reform is plausible only because they believed that all humans could recognize and accept God's truth. The activities and rhetoric of the benevolent organizations reflect their leaders' faith in the power of truth.

Another aspect of their faith in the power of truth is also evident in New School literature. Because New School Calvinists believed that truth and error could not coexist, they believed that a system of error would make every effort to suppress true religion. Throughout much of their anti-Catholic literature, in stories of Catholic obscurantism, of Catholic opposition to the Bible, of Catholic despotism, and of a Catholic conspiracy against the United States, New School Calvinists demonstrated this belief that error would necessarily seek to suppress truth. The protests against a slave power conspiracy were also part of the same pattern. Believing that any system of iniquity could not survive the light of truth, every act by Southern politicians could be portrayed as part of an inevitable clash between slavery and freedom. In this struggle, only one side could prevail.

Given their belief in the fixed, objectively valid nature of religious truth, New School Calvinists could go to great lengths to demonstrate that they were promoting universal truths. With their faith in the timeless moral truths of the Bible, they presumed that the Bible must support their moral principles. Consequently, they asserted that fermented wine or chattel slavery did not possess a Biblical sanction. They refused to see any value in non-Christian (i.e., non-Protestant) religions and circulated the most shocking stories of immorality associated with Catholicism or non-Western religions.

Their belief in the ultimate triumph of the kingdom of God was reflected most noticeably in their anti-Catholicism and their benevolent organizations. Although there is an element of optimism in this postmillennial eschatology, New School Calvinists also displayed a paradoxical combination of optimism and alarm when discussing the advent of the millennium. They believed that the forces of darkness would make every effort to oppose the kingdom of God and that a terrible struggle would precede the victory of Christ. Because the United States was destined to play a special role as the redeemer nation, it would be targeted for destruction by the forces of Antichrist.

Although it is customary for historians to refer to these movements as "antebellum reform," it is not appropriate to apply late twentieth-century standards of reform. New School adherents applied an entirely different frame of reference. Nevertheless, throughout all of their activities, they worked tirelessly to promote God's desires as they conceived of them. In their own time, and to subsequent generations, their strident efforts have aroused both admiration and controversy. When examined together, however, their ideology and reform activities reveal a consistency that endures throughout their endeavors.

Notes

Introduction

1. Nathaniel William Taylor, *Concio ad clerum: A Sermon Delivered in the Chapel at Yale College, September 10, 1828* (New Haven: Hezekiah Howe, 1828), 5; Sidney Mead, *Nathaniel William Taylor, 1786-1858: A Connecticut Liberal* (Chicago: University of Chicago Press, 1942), 221-25.

2. Nathan O. Hatch, *The Democratization of American Christianity* (New Haven, Conn.: Yale University Press, 1989); and Jon Butler, *Awash in a Sea of Faith: Christianizing the American People* (Cambridge, Mass.: Harvard University Press, 1990). Paul Conkin's recent work, *The Uneasy Center: Reformed Christianity in Antebellum America* (Chapel Hill: University of North Carolina Press, 1995), provides an overview of all reformed denominations.

3. Robert Baird, *Religion in the United States of America* (Glasglow, Scotland: Blackie and Son, 1844).

4. Clifford S. Griffin, "Religious Benevolence as Social Control," *Mississippi Valley Historical Review* 44 (December 1957): 423-44; Clifford S. Griffin, *Their Brothers' Keeper: Moral Stewardship in the United States, 1800-1865* (New Brunswick, N.J.: Rutgers University Press, 1960); Charles C. Cole, Jr., *The Social Ideas of Northern Evangelists, 1826-1860* (New York: Columbia University Press, 1954); Charles I. Foster, *An Errand of Mercy: The Evangelical United Front, 1790-1837* (Chapel Hill: University of North Carolina Press, 1960); Joseph Gusfield, *Symbolic Crusade; Status Politics and the American Temperance Movement* (Urbana: University of Illinois Press, 1963); David H. Donald, "Toward a Reconsideration of Abolitionists," in his *Lincoln Reconsidered* (New York: Alfred A. Knopf, 1956), 19-36.

5. Lois W. Banner, "Religious Benevolence as Social Control: A Critique of an Interpretation," *Journal of American History* 60 (June 1973): 23-41; Lawrence W. Kohl, "The Concept of Social Control and the History of Jacksonian America," *Journal of the Early Republic* 5 (Spring 1985): 21-33.

6. Hatch, *Democratization of Christianity*, 221-24.

7. Gilbert Barnes, *The Anti-Slavery Impulse, 1830-1844* (New York: D. Appleton-Century, 1933).

8. Alice F. Tyler, *Freedom's Ferment: Phases of American Social History to 1860* (Minneapolis: University of Minnesota Press, 1944).

9. Ronald G. Walters, *American Reformers, 1815-1860*, 2d ed. (New York: Hill and Wang, 1997), 27, 29.

10. Timothy L. Smith, "Social Reform" in *The Rise of Adventism*, ed. Edwin Gaustad (New York: Harper & Row, 1974), 18; Walters, *American Reformers*, 35; see also Timothy L. Smith, *Revivalism and Social Reform: American Protestantism on the Eve of the Civil War* (Nashville: Abingdon Press, 1957).

11. John L. Thomas, "Romantic Reform in America 1815-1865," *American Quarterly* 17 (Winter 1965): 656-81.

12. Robert H. Abzug, *Cosmos Crumbling: American Reform and the Religious Imagination* (New York: Oxford University Press, 1994).

13. Steven Mintz, *Moralists and Modernizers: America's Pre–Civil War Reformers* (Baltimore: Johns Hopkins University Press), 156 and passim.

14. George M. Marsden, *The Evangelical Mind and the New School Presbyterian Experience* (New Haven, Conn.: Yale University Press, 1970). Marsden discusses theology in more detail in "The New School Presbyterian Mind: A Study of Theology in Mid-Nineteenth Century America" (Ph.D. dissertation, Yale University, 1966).

15. Sidney Mead, *Nathaniel William Taylor, 1786-1858: A Connecticut Liberal*; see also Frank H. Foster, *A Genetic History of New England Theology* (Chicago: University of Chicago Press, 1907); and H. Shelton Smith, *Changing Conceptions of Original Sin: A Study in American Theology since 1750* (New York: Charles Scribner's Sons, 1955).

Chapter 1. The Challenge to Orthodoxy

1. *Westminster Confession*, chaps. 3 and 6. There are two versions of the *Westminster Confession*, because two chapters were added in 1942 (9 and 10). In these notes, I use the old version. To convert to the modern version add, two chapters after chapter 8.

2. Ibid., chap. 6.

3. Ibid., chaps. 16 and 9.

4. Ibid., chap. 8.

5. Ibid., chaps. 14 and 15.

6. Ibid, chap. 17. This tenet was known as "perseverance of the saints."

7. Ibid., chap. 14.

8. Ibid., chap. 3.

9. Perry Miller, *The New England Mind: The Seventeenth Century* (New York: Macmillan, 1939), 205 and passim.

10. Perry Miller may have overstated the Augustinian basis for New England Puritanism in *The New England Mind*, 3-34. Nonetheless, Augustine exerted a formidable influence on Puritan thought.

11. See the Council of Trent's Decree on Justification, especially chapters 1 and 5. The decree can be found in Joseph Neuner, *The Teachings of the Catholic Church*, ed. Karl Rahner and trans. Geoffrey Stevens (New York: Alba House, 1967).

12. Bruce Kuklick, *Churchmen and Philosophers: From Jonathan Edwards to John Dewey* (New Haven, Conn.: Yale University Press, 1985), 8-14.

13. "Doctrine of Original Sin Defended," in *Jonathan Edwards: Representative Selections*, ed. Clarence Faust and Thomas Johnson (New York: Hill and Wang, 1962), 323-27.

14. Clyde A. Holbrook, *The Ethics of Jonathan Edwards: Morality and Aesthetics* (Ann Arbor: University of Michigan Press, 1973), 54-66.

15. "The Justice of God in the Damnation of Sinners," in *Representative Selections*, 112-20; "Sinners in the Hands of an Angry God," in *Representative Selections*, 155-72.

16. "Freedom of the Will," in *Representative Selections*, 263-309, and introduction, xxiv-xlix; Perry Miller, *Jonathan Edwards* (New York: William Sloan Associates, 1949).

17. "Nature of True Virtue," in *Representative Selections*, 349-71 (the quote is on 350); "Dissertation Concerning the End for Which God Created the World," in *Representative Selections*, 340-48; Holbrook, *Ethics of Jonathan Edwards*, 97-112 and passim.

18. Clyde Holbrook uses the term "theological objectivism" to describe Edwards's insistence that all theological inquiry must seek to understand God on His own terms, rather than on man's terms, in *The Ethics of Jonathan Edwards;* other useful works on Edwards include the lengthy introduction in Faust and Johnson's *Representative Selections;* Edward H. Davidson, *Jonathan Edwards: The Narrative of a Puritan Mind* (Boston: Houghton Mifflin, 1966); and Janice Knight, "Learning the Language of God: Jonathan Edwards and the Typology of Nature," *William and Mary Quarterly* 48 (October 1991): 531-51. Nathan O. Hatch and Harry S. Stout have assembled and edited some of the best recent work on Edwards, in *Jonathan Edwards and the American Experience* (New York: Oxford University Press, 1988).

19. Henry F. May, *The Enlightenment in America* (New York: Oxford University Press, 1976), xiv and passim.

20. Leslie Stephen, *A History of English Thought in the Eighteenth Century*, 3d ed., 2 vols. (New York: G. P. Putnams Sons, 1902), 1:101-18, 134-61; Herbert M. Morais, *Deism in Eighteenth-Century America* (New York: Columbia University Press, 1934), 25-53.

21. Morais, *Deism in Eighteenth-Century America*, 125; see also Thomas Paine, *The Age of Reason, Being an Investigation of the True and Fabulous Theology* (New York: Wiley, 1944), 36.

22. Paine, *Age of Reason*, 29-30.

23. Ibid., 82-85.

24. Ibid., 194 and passim.

25. Some of the discussions of Hopkins include Joseph Haroutunian, *Piety Versus Moralism: The Passing of New England Theology* (1932; rprt. New York: Harper & Row, 1970); see also Earl A. Pope, *New England Calvinism and the Disruption of the Presbyterian Church* (New York: Garland, 1987), 31-61; Joseph Conforti, *Samuel Hopkins and the New Divinity Movement* (Grand Rapids, Mich.: Christian University Press, 1981); William K. Breitenbach, "New Divinity Theology and the Idea of Moral Accountability" (Ph.D. dissertation, Yale University, 1978); Paul K. Conkin, *The Uneasy Center: Reformed Christianity in Antebellum America* (Chapel Hill: University of North Carolina Press, 1995), 101-13; and Allen C. Guelzo, *Edwards on the Will: a Century of American Theological Debate* (Middletown, Conn.: Wesleyan University Press, 1989), 87-139; Ezra Stiles Ely made the same criticisms of Hopkins as Haroutunian in his work *A Contrast Between Hopkinsianism and Calvinism* (New York: S.S. Whitting, 1811).

26. Guelzo, *Edwards on the Will*, 87-95 and passim.

27. Guelzo, *Edwards on the Will*, 108-11, 117-23; Kuklick, *Churchmen and Philosophers*, 55-59; Conforti, *Samuel Hopkins*, 67-75.

28. In this respect, Haroutunian's *Piety Versus Moralism* remains timeless. With its exclusive focus on freedom of the will, Guelzo's *Edwards on the Will* does not address many of the more visionary aspects of Edwardsean theology.

29. Samuel Hopkins, *The System of Doctrines*, 2 vols. (Boston: Thomas & Andrews, 1793), 1:72, 78; Conforti, *Samuel Hopkins*, 110-20.

30. Hopkins, *System of Doctrines*, 1:71, 78, 344-58; Hopkins, *An Inquiry into the Nature of True Holiness* (Newport: Solomon Southwick, 1773), 19-31 and passim.

31. Hopkins, *System of Doctrines*, 1: 149.

32. Ibid., 1: 150, 155, 193; Conforti, *Samuel Hopkins*, 65-67.

33. Samuel Hopkins, *A Treatise on the Millennium* (Boston: Thomas & Andrews, 1793). For a detailed summary of Bellamy's calculations, see James W. Davidson, *The Logic of Millennial Thought in Eighteenth-Century New England* (New Haven, Conn.: Yale University Press, 1977), 192-93.

34. Hopkins, *System of Doctrines*, 2:183.

35. Hopkins, *Inquiry into the Nature of True Holiness*, 73-74; Conforti, *Samuel Hopkins*, 117-123.

36. Hopkins, *System of Doctrines*, 1:319-20.

37. Mark Valeri, *Law and Providence in Joseph Bellamy's New England: The Origins of the New Divinity in Revolutionary America* (New York: Oxford University Press, 1994), 52-54 and passim; Breitenbach, "New Divinity Theology," 125-56; see also Joseph Bellamy, *True Religion Delineated and Distinguished from All Counterfeits* (Boston: Kneeland, 1750).

38. Valeri, *Law and Providence in Joseph Bellamy's New England*, 122-133.

39. Guelzo, *Edwards on the Will*, 140-76; Edmund Morgan, *The Gentle Puritan: A Life of Ezra Stiles* (New Haven, Conn.: Yale University Press, 1962).

40. For two excellent discussions of Unitarianism, see Conrad Wright, *The Beginnings of Unitarianism in America* (Boston: Starr King Press, 1955), and Daniel

Walker Howe, *The Unitarian Conscience* (Cambridge, Mass.: Harvard University Press, 1970).

41. Wright uses the phrase "supernatural rationalism" to describe this attitude, in *Beginnings of Unitarianism*, 135-60.

42. William G. McLoughlin, *New England Dissent, 1630-1883: The Baptists and the Separation of Church and State*, 2 vols. (Cambridge, Mass.: Harvard University Press, 1971), 2:1189-99.

43. H. Shelton Smith, *Changing Conceptions of Original Sin: A Study in American Theology Since 1750* (New York: Charles Scribner's Sons, 1955), 75-85.

Chapter 2. Theology at New Haven

1. Sidney Mead, *Nathaniel William Taylor 1786-1858: A Connecticut Liberal* (Chicago: University of Chicago Press, 1942; rprt. ed., Hampden, Conn.: Archon Books, 1967), 24-37; Marie Caskey, *Chariot of Fire: Religion and the Beecher Family* (New Haven, Conn.: Yale University Press, 1978), 37-41; Stephen E. Berk, *Calvinism versus Democracy: Timothy Dwight and the Origins of American Evangelical Orthodoxy* (Hampden, Conn.: Archon Books, 1974), 49-111; Marc L. Harris, "Revelation and the American Republic: Timothy Dwight's Civic Participation," *Journal of the History of Ideas* 54 (July 1993): 449-68; see also Paul K. Conkin, *The Uneasy Center: Reformed Christianity in Antebellum America* (Chapel Hill: University of North Carolina Press, 1995), 211-19.

2. Timothy Dwight, *Theology Explained and Defended in a Series of Sermons*, 5 vols. (Middletown, Conn.: Clark & Lyman, 1818), esp. 4:455-69, 2:515-30, and 1:223-53.

3. Mead, *Taylor*, passim. Noah Porter repeated this comment in his introduction to Nathaniel William Taylor's *Lectures on the Moral Government of God*, ed. Noah Porter, 2 vols. (New York: Clark Austin & Smith, 1859). In his major work, *The Analogy of Religion Natural and Revealed*, Butler stressed the theme of God as the moral governor of the universe.

4. Mead, Nathaniel William Taylor; Allen C. Guelzo, *Edwards on the Will: A Century of American Theological Debate* (Middletown, Conn.: Wesleyan University Press, 1989), 240-72.

5. Benjamin N. Martin, "Nathaniel William Taylor," in *Yale College: A Sketch of its History*, ed. William L. Kingsley, 2 vols. (New York: Henry Holt, 1870), 1:30-31; see also Noah Porter's introduction to Taylor's *Lectures on the Moral Government of God*; and Mark. A. Noll, "Jonathan Edwards and Nineteenth-Century Theology," in *Jonathan Edwards and the American Experience*, ed. Nathan O. Hatch and Harry S. Stout (New York: Oxford University Press, 1988), 260-87.

6. [Nathaniel William Taylor], "Authority of Reason," *Quarterly Christian Spectator* 9 (March 1837): 162, quoted in Earl A. Pope, *New England Calvinism and the Disruption of the Presbyterian Church* (New York: Garland, 1987), 73.

7. Bruce Kuklick, *Churchmen and Philosophers: From Jonathan Edwards to John Dewey* (New Haven, Conn.: Yale University Press, 1985), 100-101.

8. Lyman Beecher, "The Bible a Code of Laws" in *Beecher's Works*, 3 vols. (Boston: J.P. Jewett, 1852), 2:155; Taylor, *Moral Government of God*, 1:7 and passim.

9. "Restraints on Human Depravity," *Christian Spectator* 4 (April 1822): 182-86.

10. Nathaniel William Taylor, *Essays, Lectures, Etc. upon Select Topics in Revealed Theology* (New York: Clark, Austin & Smith, 1859), 379; see also Taylor, *Moral Government of God*, 1:326-50; Taylor, *Concio ad clerum: A Sermon Delivered in the Chapel at Yale College, September 10, 1828* (New Haven, Conn.: Hezekiah Howe, 1828).

11. Lyman Beecher, *Views in Theology* (Cincinnati: Truman & Smith, 1836), 177-82.

12. Ibid., 115-16, "Moral Inability," *Christian Spectator* 5 (October 1823): 524-27; "Ability," *Presbyterian Quarterly Review* 4 (March 1856): 584-85; Douglas A. Sweeney, "Nathaniel William Taylor and the Edwardsian Tradition: A Reassessment," in *Jonathan Edwards's Writings: Text, Context, Interpretation*, ed. Stephen J. Stein (Bloomington: Indiana University Press, 1996), 148-49.

13. H. Shelton Smith, *Changing Conceptions of Original Sin: A Study in American Theology since 1750* (New York: Charles Scribner's Sons, 1955), 113-15; "Review of Taylor and Harvey on Human Depravity," *Quarterly Christian Spectator* 1 (June 1829): 343-84; Bennett Tyler, *Letters on the Origins and Progress of the New Haven Theology* (New York: Robert Carter & Ezra Collier, 1837), 15-16.

14. [Moses Stuart], "Hints on Sin and Free Agency," *The Christian Spectator* 6 (April 1, 1824): 177-82; Guelzo, *Edwards on the Will*, 273.

15. Taylor, *Essays, Etc.*, 468; Taylor, *Moral Government of God*, 1:164-72; Albert Barnes, *The Atonement in its Relations to Law and Moral Government* (Philadelphia: Perry & McMillan, 1859), 30-49. Joseph Bellamy suggested the governmental theory of the Atonement in *True Religion Delineated and Distinguished from All Counterfeits* (Boston: Kneeland, 1750), 300-46; see also William K. Breitenbach, "New Divinity Theology and the Idea of Moral Accountability" (Ph.D. dissertation, Yale University, 1978), 137-47.

16. Barnes, *Atonement*, 223; Taylor, *Moral Government of God*, 1:270-75.

17. Taylor, *Moral Government of God*, 2:147, 166, 293.

18. Beecher, "Bible a Code of Laws," in *Works*, 2:176.

19. Taylor, *Moral Government of God*, 2:255-56; "Regeneration," *Presbyterian Quarterly Review* 4 (September 1855): 226; Jeremiah Day, "Benevolence and Selfishness," *Biblical Repository* 9 (January 1843): 1-33.

20. Taylor, *Moral Government of God*, 2: 199.

21. Beecher, "Bible a Code of Laws," in *Works*, 2:176.

22. Richard Rabinowitz, *The Spiritual Self in Everyday Life: The Transformation of Personal Religious Experience in Nineteenth-Century New England* (Boston: Northwestern University Press, 1989), passim.

23. Taylor, *Essays Etc.*, 393; Beecher, "Bible a Code of Laws," in *Works*, 2:164; see also Beecher, *Views in Theology*, 205-6. The conservative Calvinist

Bennett Tyler complained that this account of regeneration amounted to "divine moral suasion," in his *Letters on the New Haven Theology*, 92.

24. Taylor, *Essays Etc.*, 390, 396, 399.

25. On eighteenth-century revivals, see Michael J. Crawford, *Seasons of Grace: Colonial New England's Revival Tradition in Its British Context* (New York: Oxford University Press, 1991); Benard A. Weisbergers' *They Gathered at the River: The Story of the Great Revivalists and Their Impact upon Religion in America* (Boston: Little Brown, 1958) remains a classic study of revivalism; see also Richard Rabinowitz, *The Spiritual Self in Everyday Life*; and George M. Marsden, *The Evangelical Mind and the New School Presbyterian Experience* (New Haven, Conn.: Yale University Press, 1970), 31-57.

26. Beecher, "Bible a Code of Laws," in *Works*, 2:189. On Protestant belief in the scientific accuracy of the Bible, see George Marsden, "Everyone One's Own Interpreter: The Bible, Science, and Authority in Mid-Nineteenth Century America," in *The Bible in America: Essays in Cultural History*, ed. Nathan O. Hatch and Mark A. Noll (New York: Oxford University Press, 1982), 79-100.

27. Beecher, "The Bible a Revelation from God to Man," and "Objections to the Inspiration of the Bible," in *Works*, 1:202-41, 242-84; David Nelson, *The Cause and Cure of Infidelity* (New York: American Tract Society, 1841), 34-73 and passim.

28. Lyman Beecher,"The Being of God," in *Works*, 1:26-33.

29. Taylor, *Moral Government of God*, 1:263-69 and passim.

30. Ibid., 1:347-48, 354-57, 391-417.

31. Taylor, *Essays Etc.*, 462; Mead, *Taylor*, 159-63 and passim; Sidney E. Ahlstrom, "The Scottish Philosophy and American Theology," *Church History* 24 (September 1955): 257-71. Lyman Beecher also expressed his faith in a knowable truth in a short discourse he delivered in "The Bible a Code of Laws," in *Works*, 2:160-63.

32. Taylor, *Essays, Etc.*, 221.

33. Beecher, *The Autobiography of Lyman Beecher*, ed. Barbara Cross (Cambridge, Mass.: The Belknap Press, 1961), 1:394. The daughter was Harriet Beecher Stowe.

34. Taylor, *Essays, Etc.*, 463.

35. George Duffield, "The Moral Obligation of the Christian Sabbath," in George Duffield and Albert Barnes, *Discourses on the Sabbath* (Philadelphia: George W. Donohue, 1836), 72; see also "The Bible Always the Same in Its Authority and Relation to Mankind," *Quarterly Christian Spectator* 4 (December 1836): 519-28.

36. John L. Thomas described these reformers as Romantic in "Romantic Reform in America 1815-1865," *American Quarterly* 17 (Winter 1965): 656-81; Ronald Walters promotes this interpretation in *American Reformers 1815-1860* (New York: Hill and Wang, 1978); on German thought, see Claude Welch, *Protestant Thought in the Nineteenth Century* (New Haven, Conn.: Yale University Press, 1972).

37. Beecher, "Bible a Code of Laws," in *Works*, 2:194.

38. Richard Hofstadter, "The Paranoid Style in American Politics," in his *The Paranoid Style in American Politics and Other Essays* (New York: Vintage Books and Random House, 1967), 3-40; Gordon Wood disagrees with the paranoid characterization, in "Conspiracy and the Paranoid Style: Causality and Deceit in the Eighteenth Century," *William and Mary Quarterly* 39 (July 1982): 401-41.

39. Daniel Walker Howe, *The Political Culture of the American Whigs* (Chicago: University of Chicago Press, 1979), 79-80, 163-64.

40. Smith, *Changing Conceptions of Original Sin*, 110-36; Lyman Beecher "The Faith Once Delivered to the Saints," in *Works*, 2:242-300; much of the early debate can be followed through the issues of the *Christian Spectator* from 1822 through 1824.

Chapter 3. Theology at Princeton and Oberlin

1. Bennett Tyler, *Letters on the Origin and Progress of the New Haven Theology* (New York: Robert Carter & Ezra Collier, 1837), 39 and passim; Joseph Harvey, *Review of a Sermon Delivered in the Chapel of Yale College* (Hartford, Conn.: Goodwin, 1829); Zebulon Crocker, *The Catastrophe of the Presbyterian Church in 1837* (New Haven, Conn.: B & W Noyes, 1838), passim; Vincent Harding, *A Certain Magnificence: Lyman Beecher and the Transformation of American Protestantism, 1775-1863* (Brooklyn, N.Y.: Carlson, 1991), 403-405, 424-25, and passim.

2. Mark A. Noll, *Princeton and the Republic, 1768-1822: The Search for a Christian Enlightenment in the Era of Samuel Stanhope Smith* (Princeton, N.J.: Princeton University Press, 1989).

3. Noll, *Princeton and the Republic*, 28-58; Mark A. Noll, "The Irony of the Enlightenment for Presbyterians in the Early Republic," *Journal of the Early Republic* 5 (Summer 1985): 149-75; Fred J. Hood, *Reformed America: The Middle and Southern Colonies, 1783-1837* (Tuscaloosa: University of Alabama Press, 1980), 10-46 and passim. Theodore D. Bozeman traces the effects of Common Sense philosophy on the Old School Presbyterians throughout the nineteenth century, in *Protestants in an Age of Science: The Baconian Ideal and Antebellum Religious Thought* (Chapel Hill: University of North Carolina Press, 1977).

4. Noll, *Princeton and the Republic*, passim.

5. John MacLean, *History of the College of New Jersey 1746-1854* (Philadelphia: J.B. Lippincott, 1877); George P. Schmidt, *Princeton and Rutgers: The Two Colonial Colleges of New Jersey* (Princeton, N.J.: Van Nostrand, 1964); Thomas Jefferson Wertenbaker, *Princeton, 1746-1896* (Princeton, N.J.: Princeton University Press, 1946), 48-80.

6. John McKay, "Archibald Alexander," in *Sons of the Prophets: Leaders in Protestantism from Princeton Seminary*, ed. Hugh T. Kerr (Princeton, N.J.: Princeton University Press, 1963), 3-21. Mark A. Noll provides a succinct analysis of Princeton theology, in his anthology *The Princeton Theology 1812-1921* (Grand Rapids, Mich.: Baker Book House, 1983).

7. For a biography of Hodge, see A.A. Hodge, *The Life of Charles Hodge*

(London: T. Nelson & Sons, 1881); see also Leonard Trinterud, "Charles Hodge," in *Sons of the Prophets*, 22-38.

8. Perry Miller, *The Life of the Mind in America, from the Revolution to the Civil War* (New York: Harcourt, Brace & World, 1965), 17. One of the most readable descriptions of Old School theology is a short book that Charles Hodge wrote for younger audiences, *The Way of Life* (Philadelphia: American Sunday School Union, 1841); Noll, *Princeton Theology*, 28-30 and passim.

9. Earl A. Pope, *New England Calvinism and the Disruption of the Presbyterian Church* (New York: Garland, 1987), passim.

10. George M. Marsden, *The Evangelical Mind and the New School Presbyterian Experience* (New Haven, Conn.: Yale University Press, 1970), 58. The term "Pelagianism" was used in Lyman Beecher's heresy trial; see "Dr. Beecher's Trial for Heresy," in *Beecher's Works* (Boston: J. P. Jewett, 1852), 3:321. For a discussion of Pelagius, see Peter Brown, *Augustine of Hippo* (Berkeley: University of California Press, 1967), 340-53.

11. Noll, *The Princeton Theology*, 30-33.

12. Among the best discussions of Finney are Charles E. Hambrick-Stowe, *Charles G. Finney and the Spirit of American Evangelicalism* (Grand Rapids, Mich.: William B. Eerdmans, 1996); William McLoughlin's introduction to Finney's *Lectures on Revivals of Religion* (Cambridge, Mass.: Belknap Press, 1960); William McLoughlin, *Modern Revivalists: Charles Grandison Finney to Billy Graham* (New York: Ronald Press, 1959); Keith Hardman, *Charles Grandison Finney, 1792-1875: Revivalist and Reformer* (Syracuse, N.Y.: Syracuse University Press, 1987); Melvin L. Vulgamore, "Social Reform in the Theology of Charles Grandison Finney" (Ph.D. dissertation, Boston University, 1963); Garth M. Rosell, "Charles Grandison Finney and the Rise of the Benevolence Empire" (Ph.D. dissertation, University of Minnesota, 1971); and Bernard A. Weisberger, *They Gathered at the River: The Story of Great Revivalists and Their Impact upon Religion in America* (Boston: Little Brown, 1958), 116-35. Leonard Sweet makes some cogent comments on Finney in "The View of Man Inherent in New Measures Revivalism," *Church History* 45 (June 1976): 206-21. Allen Guelzo argues that Finney remained within the Edwardsean tradition, in "An Heir or Rebel? Charles Grandison Finney and the New England Theology," *Journal of the Early Republic* 17 (Spring 1997): 61-94.

13. Charles G. Finney, *Memoirs of Rev. Charles G. Finney* (New York: A. S. Barnes, 1876), 42, 51.

14. Weisberger, *They Gathered at the River*, 107-21; Finney, *Memoirs*, passim; Whitney Cross, *The Burned Over District: The Social and Intellectual History of Enthusiastic Religion in Western New York* (Ithaca, N.Y.: Cornell University Press, 1950), 151-85.

15. Weisberger, *They Gathered at the River*, 109-13; *Letters of the Rev. Dr. Beecher and Rev. Mr. Nettleton on the "New Measures" in Conducting Revivals of Religion* (New York: S. & C. Carvill, 1828), 1-23, 140-73; see also McLoughlin, introduction to Finney's *Lectures on Revivals*, xxxvi-xxxvii.

16. See Finney's *Lectures on Revivals*, esp. 9-23, 140-55, and passim.

17. *Letters of Beecher & Nettleton*, 41-101 and passim.

18. Harding, *A Certain Magnificence*, 240-45; Finney, *Memoirs* 209-225; Weisberger, *They Gathered at the River*, 116-21; Lyman Beecher, *The Autobiography of Lyman Beecher*, ed. Barbara Cross, 2 vols. (Cambridge, Mass.: Belknap Press, 1961), 2:66-75.

19. Paul Johnson provides the most detailed account of the Rochester Revival, in *A Shopkeeper's Millennium: Society and Revivals in Rochester, New York, 1815-1837* (New York: Hill & Wang, 1978); see also Weisberger's discussion of Finney in *They Gathered at the River*. It should be noted, however, that Finney was most successful within the rural areas of northern New York, rather than the cities and commercial centers.

20. Weisberger, *They Gathered at the River*, 123-26, 132-33; McLoughlin, introduction to Finney's *Lectures on Revivals*, xxi-lix.

21. Finney, *Lectures on Revivals*, 13, 9, 109-11.

22. Ibid., 14, 291, xxix.

23. [Albert Dod], "Review of Finney's Sermons," *Princeton Review* 7 (July 1835): 527; see also William McLoughlin's excellent discussion of Dod's critique in his introduction to Finney's *Lectures on Revivals*, xxi-xl.

24. Weisberger, *They Gathered at the River*, 134-35.

25. Charles G. Finney, *Lectures to Professing Christians* (New York: J.S. Taylor, 1837), 215-16.

26. Ibid., 288.

27. Ibid., 160, 25-26, 58-59, and passim.

28. Ibid., 254.

29. Charles G. Finney, *Finney's Systematic Theology* [abridged] (Minneapolis: Bethany Fellowships, 1976), 60, 24, 33, and passim; see also Charles Hodge's scathing critique of Finney in "Finney's Lectures on Theology," *Princeton Review* 19 (April 1847):237-77, which was republished in his *Essays and Reviews* (New York: Robert Carter & Brothers, 1857), 245-84.

30. Finney, *Lectures to Professing Christians*, 74.

31. Vulgamore, "Charles Finney," 252-57 and passim; Finney, *Lectures to Professing Christians*, 52-79, 128-54, 175-90; Finney, *Lectures on Revivals*, 46-48; McLoughlin, introduction to Finney's *Lectures on Revivals*, xliii.

32. Rosell, "Charles Finney," 168-69.

33. Vulgamore, "Charles Finney," 246; McLoughlin, introduction to Finney's *Lectures on Revivals*, xlv.

34. Ronald G. Walters, *American Reformers 1815-1860*, 2d ed. (New York: Hill and Wang, 1997); and Timothy L. Smith, *Revivalism and Social Reform in Mid-Nineteenth Century America* (Nashville: Abingdon Press, 1957), are two leading interpreters of Finney as an optimist. Leonard Sweet questions this understanding, in "The View of Man Inherent in New Measures Revivalism"; for Finney's views on depravity see his *Systematic Theology*, 164-94.

35. John L. Thomas describes Finney as romantic, in his article "Romantic

Reform in America 1815-1865," *American Quarterly* 17 (Winter 1965): 656-81; on German thought, see Claude Welch, *Protestant Thought in the Nineteenth Century* (New Haven, Conn.: Yale University Press, 1972). See also McLoughlin's comments. For Old School comments, see Hodge, "Finney's Lectures on Theology," or Dod, "Review of Finney's Sermons." William McLoughlin makes some cogent comments in his introduction to Finney's *Lectures on Revivals*.

36. Since this is a study of the two major Calvinist denominations, I do not discuss the Methodists, who had their own perfectionist tradition.

37. See the discussion in chapter 10 below.

38. Weisberger, *They Gathered at the River*, 133-34; see George Duffield's series of articles on Finney in the 1848 and 1849 issues of the *American Biblical Repository*; Marsden, The *Evangelical Mind*, 122, 130; "The Congregational Convention," *The New Englander* 11 (February 1853): 77-78; "Perfect Love Attained," *The New Englander* 8 (November 1850): 528-42; Mark A. Noll sees Finney as one of the most significant figures of American religion, in *A History of Christianity in the United States and Canada* (Grand Rapids, Mich.: William B. Eerdmans, 1992), 174-78.

39. Robert S. Fletcher, *A History of Oberlin College from Its Foundation through the Civil War* (Oberlin, Ohio: Oberlin College, 1943), 1:445-50; "Another Development at Oberlin," *New York Observer*, December 23, 1843; "The Oberlin Lynching Case," *New York Observer*, March 6, 1841; "The Lynching Case at Oberlin," *New York Observer*, January 9, 1841.

40. Finney, *Memoirs*, 342-47 and passim.

Chapter 4. The Antelbellum Congregational and Presbyterian Communities

1. Earl A. Pope, *New England Calvinism and the Disruption of the Presbyterian Church* (New York: Garland, 1987), 347.

2. Sidney Ahlstrom, *A Religious History of the American People* (New Haven, Conn.: Yale University Press, 1972), 155-56. See also *The Cambridge and Saybrook Platforms of Church Discipline* (Boston: T. A. Marvin, 1829).

3. Ahlstrom, *Religious History of the American People*, 163-64.

4. Donald M. Scott, *From Office to Profession: The New England Ministry, 1750-1850* (Philadelphia: University of Pennsylvania Press, 1978), passim.

5. Joseph Conforti has demonstrated the reverence of New Englanders for the piety and historical memory of Jonathan Edwards in *Jonathan Edwards: Religious Tradition and American Thought* (Chapel Hill: University of North Carolina Press, 1995). I believe, however, that respect for the memory of Edwards also extended into his theological works, although they may have altered his intent. Even Taylor and Beecher used an amended version of Edwards's distinction between natural and moral ability.

6. Pope, *Disruption of the Presbyterian Church*, 276; Leo Hirrel, "The Ide-

ology of Antebellum Reform Within the New School Calvinist Community" (Ph.D. dissertation, University of Virginia, 1989), 342-46.

7. Henry K. Rowe, *History of Andover Theological Seminary* (Newton: Andover Theological Seminary, 1933), 10-155; Daniel Day Williams, *The Andover Liberals: A Study in American Theology* (1941 rpt, New York: Octagon Books, 1970), 1-10; Conforti, *Jonathan Edwards*, 112-13.

8. Rowe, *History of Andover Theological Seminary*, 71-73, 165-67 (the quote is on page 166); William A. Hallock, *Light and Love, A Sketch of the Life and Labors of Rev. Justin Edwards D.D.* (New York: American Tract Society, [N.D.]), 230-33, 331-32, 411, and 425.

9. Conforti, *Jonathan Edwards*, 108-44.

10. Zebulon Crocker, *The Catastrophe of the Presbyterian Church in 1837* (New Haven, Conn.: B & W Noyes, 1838), 239-44.

11. For an overview of Presbyterians through the twentieth century, see Lefferts A. Loetscher, *A Brief History of the Presbyterians*, 4th ed. (Philadelphia: Westminster Press, 1983).

12. Leonard J. Trinterud, *The Forming of an American Tradition: A Re-examination of Colonial Presbyterianism* (Philadelphia: Westminster Press, 1949), 17-22; see also Bryan F. Le Beau, *Jonathan Dickinson and the Formative Years of American Presbyterianism* (Lexington: University Press of Kentucky, 1997).

13. Trinterud, *Forming of an American Tradition*, 38-52.

14. Ibid., 53-121; Ahlstrom, *Religious History of the American People*, 269-75.

15. Trinterud, *Forming of an American Tradition*, 144-65.

16. Ibid., 225-27.

17. William Warren Sweet, *Religion on the American Frontier, The Presbyterians* (New York: Harper & Brothers, 1936), 99-125.

18. Ibid., 40-45, 99-125.

19. "Dr. Wilson versus the New School," *Christian Register* 14 (March 21, 1835): 126.

20. Sweet, *Religion on the American Frontier*, 40-45, 99-125.

21. John Quincy Adams, *A History of Auburn Theological Seminary, 1818-1918* (Auburn: Auburn Seminary Press, 1918), passim.

22. William S. Kennedy, *The Plan of Union or a History of the Presbyterian and Congregational Churches in the Western Reserve* (Hudson, Ohio: Pentagon Steam Press, 1856), 182 and passim.

23. Lyman Beecher, *The Autobiography of Lyman Beecher*, ed. Barbara Cross, 2 vols. (Cambridge, Mass.: Belknap Press, 1961), 2:179-86, 261-72; "To Whom Does Lane Seminary Belong and Who Endowed Lane Seminary," *The New York Observer*, April 8, 1843; Lawrence T. Lesick, *The Lane Rebels: Evangelicalism and Antislavery in Antebellum America* (Metuchen, N.J.: Scarecrow Press, 1980), 25-35.

24. Iver F. Yeager, *Church and College on the Illinois Frontier: The Beginnings of Illinois College and the United Church of Christ in Central Illinois 1829--1867* (Jacksonville, Ill.: Illinois College, 1980), 49-50.

25. George M. Marsden, *The Evangelical Mind and the New School Presbyterian Experience* (New Haven, Conn.: Yale University Press, 1970), 66.

26. Sidney Mead, *Nathaniel William Taylor, 1786-1858: A Connecticut Liberal* (Chicago: University of Chicago Press, 1942).

27. Vincent Harding, *A Certain Magnificence: Lyman Beecher and the Transformation of American Protestantism* (Brooklyn, N.Y.: Carlson, 1991), 3-21.

28. Mead, *Nathaniel William Taylor,* 33-34, 154-55, 240-41 and passim; Harding, *A Certain Magnificence,* 83-85.

29. The best biography of Lyman Beecher is Vincent Harding, *A Certain Magnificence*; other valuable works include Beecher, *Autobiography*; and Milton Rugoff, *The Beechers: An American Family in the Nineteenth Century* (New York: Harper & Row, 1981); see also James W. Frasier, *Pedagogue for God's Kingdom: Lyman Beecher and the Second Great Awakening* (Lanham, Md.: University Press of America, 1985); Stuart Henry gives a highly favorable biography of Beecher, in *Unvanquished Puritan: A Portrait of Lyman Beecher* (Grand Rapids, Mich.: W. B. Erdmans, 1976).

30. Rugoff, *The Beechers,* passim. Marie Caskey, *Chariot of Fire: Religion and the Beecher Family* (New Haven, Conn.: Yale University Press, 1978). In an effort to resolve the issues of the justice of God that had challenged his father, Edward Beecher also proposed his theory of the preexistence of souls. See Robert Merideth, *The Politics of the Universe: Edward Beecher, Abolition, and Orthodoxy* (Nashville: Vanderbilt University Press, 1963).

31. E. Bradford Davis, "Albert Barnes—1798-1870: An Exponent of New School Presbyterianism" (Th.D. dissertation, Princeton Theological Seminary, 1961), 1-72, 112 ; see also Allen Johnson and Dumas Malone, eds., *The Dictionary of American Biography* (New York: Charles Scribner's Sons, 1964), vol. 1, pt. 1, 627.

32. Davis, "Albert Barnes," 1-3.

33. See the entry on George Duffield in *The Dictionary of American Biography,* vol. 3, pt. 1, 490.

34. Robert M. York, *George B. Cheever: Religious and Social Reformer 1807--1890* (Orono: University of Maine, 1955); see also *The Dictionary of American Biography,* vol. 2, pt. 2, 48-49.

35. York, *George B. Cheever,* 151-83.

36. John H. Giltner, "Moses Stuart 1790--1852" (Ph.D. dissertation, Yale University, 1956); see also *The Dictionary of American Biography,* vo. 9, pt. 2, 174-75.

37. Williams, *The Andover Liberals,* 19-20.

38. Frank Luther Mott, *A History of American Magazines* (Cambridge, Mass.: Harvard University Press, 1938), 1:131-39, 310, 369-74, 529-35, and passim.

39. Carleton Mabee, *The American Leonardo: A Life of Samuel F. B. Morse* (New York: Alfred Knopf, 1943), 360, 398, and 168; New School General Assembly, *Minutes* (1859), 142; Beecher, *Autobiography,* 2:265.

40. Nathan O. Hatch, *The Democratization of American Christianity* (New

Haven, Conn.: Yale University Press, 1989), passim, see especially his examples of anticlerical and anti-Calvinist verses on 227-43; Paul K. Conkin, *The Uneasy Center: Reformed Christianity in Antebellum America* (Chapel Hill: University of North Carolina Press, 1995), 114-42.

41. Curtis D. Johnson, *Redeeming America: Evangelicals and the Road to the Civil War* (Chicago: Ivan R. Dee, 1993), 7-17 and passim.

42. Whitney R. Cross, *The Burned Over District: The Social and Intellectual History of Enthusiastic Religion in Western New York, 1800-1850* (Ithaca, N.Y.: Cornell University Press, 1950), 48 and passim.

43. Beecher, *Autobiography* 1:120-21. The title of this work is misleading. It is not an autobiography as such; rather, it is a collection of his correspondence, reminiscences, and other contributions, assembled by his children.

44. Robert Baird, *Religion in the United States of America* (Glasgow: Blackie and Son, 1844), passim.

45. Lois W. Banner, "The Protestant Crusade: Religious Missions, Benevolence and Reform in the United States 1790-1840" (Ph.D. dissertation, Columbia University, 1970), 45-54, 333, 336, and passim.

46. This point is discussed further in chapter 8 below. Wade C. Barclay, *History of Methodist Missions*. Vol. 2: *Early American Methodism 1769-1844* (New York: Board of Missions and Church Extension of the Methodist Church, 1950), 37.

47. Paul E. Johnson, *A Shopkeeper's Millennium: Society and Revivals in Rochester, New York, 1815-1837* (New York: Hill and Wang, 1978), 116-17; Nancy A. Hewitt, *Women's Activism and Social Change: Rochester, New York, 1822-1870* (Ithaca, N.Y.: Cornell University Press, 1984), passim.

48. Michael J. Crawford's *Seasons of Grace: Colonial New England's Revival Tradition in Its British Context* (New York: Oxford University Press, 1991) is an excellent discussion of the transatlantic aspects of eighteenth-century revivals.

49. Leigh E. Schmidt, *Holy Fairs: Scottish Communions and American Revivals in the Early Modern Period* (Princeton, N.J.: Princeton University Press, 1989), 50-69 and passim; Conkin, *The Uneasy Center*, 124-127; Loetscher, *History of the Presbyterians*, 80.

50. See, for example, Marsden, *The Evangelical Mind*, 31-59, or Ronald Walters, *American Reformers 1815--1860* (New York: Hill & Wang, 1978), 22-26 and passim.

51. On Old School attitudes toward revivals, see Samuel Miller, *Letters to Presbyterians on the Present Crisis in the Presbyterian Church* (Philadelphia: Anthony Finley, 1833), 151-64 and passim.

52. The interpretation of revivalism as a means of social control is advanced in Fred J. Hood, *Reformed America: The Middle and Southern States, 1783-1837* (Tuscaloosa: University of Alabama Press, 1980); Johnson, *A Shopkeeper's Millennium*; Charles R. Keller, *The Second Great Awakening in Connecticut* (New Haven, Conn.: Yale University Press, 1942); and Stephen E. Berk, *Calvinism versus Democracy: Timothy Dwight and the Origins of American Evangelical Ortho-*

doxy (Hampden, Conn.: Archon Books, 1974). Richard D. Sheils takes issue with these interpretations, in "The Second Great Awakening in Connecticut: Critique of the Traditional Interpretation" *Church History* 49 (December 1980): 401-15.

53. Hatch, *Democratization of American Christianity*, 221-23; also see chapter 3 above.

Chapter 5. The Role of Religion in the Republic

1. The most comprehensive account of the development of republican ideology is contained in Gordon Wood's book, *The Creation of the American Republic 1776-1787* (New York: W. W. Norton, 1969); Bernard Bailyn's *The Ideological Origins of the American Revolution* (Cambridge, Mass.: Belknap Press, 1967) is also indispensable to the understanding of republicanism; Michael F. Holt persuasively argues that the drive to preserve a republican government shaped American attitudes toward government throughout the antebellum era, in *The Political Crisis of the 1850s* (New York: John Wiley & Sons, 1978), 4-6 and passim; Daniel T. Rogers, discusses the historiography of republicanism in "Republicanism: The Career of a Concept," *Journal of American History* (June 1992): 11-38.

2. Wood, *Creation of the American Republic*, 65-70 and passim.

3. Vincent Harding, *A Certain Magnificence: Lyman Beecher and the Transformation of American Protestantism* (Brooklyn, N.Y.: Carlson, 1991), 86; "Christian Politics," *Quarterly Christian Spectator* 10 (August 1838): 422-23; "Rev. Mr. Barnes on Law," *New York Observer*, December 4, 1851. On eighteenth-century clerical concepts of republican government, see William K. Breitenbach, "New Divinity Theology and the Idea of Moral Accountability" (Ph.D. dissertation, Yale University, 1978), 43-45.

4. "Christian Politics," 427; "Barnes on Law"; see also "Restraints on Human Depravity," *Christian Spectator* 4 (April 1822): 184.

5. James McLane, "Christianity in Conflict with Politics," *American Biblical Repository*, 3d ser. 3 (January 1847): 112; "Christian Politics," 430-32; "Doctrine of the Higher Law," *The New Englander* 11 (April 1853): 161-71.

6. "Christian Politics," 432. Donald M. Scott describes many of the same attitudes toward government among New England ministers through the War of 1812. These attitudes, however, remained through the antebellum period. See *From Office to Profession: The New England Ministers, 1750-1850* (Philadelphia: University of Pennsylvania Press, 1978), 18-36.

7. Nathan O. Hatch, *The Sacred Cause of Liberty: Republican Thought and the Millennium in Revolutionary New England* (New Haven, Conn.: Yale University Press, 1977), 97-138 and passim; James M. Banner, Jr., *To the Hartford Convention: The Federalists and the Origins of Party Politics in Massachusetts, 1798-1815* (New York: Alfred A. Knopf, 1970), 26-27 and passim; William Cogswell, *The Harbinger of the Millennium* (Boston: Pierce & Parker, 1833), 130-31. Cogswell was secretary of the predominately New School American Education Society.

8. Samuel F. B. Morse, *A Foreign Conspiracy against the Liberties of the United States* (New York: Leavitt & Lord, 1835), 64; "Christian Politics," 437.

9. McLane, "Christianity in Conflict with Politics," 117.

10. Ibid., 118.

11. Banner, *To the Hartford Convention*, 148-67, 197-215

12. See Moses Stuart's letters to Daniel Webster, especially June 15, 1846, August 3, 1846, and November 19, 1843. Papers of Daniel Webster, microfilm (Dartmouth College and University Microfilms).

13. [Moses Stuart,] *Mr. Webster's Andover Address and His Political Course While Secretary of State* (Essex County: [N.P.], 1844). The title page also contains the remarks that "The Publishers have no authority to designate the authorship of the following pages, but from various circumstances, they infer the probability, that they were written by Prof. Stuart of Andover." Stuart later admitted writing the work, in *Conscience and the Constitution* (Boston: Crocker & Brewster, 1850), 6-7; see also John H. Giltner, "Moses Stuart 1780-1852," (Ph.D. dissertation, Yale University, 1956), 536-37; Fletcher Webster, ed., *The Private Correspondence of Daniel Webster*, 2 vols. (Boston: Little, Brown, 1857), 2:111.

14. Giltner, "Moses Stuart," 536-37; see also chapter 8 below.

15. Stuart, *Conscience and the Constitution*, 6-7; Giltner, "Moses Stuart," 536.

16. Stuart, *Conscience and the Constitution*, 6.

17. Robert M. York, *George B. Cheever: Religious and Social Reformer 1807-1890* (Orono: University of Maine, 1955), 115, 119; Daniel Walker Howe, *The Political Culture of the American Whigs* (Chicago: University of Chicago Press, 1979), 150-80, esp. 167.

18. Ronald P. Formisano, *The Transformation of Political Culture: Massachusetts Parties, 1827-1861* (New York: Oxford University Press, 1983), 467.

19. Richard J. Carwardine, *Evangelicals and Politics in Antebellum America* (New Haven, Conn.: Yale University Press, 1993), 28 and passim.

20. Carwardine develops this point in *Evangelicals and Politics in Antebellum America*; his work also includes a discussion of the "ethnocultural" historians.

21. Lyman Beecher, "Perils of Atheism," in *Beecher's Works*, 3 vols. (Boston: J.P. Jewett, 1852), 1:116.

22. Fred Hood, *Reformed America: The Middle and Southern States 1783-1837* (Tuscaloosa: University of Alabama Press, 1980), 48-67 and passim; "Christian Politics," 433.

23. The best account of disestablishment in New England is William McLoughlin's study *New England Dissent 1630-1833: The Baptists and the Separation of Church and State*, 2 vols. (Cambridge, Mass.: Harvard University Press, 1971).

24. Lyman Beecher, *The Autobiography of Lyman Beecher*, ed. Barbara Cross, 2 vols. (Cambridge, Mass.: Belknap Press, 1961), 1:252-53.

25. Fred Hood provides an excellent overview of the Presbyterian attitudes toward church and state, in *Reformed America*. He points to similarities between Old School and New School views on the importance of religion.

26. Ibid., 97.

27. Arthur M. Schlesinger, Jr., *The Age of Jackson* (Boston: Little Brown, 1945), 139; James R. Rohrer, "Sunday Mails and the Church State Theme in Jacksonian America," *Journal of the Early Republic* 7 (Spring 1987): 53-74; Richard R. John, "Taking Sabbatarianism Seriously: The Postal System, The Sabbath, and the Transformation of American Political Culture," *Journal of the Early Republic* 10 (Winter 1990): 517-67; Bertram Wyatt-Brown, "Prelude to Abolitionism: Sabbatarian Politics and the Rise of the Second Party System," *Journal of American History* 58 (September 1971): 329-35; Hood, *Reformed America*, 97-99.

28. Gardiner Spring, *The Sabbath: A Blessing to Mankind* (New York: American Tract Society, [N.D.]); George Duffield and Albert Barnes, *Discourses on the Sabbath* (Philadelphia: George W. Donohue, 1836); "The Perpetuity of the Sabbath," *Quarterly Christian Spectator* 4 (June 1832): 334-44.

29. Lyman Beecher, "Necessity of Revelation from God to Man," in *Works*, 1:165-66.

30. "Report of the Board of Visitors of the United States Military Academy," *Quarterly Christian Spectator* 6 (September 1834): 358-62.

31. Albert Barnes, "A Discourse Delivered in the First Presbyterian Church, Philadelphia July 10, 1836," in Duffield and Barnes, *Discourses on the Sabbath*, 105.

32. George Duffield, "The Moral Obligation of the Christian Sabbath," in Duffield and Barnes, *Discourses on the Sabbath*, 85; "Report on Sunday Mails," *Quarterly Christian Spectator* 1 (March 1829): 149-62.

33. "The Perpetuity of the Sabbath," 344.

34. Ernest Tuveson's *Redeemer Nation: The Idea of America's Millennial Role* (Chicago: University of Chicago Press, 1968) contains the fullest account of this subject; see also Ruth H. Bloch, *Visionary Republic: Millennial Themes in American Thought, 1756-1800* (Cambridge: Cambridge University Press, 1985); and Michael Barkun, *Crucible of the Millennium: The Burned Over District of New York in the 1840s* (Syracuse, N.Y.: Syracuse University Press, 1986).

35. Tuveson, *Redeemer Nation*, 34, 175, 232. Tuveson also uses the word "millenarian" to describe premillennialism. In a superb study of eighteenth-century New England millennialism, James W. Davidson suggests that the distinctions between premillennialists and postmillennialists were less than clear-cut. See *The Logic of Millennial Thought in Eighteenth Century New England* (New Haven, Conn.: Yale University Press, 1977); Whitney R. Cross gives an excellent description of the Millerites in *The Burned Over District: The Social and Intellectual History of Enthusiastic Religion in Western New York* (Ithaca, N.Y.: Cornell University Press, 1950), 287-321 and passim.

36. C.C. Goen, "Edwards New Departure in Eschatology," *Church History* 28 (March 1959): 25-40.

37. Tuveson, *Redeemer Nation*, 34; Carwardine, *Evangelicals and Politics*, 3 and passim; Ronald G. Walters, *American Reformers 1815-1861* (New York: Hill & Wang, 1978), 25-26 and passim.

38. See, for example, Samuel Hopkins, *Treatise on the Millennium* (Boston, 1793), and Albert Barnes, *Notes, Explanatory and Practical on the Book of Revelation.* (New York: Harper & Brothers, 1852).

39. Davidson, *Logic of Millennial Thought,* 129-41 and passim.

40. Jonathan Edwards, *History of the Work of Redemption,* ed. John F. Wilson, vol. 9 of *The Works of Jonathan Edwards,* ed. John E. Smith (New Haven, Conn.: Yale University Press, 1989), 462-63; Lyman Beecher, *A Plea for the West* (Cincinnati: Truman & Smith, 1835), 9-10.

41. Hollis Read, *The Hand of God in History; or Divine Providence Historically Illustrated in the Extension and Establishment of Christianity* (Hartford, Conn.: H. E. Robinson, 1851), 39.

42. George B. Cheever, *God's Hand in America* (New York: M.W. Dodd, 1841), 85-131; Tuveson, *Redeemer Nation,* passim.

43. Hatch, *Sacred Cause of Liberty,* 139-73 and passim; Ruth H. Bloch traces variations on a millennial theme across a wider spectrum of political and religious opinion, in *Visionary Republic.*

44. American Education Society, *Annual Reports,* 14th report (1833): 49; Lyman Beecher's *A Plea for the West* is also an excellent illustration of this combination of optimism and alarm in millennial thinking, especially 9-11, 30, 41-42.

45. Read, *The Hand of God in History,* 51-52; James H. Moorhead, *American Apocalypse: Yankee Protestants and the Civil War, 1860-1869* (New Haven, Conn.: Yale University Press, 1978), 10-11 and passim.

Chapter 6. The Catholic Church and the Whore of Babylon

1. The most complete study of early nineteenth-century anti-Catholicism is Ray A. Billington's *The Protestant Crusade 1800-1860: A Study of the Origins of American Nativism* (New York: Macmillan, 1938); Jenny Franchot discusses the impact of Protestant perceptions of Catholicism on antebellum literature, in *Roads to Rome: The Antebellum Protestant Encounter with Catholicism* (Berkeley and Los Angeles: University of California Press, 1994).

2. Sister Mary Augustina Ray, *American Opinion of Roman Catholicism in the Eighteenth Century* (New York: Columbia University, 1936), 266-80 and passim.

3. Francis D. Cogliano, *No King, No Popery: Anti-Catholicism in Revolutionary New England* (Westport, Conn.: Greenwood, 1995), 146-47 and passim; Ray, *American Opinion of Roman Catholicism,* 310-49, 393; Billington, *The Protestant Crusade,* 20-23.

4. Ira Leonard and Robert Parmet argue that the nativist influences were more important than religious influences, in *American Nativism 1830-1860* (New York: Van Nostrand, Reinhold, 1971); Jean Hales gives an excellent account of nativist ideology, in "The Shaping of Nativist Sentiment, 1848-1860" (Ph.D. dissertation, Stanford University, 1973).

5. Diana H. Butler describes similar anti-Catholicism among the evangelical portion of the Episcopal Church, in *Standing Against the Whirlwind: Evangelical Episcopalians in Nineteenth-Century America* (New York: Oxford University Press, 1995), 100-116, 149.

6. For example, the Old School General Assembly "almost unanimously" rejected the validity of a Roman Catholic baptism, Presbyterian General Assembly (O.S.), *Minutes* (1845), 34-37. Hodge's article was in response to this vote. [Charles Hodge], "Is the Church of Rome a Part of the Visible Church of Christ," *Princeton Review* 18 (April 1846): 320-44; also reprinted in Charles Hodge, *Essays and Reviews* (New York: Robert Carter & Brothers, 1857), 221-45.

7. Hodge, "Church of Rome," *Princeton Review*, 320-44, and in *Essays and Reviews*, 221-45.

8. Hodge, "Church of Rome," *Princeton Review*, 321-22, and in *Essays and Reviews*, 222-23.

9. James Ramsey, *The Spiritual Kingdom: An Exposition of the First Eleven Chapters of the Book of Revelation* (Richmond, Va.: Presbyterian Committee of Publication, 1873). Hodge wrote the introduction.

10. Michael E. Mooney, "Millennialism and Antichrist in New England" (Ph.D. dissertation, Syracuse University, 1982), 38-45.

11. Ibid., 38-45.

12. Ibid., 118-24, 225-28, and passim; Ray, *American Opinion of Roman Catholicism*, 120-23, 132-36.

13. Jonathan Edwards, "Notes on the Apocalypse," in *Apocalyptical Writings*, ed. Stephen J. Stein, vol. 5 of *The Works of Jonathan Edwards*, ed. John E. Smith (New Haven, Conn.: Yale University Press, 1977); Jonathan Edwards, *History of the Work of Redemption*, ed. John F. Wilson, vol. 9 of *The Works of Jonathan Edwards* (New Haven, Conn.: Yale University Press, 1989), 403-29; C.C. Goen, "Edwards' New Departure in Eschatology," *Church History* 28 (March 1959): 25-40.

14. Samuel Hopkins, *A Treatise on the Millennium* (Boston: Thomas & Andrews, 1793); George B. Cheever, "The Rise and Fall of the Papacy," *American Biblical Repository* 5 (April 1849): 321-53; George Duffield, *Dissertation on the Prophecies Relative to the Second Coming of Christ* (New York: Dayton & Newman, 1842).

15. Albert Barnes, *Notes, Explanatory and Practical on the Book of Revelation* (New York: Harper & Brothers, 1852).

16. Barnes, *Notes on Revelation*, 373; Billington, *The Protestant Crusade*, 357.

17. Barnes, *Notes on Revelation*, 422.

18. Ibid., 349; Cheever, "Rise and Fall of the Papacy," 331-35; Hopkins, *Treatise on the Millennium*, 65-98; Edwards, *Work of Redemption*, 412.

19. Moses Stuart, *Commentary on the Apocalypse* (New York: Van Nostrand & Territt, 1851).

20. Edward Beecher, "Remarks on Stuart's Commentary on the Apocalypse," *American Biblical Repository* 3 (April 1847): 272-304. Diana Butler describes a similar pattern of Biblical interpretation among evangelical Episcopalians, in *Standing Against the Whirlwind*, 100-101. Robert C. Fuller lists the Papacy as one of several antichrists in *Naming the Antichrist: The History of an American Obsession* (New York: Oxford University Press, 1995).

21. "The Apocalypse," *Presbyterian Quarterly Review* 1 (March 1853): 529-48.

22. "Popery," *Quarterly Christian Spectator* 7 (June 1835): 258-74.

23. "Roman Catholic Baptism of Bells," *Christian Spectator* 8 (August 1826): 409-12.

24. "Popery at Home," *New York Observer*, September 17, 1825.

25. William Nevin, *Thoughts on Popery* (New York: American Tract Society, [N.D.]), 51-56; Lyman Beecher, *A Plea for the West* (Cincinnati: Truman & Smith, 1835), 85.

26. Edward Beecher, *The Papal Conspiracy Exposed and Protestantism Defended in the Light of Reason, History, and Scripture* (New York: W. M. Dodd, 1855), 147; See also Samuel F.B. Morse, *A Foreign Conspiracy Against the Liberties of the United States* (New York: Leavitt, Lord, 1835), 47-48

27. E. Beecher, *Papal Conspiracy Exposed*, 148-51; Richard Hofstadter, "The Paranoid Style in American Politics," in his *The Paranoid Style in American Politics and Other Essays* (New York: Vintage Books, 1967), 21. In the opening passage, Beecher was paraphrasing Paul's letter to Timothy (1 Timothy 4: 2), where Paul warned of seducers and corrupters who would follow. Beecher thus further intimated that Catholicism was an apostasy foretold in the Bible.

28. William Strickland, *History of the American Bible Society* (New York: Harper & Brothers, 1856), 210-11 and passim; "The People's Right Defended," *Princeton Review* 3 (April 1831): 249-63.

29. On Catholic attitudes toward the Bible, see Gerald P. Fogarty, S.J., "The Quest for a Catholic Venacular Bible in America," in *The Bible in America: Essays in Cultural History*, ed. Nathan O. Hatch and Mark A. Noll (New York: Oxford University Press, 1982), 163-80; and F.J. Crehan, S.J., "The Bible in the Roman Catholic Church from Trent to the Present Day," in *The Cambridge History of the Bible*, ed., S.L. Greensdale, F.B.A. (Cambridge: Cambridge University Press, 1963), 199-237; on the Council of Trent and the Bible, see Hubert Jedin, *A History of the Council of Trent*, trans. Dom Ernest Graf, O.S.B. (London: Thomas Nelson and Sons), 52-97.

30. The earliest reference to this alleged proclamation that I can find is in a *Princeton Review* essay about an English book, *The People's Right Defended*, published under the pseudonym "Wycliff" in 1828. I can not determine precisely how this story began. See "Review of the People's Right Defended," *Princeton Review* 3 (1831): 253-54; for the alleged text of this proclamation, see [Anon.], *Twenty-two Plain Reasons For Not Being a Roman Catholic* (New York: American Tract Society, [N.D.]), 20.

31. Hollis Read, *The Hand of God in History; or Divine Providence Historically Illustrated in the Extension and Establishment of Christianity* (Hartford, Conn.: H. E. Robinson, 1851), 252-53.

32. Beecher, *Plea for the West*, 118.

33. "Review of The Religious State of Canada," *Quarterly Christian Spectator* 1 (June 1829): 286; "Review of Dwight's Travels in Germany," *Quarterly Christian Spectator* 1 (December 1829): 665; Ruth M. Elson, *Guardians of Tradition: American Textbooks in the Nineteenth Century* (Lincoln: University of Nebraska Press, 1964), passim.

34. Beecher, *Plea for the West*, 140-41; Morse, *Foreign Conspiracy*, 106 and passim.

35. George B. Cheever, *The Elements of National Greatness: An Address Before the New England Society of the City of New York* (New York: John S. Taylor, 1843), 13.

36. Morse, *Foreign Conspiracy*, 53; "Popery," 261; American Protestant Association, *Address of the Board of Managers of the American Protestant Association; with the Constitution and Organization of the Association* (Philadelphia, [N.P.], 1843), 18-20.

37. "Observations on Lower Canada," *Christian Spectator* 2 (March 1820): 133; Morse, *Foreign Conspiracy*, 27 and passim.

38. Billington, *Protestant Crusade*, 67-89.

39. Billington, *Protestant Crusade*, 73; Beecher, *A Plea For the West*, 61-66, 91; Milton Rugoff, *The Beechers: An American Family in the Nineteenth Century* (New York: Harper & Row, 1981), 152-54; Beecher, *The Autobiography of Lyman Beecher*, ed. Barbara Cross (Cambridge, Mass.: Belknap Press, 1961), 2:250-53.

40. Maria Monk, *Awful Disclosures of the Hôtel Dieu Nunnery in Montreal* (New York: Howe & Bates, 1836), 58, 111-18.

41. Billington, *Protestant Crusade*, 102-108; Alice Tyler, *Freedom's Ferment: Phases of American Social History from the Colonial Period to the Outbreak of the Civil War* (Minneapolis: University of Minnesota Press, 1944; rprt. ed., New York: Harper & Row, 1962), 372-74; Franchot, *Roads to Rome*, 135-62.

42. Billington, *Protestant Crusade*, 102; [J. Jones], *Awful Exposure of the Atrocious Plot Formed by Certain Individuals against the Clergy and Nuns of Lower Canada through the Intervention of Maria Monk* (Montreal and New York: Jones, 1836); Ralph Thompson, "The Maria Monk Affair," *Colophon* 5 (1934): pt. 17. Slocum's name appears in the statistical sections of the New School General Assembly's *Minutes* (1849, 245, and 1859, 183).

43. Billington, *Protestant Crusade*, 102-3; John J. Slocum, *A Reply to the Priests' Book* (New York: Leavitt & Lord; Boston: Crocker & Brewster, 1837), 103-12.

44. Billington, *Protestant Crusade*, 101; Thompson, "Maria Monk"; "Great Conspiracy of Religious and Literary Impostors Against Public Morals," *New York Herald*, August 12, 1836; "Maria Monk," *New York Herald*, August 18, 1836; Charles Edwards, *Reports of Chancery Cases Decided in the First Circuit of the State of New York* (New York: Gould Banks, 1843), 3:109-11; *New York Observer*, November 26, 1836. Allen Johnson and Dumas Malone, eds., *The Dictionary of American Biography* (New York: Charles Scribner's Sons, 1964), vol. 3, pt. 1 570-71. It is interesting to note that both Dwight and Bourne were also involved in antislavery activities.

45. Billington, *Protestant Crusade*, 103-4; "The Credibility of Maria Monk and Her Disclosures," *New York Observer*, May 21, 1836; "New Publication," *New York Observer*, July 9, 1836.

46. Billington, *Protestant Crusade*, 104-6; William Leete Stone, *Maria Monk and the Nunnery of the Hôtel Dieu* (New York: Howe & Bates, 1836); John

Spurlock, "The Awful Disclosures of William Leete Stone: Nativism and Nationality." Paper presented to the Society for Historians of the Early American Republic, Madison, Wis., July 1991; "Maria Monk," *New York Observer*, September 30, 1837; "Maria Monk and Her Impostitures," *Quarterly Christian Spectator* 9 (June 1837): 263-82.

47. David Brion Davis discusses the psychological dimensions of anti-Catholicism and other movements, in "Some Themes of Counter-Subversion," *Mississippi Valley Historical Review* 47 (September 1960): 205-24.

48. Monk, *Awful Disclosures*, 11-18 and passim.

49. Ibid., 56-58.

50. Ibid., 59.

51. "Letter From Spain," *New York Observer*, November 11, 1837; on convent inspections, see Billington, *Protestant Crusade*, 413-14; Ronald P. Formisano, *The Birth of Mass Political Parties: Michigan 1827-1861* (Princeton, N.J.: Princeton University Press, 1971), 257; "A Nunnery Law Wanted," *New York Observer*, November 30, 1854.

52. Ernest Tuveson, *Redeemer Nation: The Idea of America's Millennial Role* (Chicago: University of Chicago Press, 1968), 17-20; Read, *Hand of God in History*, passim; Beecher, *Plea for the West*, 9-10.

53. Richard Hofstadter included anti-Catholicism in his essay in *The Paranoid Style in American Politics*. Although the word "paranoid" may be unfortunate, he was correct in pointing to the sense of a grand conspiracy that characterized so much of the anti-Catholic literature.

54. Beecher, *Plea For the West*, 44-45.

55. Ibid., 120.

56. Ibid., passim; Morse, *Foreign Conspiracy*, passim.

57. "Popery," 268-69; *Home Missionary* 14 (December 1841):194; Beecher, *Plea For the West*, 68, 72.

58. "Power of Romanism in the United States," *New York Observer*, February 11, 1843.

59. Morse, *Foreign Conspiracy*, 64.

60. Read, *Hand of God in History*, 53.

61. Morse, *Foreign Conspiracy*, 124.

62. Billington, *Protestant Crusade*, 120, 166-92, and passim; American Protestant Association, *Address of the Board of Managers*; American Tract Society, *Sketch of the Origin and Character of the Principal Series of Tracts of the American Tract Society* (New York: American Tract Society, 1859); Harvey G. Neufeldt, "The American Tract Society, 1825-1865: An Examination of Its Religious, Economic, Social, and Political Ideas" (Ph.D. dissertation, Michigan State University, 1971), 204-9 and passim.

63. Elson, *Guardians of Tradition*, 47-52 and passim; Sister Marie Lenore Fell, *The Foundations of Nativism In American Textbooks, 1783-1860* (Washington D.C.: Catholic University Press, 1941); Billington, *Protestant Crusade*, 142-65 and passim.

64. George B. Cheever, *The Right of the Bible in Our Public Schools* (New York: Robert Carter & Brothers, 1854), 77.

65. Billington, *Protestant Crusade*, 292-95.

66. Billington, *Protestant Crusade*, 300-5.

Chapter 7. The Temperance Crusade

1. Among the most influential reinterpretations of the temperance cause are Norman Clark, *Deliver Us From Evil: An Interpretation of American Prohibition* (New York: W. W. Norton, 1976); Ian Tyrrell, *Sobering Up: From Temperance to Prohibition in Antebellum America, 1800-1860* (Westport, Conn.: Greenwood, 1979); W. J. Rorabaugh, *The Alcoholic Republic* (New York: Oxford University Press, 1979); and Jed Dannenbaum, *Drink and Disorder: Temperance Reform in Cincinnati from the Washingtonian Revival to the W.C.T.U.* (Urbana: University of Illinois Press, 1984). Joseph Kett has discussed all but the last work in his essay "Review Essay/Temperance and Intemperance as Historical Problems," *Journal of American History* 67 (March 1981): 878-85. Joseph R. Gusfield portrays temperance as an effort by a status-conscious middle class, in *Symbolic Crusade: Status Politics and the American Temperance Movement* (Urbana: University of Illinois Press, 1963).

2. John Allen Krout, *The Origins of Prohibition* (New York: Alfred A. Knopf, 1925), 26-50.

3. Rorabaugh, *The Alcoholic Republic*, 179-83.

4. Paul Johnson, *A Shopkeeper's Millennium: Society and Revivals in Rochester, New York, 1815-1837* (New York: Hill & Wang, 1978), 55-61 and passim; Dannenbaum, *Drink and Disorder*, 3-6.

5. Krout, *Origins of Prohibition*, 1-25.

6. Rorabaugh, *Alcoholic Republic*, 10, 20-21.

7. Tyrrell, *Sobering Up*, 33-54; Krout *Origins of Prohibition*, 90-93.

8. Krout, *Origins of Prohibition*, 108-10; Tyrrell, *Sobering Up*, 68-78.

9. As president of the American Temperance Society and later as president of Andover Seminary, Justin Edwards exerted a strong influence on the temperance movement and antebellum religion in general. Although he considered himself to be a staunch Calvinist, apparently his sympathies leaned toward New Haven. In 1827, Edwards received an honorary Doctor of Divinity from Yale College, and later he encouraged two of his sons to study at Yale. Edwards maintained friendly relations with such strongly New School organizations as the Home Missionary Society and the American Board of Commissioners for Foreign Missions. While president of Andover, he brought such New School ministers as Calvin Stowe, E.P. Barrows, and Thomas Skinner to the faculty. See William A. Hallock, *Light and Love: A Sketch of the Life and Labors of the Rev. Justin Edwards D.D.* (New York: American Tract Society, 1855), 233, 305-6, 331-32, 425, and passim.

10. Lyman Beecher, *Six Sermons on the Nature, Occasions, Signs, Evils, and Remedy of Intemperance* (Boston: T.R. Marvin, 1828).

11. Krout points out that five of the sixteen original members of the American Temperance Society were also members of the Congregationalist-oriented American Board of Commissioners for Foreign Missions, in *Origins of Prohibition*, 108-9.

12. Wade C. Barclay, *History of Methodist Missions*. Vol. 2: *Early American Methodism* (New York: Board of Missions and Church Extension of the Methodist Church, 1950), 37.

13. Garwin E. Lane explained the distinction, in *Temperance a Christian Duty, Abstinence a Christian Liberty* (Albany: Gray & Sprague, 1851).

14. Albert Barnes, *Barnes on the Traffic in Ardent Spirits* (New York: American Tract Society, [N.D.]), 1.

15. "The Philosophy and Influence of Habit in its Relation to Intemperance," *Quarterly Christian Spectator* 6 (September 1834): 370-81.

16. Ibid., 370-381; Justin Edwards, *Temperance Manual* (New York: American Tract Society, [185?]), 27-29; American Temperance Society, *Annual Reports* (New York: American Temperance Society), 4th report (1831): 13.

17. Temperance Society, *Annual Reports*, 6th report (1833): 18.

18. "The Philosophy of Habit," 370-81; see also Heman Humphrey, *Parallel Between Intemperance and the Slave Trade: An Address Delivered at Amherst College, July 4, 1828* (Amherst, Mass.: J. S. and C. Adams), 1828.

19. Edwards, *Temperance Manual*, 7-8, 34-36; Temperance Society, *Annual Reports*, 6th report (1833): 45.

20. [Justin Edwards], *On the Traffic in Ardent Spirits* (New York: American Tract Society, [N.D.]), 4; Krout, *Origins of Prohibition*, 234-36; "Another Jail to Let," *New York Observer*, January 28, 1837; "Discourse on Intemperance," *Quarterly Christian Spectator* 1 (November 1827): 599.

21. See, for example, *The Poor Man's House Repaired* (New York: American Tract Society, [N.D.]); [Job F. Halsey], *Who Slew All These?* (New York: American Tract Society, [N.D.]); "The Intemperate," *New York Observer*, December 7, 1833; Krout, *Origins of Prohibition*, 254-55.

22. Edwards, *Temperance Manual*, 74-75; see also "Confessions of a Rum Seller," *New York Observer*, June 11, 1831.

23. [Baxter Dickinson], *Alarm to Distillers and Their Allies*, (New York: American Tract Society, [N.D.]), 2. Dickinson was an Andover graduate who taught at Lane Seminary from 1835 to 1839 and at Auburn Seminary from 1839 to 1847; Temperance Society, *Annual Reports*, 5th report (1832): 25.

24. George B. Cheever, *The True History of Deacon Giles Distillery* (New York: [N.P.], 1844).

25. Krout, *Origins of Prohibition*, 259-60; Robert M. York, *George B. Cheever: Religious and Social Reformer, 1807-1890* (Orono: University of Maine, 1955), 73-79.

26. Krout, *Origins of Prohibition*, 182-222; Tyrrell, *Sobering Up*, 159-90. Because this study concerns religiously oriented reform, I do not cover the Washingtonians. Tyrrell and Krout give excellent accounts.

27. Temperance Society, *Annual Reports*, 6th report, (1833): 66; see also "Licensing of Dram Shops," *New York Observer*, December 21, 1833.

28. The best accounts of the prohibition campaigns in the antebellum era are Krout, *The Origins of Prohibition*, and Tyrrell, *Sobering Up*.

29. John Marsh, *The Temperance Battle Not Man's But God's* (New York: American Temperance Union, 1858), 15-16; see also Albert Barnes, *The Throne of Iniquity* (New York: National Temperance Society, [1851]), 14 and passim.

30. "Remarks on the Wine Traffic," *New York Observer*, March 14, 1840; "Stuart's Prize Essay," *New York Observer*, March 5, 1831.

31. Moses Stuart, *Essay on the Prize Question* (New York: John P. Haven, 1830).

32. In his work, *The Bible Rule of Temperance*, George Duffield said that he had published a tract in 1835 suggesting the possibility of unfermented wine (p. 86).

33. Eliphalet Nott, *Lectures on Temperance*, (New York: A.M. Moffort, 1858), 83-182 and passim (these lectures were originally published in 1839, with numerous re-editions); Krout, *Origins of Prohibition*, 165-167.

34. Nott, *Lectures on Temperance*, 133-35; Rev. R[alph] Crampton, *The Wine of the Bible and the Bible Use of Wine* (New York: John Abray, 1859), 8-9; John H. Giltner, "Moses Stuart 1780-1852" (Ph.D. dissertation, Yale University, 1956), 518-23.

35. "Excess in Intoxicating Drink," *New York Observer*, April 2, 1842.

36. [John MacLean], "Bacchus and Anti-Bacchus," *Princeton Review* 13 (April, October 1841): 267-306, 471-523.

37. Ibid., 269-71.

38. Ibid., 268.

39. Ibid., 522-23.

40. "Temperance Societies and the Lord's Supper," *New York Observer*, December 18, 1841; "Review of Mr. Delavan's Letters, *New York Observer*, February 19, 1842 and passim; Krout, *Origins of Prohibition*, 166-67; Glen C. Altschuler and Jan M. Saltzgaber, eds., *Revivalism, Social Conscience and Community in the Burned-Over District: The Trial of Rhoda Bement* (Ithaca, N.Y.: Cornell University Press, 1983), 100-2.

41. "Wine at the Communion," *New York Observer*, February 5, 1842. James Alexander was the son of Archibald Alexander.

42. "Mr. Delavan's Hobby," *New York Observer*, August 31, 1854.

43. "The Wine Question," *New York Observer*, April 30, 1842; "How to Flavor Wine," *New York Observer*, June 12, 1851; see also E. Douglas Branch, *The Sentimental Years* (New York: D. Appleton-Century, 1934), 231.

44. Moses Stuart, *Scriptural View of the Wine Question in a Letter to the Rev. Dr. Nott* (New York: Leavitt, Trow, 1848); Giltner, "Moses Stuart," 518-23. Some postwar proponents of the two-wine theory included William Patton, *The Laws of Fermentation and the Wines of the Ancients* (New York: National Temperance Society and Publication House, 1877); C.E. Ferrin, *The Wine Text of*

the Bible (New York: Lowell Adam, Wesson, 1877); R.N. Davies, *The Teaching of the Sacred Scriptures Concerning Wine and Other Liquor* (Cincinnati: Cranston & Stowe, 1887); Crampton, *Wine of the Bible*, 19.

45. Krout, *Origins of Prohibition*, 159-62; American Temperance Union, *Report of the Executive Committee*, 1840.

46. Krout, *Origins of Prohibition*, 159-62.

47. Duffield, *The Bible Rule of Temperance*, 86; Stuart, *Scriptural View of the Wine Question*; Giltner, "Moses Stuart," 518-23; Albert Barnes, *Notes, Explanatory and Practical, on the Gospel* [John], 2 vols. (New York: Harper & Bros. 1855), 2:201-2.

48. Presbyterian General Assembly (O.S.), *Minutes* (1842), 16; "The Old School General Assembly," *New York Observer*, May 28, 1842; Eliphalet Nott was probably the most important exception to this generalization. See Codman Hislop, *Eliphalet Nott* (Middletown, Conn.: Wesleyan University Press, 1971). Nott's role in the 1838 General Assembly was described in the May 26, 1838, issue of the *New York Observer*; Nott's name repeatedly appears in the Old School General Assembly *Minutes*, within the Albany Presbytery.

Chapter 8. Chattel Slavery

1. David Brion Davis, *The Problem of Slavery in Western Culture* (Ithaca, N.Y.: Cornell University Press, 1966), 91-97 and passim.

2. Charles Hodge, "Slavery," in *Essays and Reviews* (New York: Robert Carter and Brothers, 1857), 473-511, the same article appeared in the *Princeton Review* 7 (April 1836): 268-305; George Junkin, *The Integrity of Our National Union Vs. Abolitionism* (Cincinnati: B. P. Donoge, 1843), 75-78; Nathan L. Rice, *Lectures on Slavery* (Cincinnati: J.A. James, 1845).

3. For an excellent discussion of anarchism and radical abolitionism, see Lewis Perry, *Radical Abolitionism, Anarchy and the Moral Government of God in Antislavery Thought* (Ithaca, N.Y.: Cornell University Press, 1973).

4. James Brewer Stewart emphasizes the role of evangelicals, in *Holy Warriors: The Abolitionists and American Slavery* (New York: Hill & Wang, 1976).

5. See chapter 2 above.

6. Quoted in Robert H. Abzug, *Passionate Liberator, Theodore Dwight Weld and the Dilemma of Reform* (New York: Oxford University Press, 1980), 88.

7. Samuel Hopkins, *A Dialogue Concerning the Slavery of the Africans* (Norwich: Judah P. Spooner); Joseph A. Conforti, *Samuel Hopkins and the New Divinity Movement* (Grand Rapids, Mich.: Christian University Press, 1981), 126-48.

8. Charles Beecher, *The God of the Bible Against Slavery* (New York: American Antislavery Society, [N.D.]), 8.

9. Harriet Beecher Stowe, *The Key to Uncle Tom's Cabin*, with a preface by William Loren Katz (New York: Arno Press, 1968), 481.

10. Henry Ward Beecher, *Patriotic Addresses in America and England* (New York: Fords, Howard & Hulbert, 1887), 184-85; Stowe, *The Key to Uncle Tom's Cabin*, 481; Jonathan Blanchard, in Jonathan Blanchard and Nathan L. Rice, *A*

Debate on Slavery . . . Upon the Question: Is Slaveholding in Itself Sinful, and the Relation Between Master and Slave Sinful (Cincinnati: Wm. H. Moore, 1846), 176.

11. Charles Beecher, *The God of the Bible*, 8.

12. E[lijah] P[orter] Barrows, *A View of the American Slavery Question* (New York: John Taylor, 1836), 21-22, Barrows's name later appears in the New School General Assembly *Minutes* as a professor at Western Reserve College (1851, 94, and 1852, 242).

13. Leonard Bacon, *Slavery Discussed in Occasional Essays* (New York: Baker and Scribner's, 1846); Charles Hodge "Slavery," in *Essays and Reviews*, 473-511, and in *Princeton Review*, 268-305; Rice, *Lectures on Slavery*, passim.

14. The first minister to use the term *malum in se* was Edward Royall Tyler, in his short book *Slaveholding a Malum In Se or Invariably Sinful* (Hartford, Conn.: S.S. Cowles, 1839).

15. Barrows, *View of the Slavery Question*, 40, 43; see also John H. Giltner, "Moses Stuart, 1780-1852" (Ph.D. dissertation, Yale University, 1956), 526-28.

16. Bacon, *Slavery Discussed in Occasional Essays*, 57-79; James G. Birney, *American Churches: The Bulwark of Slavery* (Newburyport, Mass.: Charles Whipple, 1842), 31-33; Parker Pillsbury, *Acts of the Antislavery Apostles* (Concord, N.H.: Clague, Wegman, Schlicht, 1883), 389-91 and passim; John R. McKivigan, *The War Against Proslavery Religion: Abolitionism and the Northern Churches 1830-1865* (Ithaca, N.Y.: Cornell University Press, 1984), passim; Victor B. Howard, *Conscience and Slavery: The Evangelistic Calvinist Domestic Missions, 1837-1861* (Kent, Ohio: Kent State University Press, 1991), 40-54, 63-72, and passim; Lawrence Lessick, *The Lane Rebels: Evangelicalism and Antislavery in Antebellum America* (Metuchen, N.J.: Scarecrow Press, 1980), 121-25 and passim.

17. David Brion Davis, "The Emergence of Immediatism in British and American Antislavery Thought," *Mississippi Valley Historical Review* 49 (September 1962): 209-30; Anne C. Loveland, "Evangelicalism and 'Immediate Emancipation' in American Antislavery Thought," *Journal of Southern History* 32 (May 1966): 172-88.

18. The actual condition of slaves has been the focus of considerable research and debate. Peter J. Parish's *Slavery: History and Historians* (New York: Harper & Row, 1989) is an excellent introduction to this topic. Eugene Genovese's *Roll Jordan Roll: The World the Slaves Made* (New York: Vintage Books, 1972) is another invaluable study. John W. Blassingame presents a comparatively severe picture of slave life, in *The Slave Community: Plantation Life in the Antebellum South*, rev. ed. (New York: Oxford University Press, 1979). Robert Fogel and Stanley Engerman suggest that the physical privations of slavery have been exaggerated in their controversial work, in *Time on the Cross: The Economics of American Negro Slavery* (Boston: Little Brown, 1974).

19. H.W. Beecher, *Patriotic Addresses*, 185.

20. Theodore Dwight Weld, *American Slavery as It Is* (New York: American Antislavery Society, 1839); Abzug, *Passionate Liberator*, 210-14.

21. Weld, *Slavery as It Is*, 111.

22. Theodore Dwight Weld, *Slavery and the Internal Slave Trade* (London: Thomas Ward, 1841), 74, 76.

23. Ibid., 96.

24. Ronald G. Walters, "The Erotic South: Civilization and Sexuality in American Abolitionism," *American Quarterly* 25 (May 1973): 155-201; Ronald G. Walters, *The Antislavery Appeal: American Abolitionism after 1830* (Baltimore: Johns Hopkins University Press, 1976), 76-82. Eugene Genevose presents a good, sensitive discussion of this aspect of slavery in *Roll Jordan Roll*, 413-31.

25. George Bourne, *Picture of Slavery in the United States of America* (Boston: Isaac Knapp, 1838), 91-95.

26. Weld, *Slavery and the Internal Slave Trade*, 137; see also John W. Christie and Dwight L. Dumond, *George Bourne and The Book and Slavery Irreconcilable* (Wilmington: Historical Society of Delaware, 1969).

27. Joan D. Hedrick, *Harriet Beecher Stowe: A Life* (New York: Oxford University Press, 1994), 153-57 and passim; Charles H. Foster, *The Rungless Ladder: Harriet Beecher Stowe and New England Puritanism* (Durham, N.C.: Duke University Press, 1954), 95.

28. For Stowe's views of Augustine St. Clare, see *The Key to Uncle Tom's Cabin*, 61-68.

29. Harriet Beecher Stowe, *Uncle Tom's Cabin; or Life among the Lowly*, with an introduction by Dwight L. Dumond (New York: Collier Books, 1962), chaps. 1 and 21. Because of the innumerable editions of this work, I have referred to chapters rather than pages.

30. Ibid., chaps. 16 and 29 and passim; Stowe, *Key to Uncle Tom's Cabin*, 57-61.

31. Stowe, *Uncle Tom's Cabin*, chaps. 31 and 42.

32. Ibid., chaps. 31 and 42.

33. Milton Rugoff, *The Beechers: An American Family in the Nineteenth Century* (New York: Harper & Row, 1974), 47-53; Foster, *The Rungless Ladder*, 93-99.

34. Lawrence Buell, "Calvinism Romanticized: Harriet Beecher Stowe, Samuel Hopkins, and *The Minister's Wooing*," *ESQ: A Journal of the American Renaissance* 23 (Fall 1978): 119-32; Foster, *The Rungless Ladder*, 86-126.

35. Stowe, *Uncle Tom's Cabin*, chap. 10.

36. Rice, *Lectures on Slavery*, passim; some of the *New York Observer's* articles on slavery include "A Slaveholder Disciplined," January 13, 1847; "The Slave Market and the Sick Slave," August 21, 1848; "Antislavery Feeling in the Slave-Holding States," March 10, 1849; "Slavery and the Remedy," April 28, 1849; "Religion Among Slaves," February 24, 1853; "The Bible and Slavery," October 4, 1855; "Antislavery in the Slave States," November 23, 1844; "Southern Sentiments on Slavery," July 19, 1845.

37. Junkin, *The Integrity of Our National Union*, 14-71 and passim; Hodge, "Slavery," 473-511; Thornton Stringfellow, "Scripture on Slavery," in *Cotton is King and Pro-Slavery Arguments*, ed. E.N. Elliot (Augusta, Ga.: Pritchard, Abbott & Loomis, 1860), 461-508; Rice, *Lectures on Slavery*, passim.

38. George B. Cheever, *The Guilt of Slavery and the Crime of Slaveholding* (Boston: John P. Jewett, 1860), 27.

39. Hopkins, *Dialogue Concerning the Slavery of Africans*, 30-35; Bourne, *The Book and Slavery Irreconcilable*; Angela Grimke, *Appeal to the Christian Women of the South* (New York: American Antislavery Society, 1836), 2-10 and passim; Theodore Dwight Weld, *The Bible Against Slavery: An Inquiry into The Patriarchal and Mosiac Systems on the Subject of Human Rights* (New York: American Antislavery Society, 1838); Albert Barnes, *An Inquiry into the Scriptural Views of Slavery* (Philadelphia: Parry & McMillan, 1857).

40. Barnes, *Scriptural Views of Slavery*, 260-66 and passim; Edward Bradford Davis, "Albert Barnes: 1798-1870: An Exponent of New School Calvinism" (Th.D. dissertation, Princeton Seminary, 1961), 302-4.

41. Cheever, *Guilt of Slavery*, 355-57.

42. Ibid., 237-47; Barnes, *Scriptural Views of Slavery*, 140-43; Bacon, *Slavery Discussed in Occasional Essays*, 32; Moses Stuart, *Conscience and the Constitution*, (Boston: Crocker & Brewster, 1850), 30-32.

43. Bacon, *Slavery Discussed in Occasional Essays*, 180 and passim. Bacon is an excellent example of the fact that not all New School Calvinists were militant antislavery activists, even though virtually all militants within the Presbyterian and Congregational churches were New School adherents. See Timothy J. Lehr, "Leonard Bacon and the Myth of the Good Slaveholder," *New England Quarterly* 49 (June 1976): 194-213.

44. John McKivigan, *The War against Proslavery Religion*, passim; see also Howard, *Conscience and Slavery*, passim.

45. Russell B. Nye, *Fettered Freedom: Civil Liberties and the Slavery Controversy, 1830-1860* (East Lansing: Michigan State University Press, 1963), gives the best account of the repression of the slavery debate.

46. Leonard Richards, *Gentlemen of Property and Standing: Anti-Abolition Mobs in Jacksonian America* (New York: Oxford University Press, 1970); Harriet Martineau, *The Martyr Age of the United States* (Boston: Weeks, Jordan, 1839).

47. Barrows, *View of the Slavery Question*, 33. Barrows is paraphrasing John 3: 19-20.

48. Nye, *Fettered Freedom*, 282-92; Stewart, *Holy Warriors*, 77.

49. David Brion Davis, *The Slave Power Conspiracy and the Paranoid Style* (Baton Rouge: Louisiana State University Press, 1969).

50. Charles Beecher, *The Duty of Disobedience to Wicked Laws* (Newark, N.J.: J.M. McIlvaine, 1851), 16; H.W. Beecher, *Patriotic Addresses*, 188-89; "The Fugitive Slave Law," *The New Englander* 8 (November 1850): 615-45; David Potter, *The Impending Crisis, 1848-1861* (New York: Harper & Row, 1976), 131-34; Ralph Alan Keller, "Northern Protestant Churches and the Fugitive Slave Law of 1850" (Ph.D. dissertation, University of Wisconsin, 1969).

51. Keller, "Protestant Churches and the Fugitive Slave Law," 123-27; Giltner, "Moses Stuart," 536-44; Stuart, *Conscience and the Constitution*. In 1835, Stuart expressed similar views about the Bible and slavery.

52. Henry Ward Beecher, *Defence of Kansas* (Washington, D.C.: Buell & Blanchard, 1856), 2.

53. William Goodell, ed., *American Jubilee*, March, 1854.

Chapter 9. Benevolence, the Social Order, and the Kingdom of God

1. Henry F. May, *Protestant Churches and Industrial America* (New York: Harper & Brothers, 1949), 39-90 and passim.

2. Lois Banner's excellent study, "The Protestant Crusade: Missions, Benevolence, and Reform in the United States, 1790-1840" (Ph.D. dissertation, Columbia University, 1970), provides a wealth of information about these organizations.

3. William P. Strickland, *History of the American Bible Society* (New York: Harper & Brothers, 1856); American Bible Society, *Annual Reports*; Peter J. Wosh, "Bibles, Benevolence, and Emerging Bureaucracy: The Persistence of the American Bible Society, 1816-1890" (Ph.D. dissertation, New York University, 1988).

4. American Tract Society, *Annual Reports*; Harvey G. Neufeldt, "The American Tract Society, 1825-1865: An Examination of Its Religious, Economic, Social, and Political Ideas" (Ph.D. dissertation, Michigan State University, 1971); Banner, "Protestant Crusade," 333-35; Diana H. Butler, *Standing Against the Whirlwind: Evangelical Episcopalians in Nineteenth-Century America* (New York: Oxford University Press, 1995), 153-55.

5. Edwin William Rice, *The Sunday School Movement and the American Sunday School Union 1817-1917* (Philadelphia: American Sunday School Union, 1917); Frederick A. Packard, *Letters on the Design and Importance of the American Sunday School Union in New England* (Philadelphia: American Sunday School Union, 1838); American Sunday School Union, *Annual Reports*.

6. American Education Society, *Annual Reports*, 30th report, (1846): 12-13 and passim.

7. Collin B. Goodykoontz, *Home Missions on the American Frontier, with Particular Reference to the American Home Missionary Society* (Caldwell, Idaho: Claxton Press, 1939); *Relations of the Presbyterian Church to the Work of Home Missions: Report of the General Assembly's Commission of Investigation* (New York: John A. Gray, 1860); American Home Missionary Society, *Annual Reports*, passim.

8. Victor B. Howard provides a detailed discussion of slavery in the American Home Missionary Society, in *Conscience and Slavery: The Evangelistic Calvinist Domestic Missions, 1837-1861* (Kent, Ohio: Kent State University Press, 1990).

9. Clifton J. Philips, *Protestant America and the Pagan World: The First Half Century of the American Board of Commissioners for Foreign Missions 1810-1860* (Cambridge, Mass.: Harvard University Press, 1969); William R. Hutchison, *Errand to the World; American Protestant Thought and Foreign Missions* (Chicago: University of Chicago Press, 1987); American Board of Commissioners for Foreign Missions, *Annual Reports*.

10. Hutchison, *Errand to the World*, 77-90 and passim.

11. Joan Brumberg gives an account of the hardships of the Baptist missionary Adoniram Judson in *Mission for Life: The Story of the Family of Adoniram Judson* (New York: Free Press, 1980).

12. Carroll Smith-Rosenberg, *Religion and the Rise of the American City: The New York City Mission Movement, 1812-1870* (Ithaca, N.Y.: Cornell University Press, 1971), 255.

13. Isaac S. Hartley, *Memorial of Robert Milham Hartley* (privately published, 1882; rprt. New York: Arno Press, 1976), 67-68, 530. Hartley's funeral services were conducted in the New School Madison Square Presbyterian Church.

14. Roy Lubove, "The New York Association for Improving the Condition of the Poor: The Formative Years," *New York Historical Society Quarterly* 43 (July 1959): 307-27; New York Association for Improving the Condition of the Poor, *Annual Reports*, 1st report (1845): 17-18, 4th report (1847): 12-17.

15. George M. Marsden, *The Evangelical Mind and the New School Presbyterian Experience* (New Haven, Conn.: Yale University Press, 1970), 73-75; [Charles Hodge], "Review of a Plea for Voluntary Societies," *Princeton Review* 9 (January 1837): 112-14; Samuel Miller, *Letters to Presbyterians on the Present Crisis in the Presbyterian Church* (Philadelphia: Anthony Finley, 1833), 78; Samuel J. Baird, *A History of the New School and the Questions Involved in the Disruption of the Presbyterian Church in 1838* (Philadelphia: Claxton, Rumsen & Hoffelfinger, 1868), 282-326.

16. Banner, "Protestant Crusade," 333-35; Butler, *Standing Against the Whirlwind*, 46-48, 75.

17. American Tract Society, *Annual Reports*, 26th report (1851): 66, 2d report (1827): 24; other examples of the belief in the efficacy of tracts can be found in "Labors of a Tract Visitor," *New York Observer* May 23 1840-August 8, 1840.

18. "A More Excellent Way," *Christian Spectator* 6 (September 1824): 471; American Board of Commissioners for Foreign Missions, *Moral Conditions and Prospects of the Heathen* (Boston: Crocker & Brewster, 1833).

19. Phillips, *Protestant America and the Pagan World*, 270.

20. *Tahiti Without the Gospel* (Philadelphia: American Sunday School Union, 1833), 217-18, 225.

21. Ray A. Billington, *The Protestant Crusade 1800-1860: A Study of the Origins of American Nativism* (New York: Macmillan, 1938), 118-41 and passim; American Tract Society, *Sketch of the Origin and Character of the Principal Series of Tracts of the American Tract Society* (New York: The American Tract Society, 1859); William Nevin *Thoughts on Popery* (New York: American Tract Society, [N.D.]); Neufeldt, "American Tract Society," 204-9. Almost every second or third issue of the *Home Missionary* contains an article on Catholicism.

22. American Board of Commissioners for Foreign Missions, *Annual Reports*, 28th report (1837): 55.

23. Ibid., 31st report (1840): 32-37; Phillips, *Protestant America and the Pagan World*, 115-18; Charles De Varigny, *Fourteen Years in the Sandwich Islands*

1855-1868, trans. Alfons L. Korn (Honolulu: University Press of Hawaii, 1981), 47-51.

24. Mary Zwiep, *Pilgrim Path: The First Company of Women Missionaries to Hawaii* (Madison: University of Wisconsin Press, 1991).

25. Hutchison, *Errand to the World*, 86; Rufus Anderson, *The Hawaiian Islands: Their Progress and Condition under Missionary Labors* (Boston: Gould and Lincoln, 1864), 229-230.

26. Hutchison, *Errand to the World*, 86-87.

27. Anderson, *The Hawaiian Islands*, 229-30.

28. Anderson, *Hawaiian Islands*, passim; Sylvester K. Stevens, *American Expansion in Hawaii. 1842-1898* (Harrisburg, Penn.: Archives Publishing, 1945), 25-33.

29. Bradford Smith, *Yankees in Paradise: The New England Impact on Hawaii* (Philadelphia: J.B. Lippincott, 1956), 281-89.

30. Hutchison, *Errand to the World*, 77-90.

31. [Rufus Anderson], *Memorial of the First Fifty Years of the American Board of Commissioners for Foreign Missions* (Boston: American Board of Commissioners for Foreign Missions, 1862), 250-51 and passim; Rufus Anderson, *History of the Sandwich Islands Missions* (Boston: Congregational Publishing, 1870), 173 and passim; see also Anderson's 1864 account of the Sandwich Islands, *The Hawaiian Islands*, passim, especially the passages quoted above.

32. William G. McLoughlin, *Cherokees and Missionaries, 1789-1839* (New Haven, Conn.: Yale University Press, 1984), provides a full account of this topic.

33. New York Association for Improving the Condition of the Poor, *Annual Reports*, 6th report (1849): 16, 14th report (1857): 14-16.

34. The instructions, contained in various *Annual Reports*, advised visitors to exercise the most careful discrimination in dispensing assistance. See also New York Association for Improving the Condition of the Poor, *Annual Reports*, 1st report (1845): 17-18, 4th report (1847): 12-17; Hartley, *Memorial of Hartley*, 186.

35. New York Association for Improving the Condition of the Poor, *Annual Reports*, 13th report (1856): 87, 10th report (1853): 33-35. An extract from the tenth report, denouncing indiscriminate charity using Scripture, was republished in the fourteenth through sixteenth reports.

36. Ibid. 5th report (1848): 15; 6th report (1849): 20-21.

37. Ibid., 12th report (1855): 33; 13th report. (1856): 18.

38. Ibid., 23d report (1866): 38-39.

39. Hartley, *Memorial of Hartley*, 343.

40. New York Association for Improving the Condition of the Poor, *Annual Reports* 9th report (1852): 38-39, 10th report (1853): 30, 13th report (1856): 42-51, 14th report (1857): 18-26, 25th report (1868): 31-42; Hartley, *Memorial of Hartley*, 200-3, 216-22; Smith-Rosenberg, *Religion and the Rise of the American City*, 266-70.

41. Timothy L. Smith argues that antebellum concern over the urban poor

provided the origins of the Social Gospel, in *Revivalism and Social Reform in Mid-Nineteenth Century America* (Nashville: Abingdon Press, 1957), 151-67 and passim.

42. American Board of Commissioners for Foreign Missions, *Annual Reports*, 21st report (1830): 105, 21st report (1830): 105.

Chapter 10. The Closing Years of Antebellum Reform

1. Earl A. Pope's excellent work, *New England Calvinism and the Disruption of the Presbyterian Church* (New York: Garland, 1987), is the most thorough analysis of the Presbyterian schism; George M. Marsden, *The Evangelical Mind and the New School Presbyterian Experience* (New Haven, Conn.: Yale University Press, 1970) is another valuable account; Leo Hirrel, "The Ideology of Antebellum Reform Within the New School Calvinist Community" (Ph.D. dissertation, University of Virginia, 1989), 317-54, contains a more detailed discussion of this topic.

2. Marsden, *Evangelical Mind*, 62-63; Pope, *Disruption of the Presbyterian Church*, 321-24: [Charles Hodge], "The General Assembly of 1837," *Princeton Review* 9 (July 1837): 407-85; the *New York Observer* carried a detailed account of this Assembly in its May 27 through June 24, 1837, issues, with some articles following throughout that summer.

3. Vincent Harding, *A Certain Magnificence: Lyman Beecher and the Transformation of American Protestantism, 1775-1863* (Brooklyn, N.Y.: Carlson, 1991), 430-31; Marsden, *Evangelical Mind*, 64; Pope, *Disruption of the Presbyterian Church*, 333-35.

4. Marsden, *Evangelical Mind*, 64-66; Harding, *A Certain Magnificence*, 434-37; Pope, *Disruption of the Presbyterian Church*, 342-47; Presbyterian General Assembly, *Minutes*, (1838), 6-8, 19-21 33-40, 48-51; the *New York Observer* provided a detailed account of these events in its May 26, 1838, issue and in subsequent issues.

5. Marsden's excellent book provides a solid discussion of the rise of denominationalism, *The Evangelical Mind*, 104-41 (the quotation is on 128); see also Lois Banner's fine work, "The Protestant Crusade: Missions, Benevolence, and Reform in the United States, 1790-1840" (Ph.D. dissertation, Columbia University, 1970), 350-80.

6. *Relations of the Presbyterian Church to the Work of Home Missions: Report of the General Assembly's Commission of Investigation* (New York: John A. Gray, 1860); "The General Assembly," *Presbyterian Quarterly Review* 2 (September 1853): 307-17; Marsden, *Evangelical Mind*, 130.

7. "The Albany Convention and the New Englander," *Presbyterian Quarterly Review* 1 (March 1853): 630.

8. "The Spirit of American Presbyterianism," *Presbyterian Quarterly Review* 1 (1853): 473-523; 2 (1854): 206-46; 3 (1855): 122-54, 467-503, 648-85; and "Old and New Theology," *Presbyterian Quarterly Review* 3 (1855): 89-121, 353-71, 630-47; 4 (1856): 213-46, 578-620.

9. "Old and New Theology," 4:585 and passim.

10. "The Princeton Review's Criticism on `Barnes on the Atonement,'" *Presbyterian Quarterly Review* 8 (October 1859): 311-36; Albert Barnes, *The Atonement in Relation to Law and Moral Government* (Philadelphia: Parry & McMillan, 1859); "Barnes on the Atonement," *Princeton Review* 31 (July 1859): 464-88.

11. George Duffield's articles are scattered throughout the *American Biblical Repository* 3d ser. 4 (1848): 212-52, 412-52, 711-46, and 5 (1849): 96-129; "Albany Convention and the New Englander," 632-35.

12. Marsden provides a detailed discussion of Smith in *Evangelical Mind*, 157-81.

13. Henry Boynton Smith, "Faith and Philosophy" in *Faith and Philosophy: Discourses and Essays* (New York: Scribner, Armstrong, 1877), 46.

14. Smith, "The Idea of Christian Theology as a System" in *Faith and Philosophy*, 160.

15. Barbara M. Cross, *Horace Bushnell: Minister to a Changing America* (Chicago: University of Chicago Press, 1958); David L. Smith, *Symbolism and Growth: The Religious Thought of Horace Bushnell* (Chico, Calif.: Scholars Press, 1981).

16. Horace Bushnell, "Preliminary Dissertation on the Nature of Language as Related to Thought and Spirit," in *God in Christ: Three Discourses Delivered at New Haven, Cambridge, and Andover, with a Preliminary Dissertation on Language* (Hartford, Conn.: Brown & Parsons, 1849), 9-117.

17. Bushnell, *God in Christ*, 137-40, 146-47, 172-77, 213-15, 234-35, and passim; D. Smith, *Symbolism and Growth*, 139-74.

18. Louise L. Stevenson, *Scholarly Means to Evangelical Ends: The New Haven Scholars and the Transformation of Higher Learning in America, 1830-1890* (Baltimore: Johns Hopkins University Press, 1986).

19. Horace Bushnell, *Christian Nurture*, with an introduction by John M. Mulder (Grand Rapids, Mich.: Baker Book House, 1979); Calvin Stowe, "The Principles of Presbyterianism and the Reasons for Upholding Them," *American Biblical Repository* 2d ser. 12 (October 1844): 290. Although he is well remembered for his famous wife (Harriet Beecher Stowe) and father-in-law, Calvin Stowe was a well-respected Bible scholar at Lane and Andover Seminaries in his own right. He provided invaluable assistance to Lyman Beecher during Beecher's heresy trial.

20. Albert Barnes, *Notes Explanatory and Practical on the First Epistle of Paul to the Corinthians* (New York: Harper & Brothers, 1841), 222.

21. Donna A. Behnke, *Religious Issues in Nineteenth-Century Feminism* (Troy, N.Y.: Whitson, 1982); Nancy Cott, "In the Bonds of Womanhood: Perspectives on Female Experience and Consciousness in New England, 1780-1830" (Ph.D. dissertation, Brandeis University, 1974), 129-35. Cott's dissertation contains a much fuller discussion of ministers' sermons than does her book of the same title. See also Blanche Hersh, *The Slavery of Sex: Feminist-Abolitionists in America* (Urbana: University of Illinois Press, 1978), 137-45.

22. M[ilo] J. Hickok, "The Mission of Women under the Gospel," *The*

American National Preacher, 26 (August 1852): 180; Hickok's name appears in the New School General Assembly *Minutes* for 1852, 219.

23. Behnke, *Religious Issues in Nineteenth-Century Feminism*, 279-82; see also Horace Bushnell, *Women's Suffrage: The Reform Against Nature* (New York: Charles Scribner, 1869).

24. "The General Assembly," *Presbyterian Quarterly Review* 2 (September 1853): 308-10; American Education Society, *Annual Reports* 42d report (1858): 16-17.

25. Julian Sturtevant, "The American Colporteur System," *American Biblical Repository* 2d ser. 12 (July 1844): 214-43; New School General Assembly, *Minutes*, (1854): 532-34, (1855): 48-49 and passim; Marsden, *Evangelical Mind*, 137-41. Sturtevant was a member of the so-called Yale band who helped create Illinois College. Sturtevant served as president of the college and was accused of heresy along with Edward Beecher.

26. See discussion in chapter 7 above.

27. Tyler Anbinder, *Nativism and Slavery: The Northern Know Nothings and the Politics of the 1850s* (New York: Oxford University Press, 1992).

28. Ronald Formisano, *The Birth of Mass Political Parties: Michigan 1827-1861* (Princeton, N.J.: Princeton University Press, 1971), 239, 256-57, 271-72; Michael F. Holt, *Forging a Majority: The Formation of the Republican Party in Pittsburgh, 1848-1860* (New Haven, Conn.: Yale University Press, 1969), "The Politics of Impatience: The Origins of Know-Nothingism," *Journal of American History* 60 (September 1973): 309-31, and *The Political Crisis of the 1850s* (New York: John Wiley & Sons, 1978), 161. Holt describes Republican tactics as using Catholics as a "negative reference group."

29. Some of the best discussions of the political slavery controversy include David M. Potter, *The Impending Crisis, 1848-1861* (New York: Harper & Row, 1976); Richard H. Sewell, *Ballots for Freedom: Antislavery Politics in the United States 1837-1860* (New York: Oxford University Press, 1976); James Brewer Stewart, *Holy Warriors; The Abolitionists and American Slavery* (New York: Hill & Wang, 1976); and William E. Gienapp *The Origins of the Republican Party, 1852-1856* (New York: Oxford University Press, 1987).

30. For an excellent discussion of the reaction of Northern Protestant clergy to the Civil War, see James H. Moorhead, *American Apocalypse: Yankee Protestants and the Civil War 1860-1869* (New Haven, Conn.: Yale University Press, 1978).

In Retrospect

1. Sidney E. Ahlstrom, ed., *Theology in America: The Major Protestant Voices From Puritanism to Neo-Orthodoxy* (Indianapolis: Bobbs-Merrill, 1967), 211; Daniel Day Williams, *The Andover Liberals: A Study in American Theology* (1941; rprt. New York: Octagon Books, 1970); Bruce Kuklick, *Churchmen and Philosophers: From Jonathan Edwards to John Dewey* (New Haven, Conn.: Yale University Press, 1985), 216-30.

Bibliography

Primary Sources

Manuscript Collections

"Papers of Albert Barnes," Presbyterian Historical Society, Philadelphia.
"Papers of Daniel Webster." Microfilmed by University Microfilms in collaboration with Dartmouth College, 1971.

Annual Reports of Organizations

American Bible Society. New York. *Annual Reports*, 1816-60.
American Board of Commissioners for Foreign Missions. New York. *Annual Reports*, 1810-60.
American Education Society. Andover, Mass. *Annual Reports*, 1816-60.
American Home Missionary Society. New York. *Annual Reports*, 1826-60.
American Sunday School Union. Philadelphia. *Annual Reports*, 1824-60.
American Temperance Society. Andover, Mass. *Annual Reports*, 1829, 1833-36.
American Temperance Union. Philadelphia. *Annual Reports*, 1838-59.
American Tract Society. New York. *Annual Reports*, 1826-60.
New York Association for Improving the Conditions of the Poor. New York. *Annual Reports*, 1843-60.

Magazines and Newspapers

American Biblical Repository [title varies]. Andover & New York, 1836-50.
Christian Spectator. New Haven, Conn., 1819-28.
Goodell, William, ed. *American Jubilee*. New York, 1854-55.
The New Englander. New Haven, Conn., 1843-60.
The New York Observer. New York, 1823-60.
Presbyterian General Assembly [New School]. New York. *Minutes*. 1838-60.

Presbyterian General Assembly [Old School]. Philadelphia. *Minutes.* 1825-60.
The Princeton Review [title varies]. Princeton, 1825-60.
Presbyterian Quarterly Review. Philadelphia, 1852-60.
Quarterly Christian Spectator. New Haven, Conn., 1829-38.

Books and Pamphlets

American Bible Society. *The Manual of the American Bible Society.* New York: American Bible Society Press, 1871.

American Board of Commissioners for Foreign Missions. *Moral Conditions and Prospects of the Heathen.* Boston: Crocker and Brewster, 1833.

American Protestant Association. *Address of the Board of Managers of the American Protestant Association with the Constitution and Organization of the Association.* Philadelphia: [N.P.], 1843.

American Sunday School Union. *Considerations Touching the Principles and Objects of the American Sunday School Union.* Philadelphia: American Sunday School Union, 1845.

———. *Constitution of the American Sunday School Union, with the By-laws of the Board.* Philadelphia: American Sunday School Union, 1849.

American Tract Society. *The Address of the Executive Committee of the American Tract Society to the Christian Public.* New York: D. Fanshaw, 1825.

———. *The American Colporteur System.* New York: American Tract Society, 1836.

———. *Sketch of the Origin and Character of the Principal Series of Tracts of the American Tract Society.* New York: The American Tract Society, 1859.

Anderson, Rufus. *The Hawaiian Islands: Their Progress and Condition under Missionary Labors.* Boston: Gould & Lincoln, 1864.

———. *History of the Sandwich Island Missions.* Boston: Congregational Publishing Company, 1870.

———. *Memorial Volume of the First Fifty Years of the American Board of Commissioners for Foreign Missions.* Boston: American Board of Commissioners for Foreign Missions, 1862.

Bacon, Leonard. *A Discourse on the Traffic in Spirituous Liquors.* New Haven, Conn.: B.L. Hamlen, 1838.

———. *A Plea for Africa.* New Haven, Conn.: T.G. Woodward, 1825.

———. *Slavery Discussed in Occasional Essays.* New York: Baker and Scribner's, 1846.

———. *Total Abstinence from Ardent Spirits, an Address Delivered by Request of the Young Men's Temperance Society of New Haven.* New Haven, Conn.: Sidney's Press, 1829.

Baird, Robert. *Religion in the United States of America.* Glasglow: Blackie and Son, 1844.

Baird, Samuel. *A History of the New School and of the Questions Involved in the Disruption of the Presbyterian Church in 1838.* Philadelphia: Claxton, Rumsen & Hoffelfinger, 1868.

Barnes, Albert. *The Atonement in its Relations to Law and Moral Government.* Philadelphia: Parry & McMillan, 1859.

―――. *Barnes on the Traffic in Ardent Spirits.* New York: American Tract Society, [N.D.].

―――. *The Casting Down of Thrones, A Discourse on the Present State of Europe.* Philadelphia: William Sloanmaker, 1848.

―――. *The Church and Slavery.* Philadelphia: Parry & McMillan, 1857.

―――. *The Connexion of Temperance with Republican Freedom.* Philadelphia: Boyle & Benedict, 1835.

―――. *Home Missions, A Sermon in Behalf of the American Home Missionary Society.* New York: American Home Missionary Society, 1849.

―――. *The Gospel Necessary in our Country.* Washington, D.C.: Kirkwood and McStill, 1852.

―――. *An Inquiry into the Scriptural Views of Slavery.* Philadelphia: Parry & McMillan, 1857.

―――. *Life at Threescore and Ten.* New York: American Tract Society, 1871.

―――. *Notes, Explanatory and Practical on the Book of Revelation.* New York: Harper & Brothers, 1852.

―――. *Notes, Explanatory and Practical, on the Epistle to the Romans.* New York: Leavitt & Lord, 1835.

―――. *Notes, Explanatory and Practical on the First Epistle of Paul to the Corinthians.* New York: Harper & Brothers, 1841.

―――. *Notes, Explanatory and Practical, on the Gospel.* New York: Harper & Brothers, 1855.

―――. *The Throne of Iniquity.* New York: National Temperance Society, [N.D.].

―――. *The Way of Salvation.* Philadelphia: William F. Geddes, 1830.

Barrows, E[lijah] P[orter]. *A View of the American Slavery Question.* New York: John Taylor, 1836.

Beecher, Charles. *The God of the Bible Against Slavery.* New York: American Anti-Slavery Society, 1855.

―――. *The Duty of Disobedience to Wicked Laws: A Sermon on the Fugitive Slave Law.* Newark: J.M. McIlvaine, 1851.

Beecher, Edward. *The Papal Conspiracy Exposed, and Protestantism Defended, in the Light of Reason, History and Scripture.* New York: M.W. Dodd, 1855.

Beecher, Henry Ward. *Defence of Kansas.* Washington, D.C.: Buell & Blanchard, 1856.

―――. *Patriotic Addresses In America and England, from 1850 to 1885, on Slavery, the Civil War, and the Development of Civil Liberty in the United States.* Edited by John R. Howard. New York: Fords, Howard & Hulbert, 1887.

Beecher, Lyman. *The Autobiography of Lyman Beecher.* 2 vols. Edited by Barbara Cross. Cambridge, Mass.: Belknap Press, 1961.

―――. *Beecher's Works.* 3 vols. Boston: J.P. Jewett & Co., 1852.

―――. *A Plea for the West.* Cincinnati: Truman & Smith, 1835.

―――. *The Practicality of Suppressing Vice, By Means of Societies Instituted for that Purpose.* New London, Conn.: Samuel Green, 1804.

————. *A Reformation of Morals Practicable and Indispensable*. Andover, Mass.: Fagg, 1814.

————. *The Remedy for Dueling*. Sag-Harbor, N.Y.: Alden Spooner, 1807.

————. *Six Sermons on the Nature, Occasions, Signs, Evils, and Remedy of Intemperance*. Boston: T.R. Marvin, 1828.

————. *Views in Theology*. Cincinnati: Truman & Smith, 1836.

Bellamy, Joseph. *True Religion Delineated and Distinguished From all Counterfeits*. Boston: Kneeland, 1750.

Birney, James Gillespie. *The American Churches, the Bulwarks of American Slavery*. Newburyport, Mass.: Charles Whipple, 1842.

————. *A Letter on the Political Obligations of Abolitionists*. Boston: Dow & Jackson, 1839.

————. *Letter to the Ministers and Elders on the Sin of Holding Slaves and the Duty of Immediate Emancipation*. New York: W. Benedict & Co., 1834.

Blanchard, Jonathan, and Nathan L. Rice. *A Debate on Slavery . . . upon the Question: Is Slaveholding in Itself Sinful and the Relation Between Master and Slave Sinful*. Cincinnati: Wm. H. Moore, 1846.

Bourne, George. *An Address to the Presbyterian Church Enforcing the Duty of Excluding All Slaveholders from the Communion of Saints*. New York: [N.P.], 1833.

————. *The American Text-Book of Popery Being an Authentic Compend of the Bulls, Canons and Decretals of the Roman Hierarchy*. Philadelphia: Griffith & Simon, 1846.

————. *The Book and Slavery Irreconcilable*. Philadelphia: J.M. Sanderson, 1816.

————. *Picture of Slavery in the United States of America*. Boston: Isaac Knap, 1838.

Bushnell, Horace. *Christian Nurture*, Introduction by John M. Mulder. Grand Rapids, Mich.: Baker Book House, 1979.

————. *God in Christ: Three Discourses Delivered at New Haven, Cambridge, and Andover, with a Preliminary Dissertation on Language*. Hartford, Conn.: Brown & Parsons, 1849.

————. *Women's Suffrage: The Reform Against Nature*. New York: Charles Scribner, 1869.

The Cambridge and Saybrook Platforms of Church Discipline. Boston: T.R. Marvin, 1829.

Cheever, George B. *The Commission from God: or the Missionary Enterprise, Against the Sin of Slavery; and the Responsibility of the Church and Ministry for its Fulfillment*. Boston: J.P. Jewett, 1858.

————. *The Elements of National Greatness, an Address before the New England Society of the City of New York*. New York: John S. Taylor, 1843.

————. *God Against Slavery*. New York: Joseph H. Ladd, 1857.

————. *God's Hand in America*. New York: M.W. Dodd, 1841.

————. *The Guilt of Slavery and the Crime of Slaveholding, Demonstrated from the Hebrew and Greek Scriptures*. Boston: J.P. Jewett, 1860.

————. *The Curse of God Against Political Atheism: With Some of the Lessons of the Tragedy at Harpers Ferry*. Boston: Walker, Wise, 1859.

————. *The Right of the Bible in our Public Schools*. New York: Robert Carter & Brothers, 1854.

————. *Some Principles According to which the World Is Managed, Contrasted with the Government of God and the Principles Exhibited for Man's Guidance in the Bible*. Boston: Perkins and Marvin, 1833.

————. *The True History of Deacon Giles' Distillery*. New York: [N.P.], 1844.

Cogswell, William. *The Harbinger of the Millennium*. Boston: Pierce & Parker, 1833.

————. *Theological Class Book: Containing a System of Divinity in the Form of Questions and Answers*. Boston: Crocker & Brewster, 1832.

Crampton, R[alph]. *The Wine of the Bible and the Bible Use of Wine*. New York: John A. Gray, 1859.

Crocker, Zebulon. *The Catastrophe of the Presbyterian Church in 1837*. New Haven, Conn.: B & W Noyes, 1838.

Davies, R.N. *The Teaching of the Sacred Scripture on Wine and Other Liquor*. Cincinnati: Cranston and Stowe, 1887.

Dickinson, Austin. *Bible Argument for Temperance*. New York: American Tract Society, [N.D.].

————. *Appeal to the American Youth on Temperance*. New York: American Tract Society, [N.D.].

[Dickinson, Baxter]. *Alarm to Distillers and Their Allies*. New York: American Tract Society, [N.D.].

Duffield, George. *The Bible Rule of Temperance*. New York: National Temperance Society, 1866.

————. *Dissertation on the Prophecies Relative to the Second Coming of Christ*. New York: Dayton & Newman, 1842.

————. *A Sermon on American Slavery: Its Nature and the Duties of Christians in Relation to It*. Detroit: J.S. & S.A. Bagg, 1840.

Duffield, George, and Albert Barnes. *Discourses on the Sabbath*. Philadelphia: George W. Donohue, 1836.

Dwight, Timothy. *Theology Explained and Defended in a Series of Sermons*. 5 vols. Middletown, Conn.: Clark & Lyman, 1818.

Edwards, Jonathan. *Apocalyptic Writings*. Edited by Stephen J. Stein. Vol. 5 in *Works of Jonathan Edwards*, ed. John E. Smith. New Haven, Conn.: Yale University Press, 1977.

————. *History of the Work of Redemption*. Edited by John F. Wilson. Vol. 9 in *Works of President Edwards*, ed. John E. Smith. New Haven, Conn.: Yale University Press, 1989.

Edwards, Justin. *Letters to the Friends of Temperance in Massachusetts*. Boston: Seth Blias, 1836.

————. *On the Traffic in Ardent Spirits*. New York: American Tract Society, [N.D.].

————. *Temperance Manual*. New York: American Tract Society, [N.D.].

Elliot, E.N., ed. *Cotton Is King Comprising the Writings of Hammond, Harper,*

Christy, Stringfellow, Hodge, Bledsoe, and Cartwright, on This Important Subject. Augusta, Ga.: Pritchard, Abbott & Loomis, 1860.

Ely, Ezra Stiles. *A Contrast Between Hopkinsianism and Calvinism.* New York: S.S. Whitting, 1811.

Eveleth, Ephraim. *History of the Sandwich Islands.* Philadelphia: American Sunday School Union, 1839.

Ferrin, C.E. *The Wine Text of the Bible.* New York: Lowell, Adam, Wesson, 1877.

Finney, Charles G. *Finney's Systematic Theology* [abridged]. Minneapolis: Bethany Fellowships, 1976.

———. *Lectures on Revivals of Religion.* Edited by William G. McLoughlin. Cambridge, Mass.: Belknap Press, 1960.

———. *Memoirs of Rev. Charles G. Finney.* New York: A.S. Barnes, 1876.

———. *Lectures to Professing Christians.* New York: J.S. Taylor, 1837.

———. *The Promise of the Spirit.* Compiled and edited by Timothy L. Smith. Minneapolis: Bethany Fellowships, 1980.

Fitch, Eleazar T. *An Inquiry into the Nature of Sin In Which the Views Advanced in "Two Discourses on the Nature of Sin" are Pursued, and Vindicated from the Objections Stated in the Christian Advocate.* New Haven, Conn.: A. H. Mattly, 1827.

———. *National Prosperity Perpetuated: A Discourse Delivered in the Chapel of Yale College on the Day of the Annual Thanksgiving.* New Haven, Conn.: Treadway & Adams, 1828.

———. *Two Discourses on the Nature of Sin.* New Haven, Conn.: Treadway & Adams, 1826.

Fleming, Robert. *Apocalyptical Key, A Discourse on the Rise and Fall of Antichrist or the Pouring out of the Vials.* Covington, Kentucky: R.C. Langdon, 1844.

Gillett, Ezra H. *History of the Presbyterian Church in the United States of America.* 2 vols. Philadelphia: Presbyterian Publication Committee, 1864.

Goodell, William. *Slavery and Anti-Slavery; A History of the Great Struggle in Both Hemispheres; With a View of the Slavery Question in the United States.* New York: William Goodell, 1853.

Graham, William. *The Cause and Manner of the Trial and Suspension of the Rev. William Graham; by the New School Synod of Cincinnati.* Cincinnati: [N.P.], 1845.

Grimke, Angela. *Appeal to Christian Women of the South.* New York: American Antislavery Society, 1836.

Guide to the Savior. Philadelphia: American Sunday School Union, 1846.

Hallock, William A. *Light and Love: A Sketch of the Life and Labors of Rev. Justin Edwards D.D.* New York: American Tract Society, 1855.

[Halsey, Job F.] *Who Slew All these?.* New York: American Tract Society, [N.D.].

Hartley, Isaac S. *Memorial of Robert M. Hartley.* Privately published, 1882; rprt. New York: Arno Press, 1976.

Harvey, Joseph. *An Examination of the Arminian and Pelagian Theory of Moral Agency as Recently Advocated by Dr. Beecher in His Views in Theology.* New York: Ezra Collier, 1837.

————. *A Review of a Sermon Delivered in the Chapel of Yale College.* Hartford: Goodwin, 1829.

————. *An Appeal to Christians on the Immorality of Using or Vending Distilled Liquors as an Article of Luxury or Diet.* Middletown, Conn.: William D. Starr, 1831.

Hickok, M[ilo] J. "The Mission of Woman Under the Gospel." *The National Preacher.* 26 (August 1852): 169-84.

History of Popery. Introduction by Samuel Miller. New York: John P. Haven, 1834.

History of the Proceedings of the Carlisle Presbytery in Relation to a Work Entitled Duffield on Regeneration in a Series of Letters from a Person Present to His Friend. Philadelphia: Wm. F. Geddes, 1832.

Hodge, Charles. *Essays and Reviews.* New York: Robert Carter and Brothers, 1857.

————. *Systematic Theology.* 3 vols. New York: C. Scribner's, 1872-73.

————. *The Way of Life.* Philadelphia: American Sunday School Union, 1841.

Hopkins, Samuel. *A Dialogue Concerning the Slavery of the Africans.* Norwich, Conn.: Judah P. Spooner, 1776.

————. *An Inquiry into the Nature of True Holiness.* Newport, R.I.: Soloman Southwick, 1773.

————. *The System of Doctrines.* 2 vols. Boston: Thomas & Andrews, 1793.

————. *A Treatise on the Millennium.* Boston: Thomas & Andrews, 1793.

Hughes, John A., and John Breckinridge. *A Discussion of the Question, Is the Roman Catholic Religion Inimical to Civil or Religious Liberty? And of the Question, Is the Presbyterian Religion Inimical to Civil or Religious Liberty?* Philadelphia: Carey, Lea, and Blanchard, 1836.

Humphrey, Heman. *Parallel Between Intemperance and the Slave Trade: An Address Delivered at Amherst College, July 4, 1828.* Amherst, Mass.: J.S. and C. Adams, 1828.

[Jones, J.] *Awful Exposure of the Atrocious Plot Formed by Certain Individuals Against the Clergy and Nuns of Lower Canada Through the Intervention of Maria Monk.* Montreal: Jones, 1836.

Junkin, George. *The Integrity of Our National Union versus Abolitionism: An Argument from the Bible.* Cincinnati: B.P. Donoge, 1843.

Kennedy, William S. *The Plan of Union: or A History of the Presbyterian and Congregational Churches of the Western Reserve.* Hudson, Ohio: Pentagon Steam Press, 1856.

Kitteridge, Jonathan. *Address on the Effects of Ardent Spirits.* New York: American Tract Society [N.D.].

Knox College by Whom Founded and Endowed. Chicago: Press & Tribune, 1860.

Lane, Garwin E. *Temperance a Christian Duty, Abstinence a Christian Liberty.* Albany, N.Y.: Gray & Sprague, 1851.

Letters of the Rev. Dr. Beecher and Rev. Mr. Nettleton on the "New Measures" in Conducting Revivals of Religion. New York: S. & C. Carvill, 1828.

Marsh, John. *The Temperance Battle Not Man's But God's*. New York: American Temperance Union, 1858.

Martineau, Harriet. *The Martyr Age of the United States*. Boston: Weeks, Jordan, 1839.

Miller, Samuel. *Letters to Presbyterians on the Present Crisis in the Presbyterian Church*. Philadelphia: Anthony Finley, 1833.

Monk, Maria. *The Awful Disclosures of Maria Monk*. New York: Howe & Bates, 1836.

Morse, Samuel F.B. *A Foreign Conspiracy Against The Liberties of the United States*. New York: Leavitt & Lord, 1835.

————. *Imminent Dangers to the Free Institutions of the United States Through Foreign Immigration*. New York: E.B. Clayton, 1835.

Nelson, David. *The Cause and the Cure for Infidelity*. New York: American Tract Society, 1841.

Nevin, William. *Thoughts on Popery*. New York: American Tract Society, [N.D.].

Nott, Eliaphlet. *Lectures on Temperance*. New York: A. M. Moffort, 1858.

On the Objections Commonly Urged Against the Holy Bible. New York: American Tract Society, [N.D.].

Packard, Frederick A. *Letters on the Design and Importance of the American Sunday School Union in New England*. Philadelphia: American Sunday School Union, 1838.

Paine, Thomas. *The Age of Reason Being an Investigation of the True and Fabulous Theology*. New York: Wiley, 1944.

Patton, William. *The Laws of Fermentation and the Wines of the Ancients*. New York: National Temperance Society and Publication House, 1877.

Pillsbury, Parker. *Acts of the Antislavery Apostles*. Concord, N.H.: Clague, Wegman, Schlicht, 1883.

The Poor Man's House Repaired. New York: American Tract Society, [N.D.].

Ramsey, James B. *The Spiritual Kingdom, An Exposition of the First Eleven Chapters of the Book of Revelation*. Richmond, Va.: Presbyterian Committee of Publication, 1873.

Read, Hollis. *The Hand of God in History, or Divine Providence Historically Illustrated in the Extension and Establishment of Christianity*. Hartford: H. E. Robinson, 1851.

Report of the Trial of the Cause of John Taylor vs. Edward C. Delavan, Prosecuted for an Alleged Libel, Tried at the Albany Circuit April 1840. Albany, N.Y.: Hoffman, White & Vissher, 1840.

Relations of the Presbyterian Church to the Work of Home Missions: Report of the General Assembly's Commission of Investigation. New York: John A. Gray, 1860.

Rice, Nathan L. *Lectures on Slavery*. Cincinnati: J. A. James, 1845.

Slocum, John J. *A Reply to the Priests Book*. New York: Leavitt & Lord; Boston: Crocker & Brewster, 1837.

Smith, Henry Boynton. *Faith and Philosophy: Discourses and Essays.* New York: Scribner & Armstrong, 1877.

The Spirit of Popery. New York: American Tract Society, [1840].

Spring, Gardiner. *The Sabbath a Blessing to Mankind.* New York: American Tract Society, [N.D.].

Stowe, Harriet Beecher. *The Key To Uncle Tom's Cabin.* Preface by William Loren Katz. New York: Arno Press, 1968.

———. *Uncle Tom's Cabin; or Life Among the Lowly.* Introduction by Dwight L. Dumond. New York: Collier Books, 1962.

Strickland, William P. *History of the American Bible Society.* New York: Harper & Brothers, 1856.

Stone, William Leete. *Maria Monk and the Nunnery of the Hotel Dieu.* New York: Howe & Bates, 1836.

Stuart, Moses. *A Commentary on the Apocalypse.* New York: Van Nostrand & Terrett, 1851.

———. *Conscience and the Constitution.* Boston: Crocker & Brewster, 1850.

———. *Essay on the Prize Question.* New York: John P. Haven, 1830.

———. *Mr. Webster's Andover Address and His Political Course while Secretary of State.* Essex, Mass.: [N.P.], 1844.

———. *Scriptural View of the Wine Question in a Letter to the Rev. Dr. Nott.* New York: Leavitt, Trow, 1848.

———. *Two Discourses on the Atonement.* Andover, Mass.: Mark Newman, 1828.

Tahiti Without the Gospel. Philadelphia: American Sunday School Union, 1833.

Tappan, Lewis. *Letters Respecting a Book "Dropped from the Catalogue" of the American Sunday School Union in Compliance with the Dictation of the Slave Power.* New York: American and Foreign Antislavery Society, 1848.

Taylor, Nathaniel William. *Concio ad clerum: A Sermon Delivered in the Chapel at Yale College, September 10, 1828.* New Haven, Conn.: Hezekiah Howe, 1828.

———. *Essays, Lectures, Etc. Upon Select Topics in Revealed Theology.* New York: Clark, Austin & Smith, 1859.

———. *Lectures on the Moral Government of God.* Edited by Noah Porter. 2 vols. New York: Clark, Austin, & Smith, 1859.

———. *Practical Sermons.* New York: Clark, Austin, & Smith, 1858.

Trial of Albert Barnes Before the Synod of Philadelphia on a Charge of Heresy Preferred Against Him by the Rev. George Junkin. New York: Van Nostrand & Dwight, 1836.

Twenty-two Plain Reasons for Not Being a Roman Catholic. New York: American Tract Society, [N.D.].

Tyler, Bennett. *Letters on the Origins and Progress of the New Haven Theology.* New York: Robert Carter & Ezra Collier, 1837.

Tyler, Edward Royall. *Slaveholding a Malum In Se or Invariably Sinful.* Hartford: S.S. Cowles, 1839.

Varigny, Charles de. *Fourteen Years in the Sandwich Islands 1855-1868.* Translated by Alfons L. Korn. Honolulu: University Press of Hawaii, 1981.

Weld, Theodore Dwight. *American Slavery as It Is, Testimony of a Thousand Witnesses*. New York: American Anti-Slavery Society, 1839.
————. *The Bible Against Slavery, An Inquiry into the Patriarchial and Mosiac Systems on the Subject of Human Rights*. New York: American Anti-Slavery Society, 1838.
————. *Slavery and the Internal Slave Trade*. London: Thomas Ward, 1841.

Secondary Sources

Articles

Banner, Lois. "Religious Benevolence as Social Control: A Critique of an Interpretation." *Journal of American History* 60 (June 1973): 23-41.
Breitenbach, William. "The Consistent Calvinism of the New Divinity Movement." *William and Mary Quarterly* 41 (April 1984): 241-64.
Buell, Lawrence, "Calvinism Romanticized: Harriet Beecher Stowe, Samuel Hopkins, and *The Minister's Wooing*." *ESQ: A Journal of the American Renaissance*. 23 (Fall 1978): 119-32.
Cherry, Conrad. "Nature and the Republic: The New Haven Theology." *New England Quarterly* 51 (December 1978): 509-26.
Crehan, F.J., S.J. "The Bible in the Roman Catholic Church from Trent to the Present Day." In *The Cambridge History of the Bible*, ed. S.L. Greensdale. 3:199-237. Cambridge: Cambridge University Press, 1963.
Davis, David Brion. "The Emergence of Immediatism in British and American Antislavery Thought." *Mississippi Valley Historical Review* 49 (September 1962): 209-30.
————. "Some Themes of Counter-Subversion." *Mississippi Valley Historical Review* 47 (September 1960): 205-24.
Goen, C. C. "Edwards' New Departure in Eschatology." *Church History* 28 (March 1959): 25-40.
Griffin, Clifford S. "Religious Benevolence As Social Control." *Mississippi Valley Historical Review* 44 (December 1957): 423-44.
Guelzo, Allen C. "An Heir or Rebel? Charles Grandison Finney and the New England Theology." *Journal of the Early Republic* 17 (Spring 1997): 61-94.
Harris, Marc L. "Revelation and the American Republic: Timothy Dwight's Civic Participation." *Journal of the History of Ideas* 54 (July 1993): 449-68.
Hightower, Raymond. "Joshua L. Wilson, Frontier Controversialist." *Church History* 3 (December 1934): 300-16.
Holt, Michael F. "The Politics of Impatience: The Origins of Know-Nothingism." *Journal of American History* 60 (September 1973): 309-31.
John, Richard R. "Taking Sabbatarianism Seriously: The Postal System, the Sabbath, and the Transformation of American Political Culture." *Journal of the Early Republic* 10 (Winter 1990): 517-67.
Kett, Joseph F. "Temperance and Intemperance as Historical Problems." *Journal of American History* 67 (March 1981): 878-85.

Kohl, Lawrence F. "The Concept of Social Control and the History of Jacksonian America." *Journal of the Early Republic* 5 (Spring 1985): 21-33.

Knight, Janice. "Learning the Language of God: Jonathan Edwards and the Typology of Nature." *William and Mary Quarterly* 41 (April 1984): 241-64.

Lehr, Timothy J. "Leonard Bacon and the Myth of the Good Slaveholder." *New England Quarterly* 49 (June 1976) 194-213.

Loveland, Anne C. "Evangelicalism and 'Immediate Emancipation' in American Antislavery Thought." *Journal of Southern History* 32 (May 1966): 172-88.

Lubove, Roy. "The New York Association for Improving the Condition of the Poor: The Formative Years." *New York Historical Society Quarterly* 43 (July 1959): 307-27.

Mead, Sidney E. "Lyman Beecher and Connecticut Orthodoxy's Campaign Against the Unitarians, 1819-1826." *Church History* 9 (1940): 218-34.

Moorhead, James. "Social Reform and the Divided Conscience of Antebellum Protestantism." *Church History* 48 (December 1979): 416-30.

Noll, Mark A. "The Irony of the Enlightenment for the Presbyterians in the Early Republic." *Journal of the Early Republic* 5 (Summer 1985): 149-75.

Rogers, Daniel T. "Republicanism: The Career of a Concept." *Journal of American History* 79 (June 1992): 11-38.

Rohrer, James R. "Sunday Mails and the Church-State Theme in Jacksonian America." *Journal of the Early Republic* 7 (Spring 1987): 53-74.

Sandeen, Ernest R. "The Princeton Theology, One Source of Biblical Literalism in American Protestantism." *Church History* 31 (September 1962): 307-21.

Shiels, Richard D. "The Second Great Awakening In Connecticut: A Critique of the Traditional Interpretation." *Church History* 49 (December 1980): 401-15.

Smith, Elwyn A. "The Role of the South in the Presbyterian Schism of 1837-38." *Church History* 29 (March 1960): 44-61.

Sweet, Leonard I. "The View of Man Inherent in New Measures Revivalism." *Church History* 45 (June 1976): 206-21.

Thomas, John L. "Romantic Reform in America 1815-1865." *American Quarterly* 17 (Winter 1965): 656-81.

Thompson, J. Earl. "Abolition and Theological Education at Andover." *New England Quarterly*. 47 (June 1974): 238-61.

Thompson, Ralph. "The Maria Monk Affair." *Colophon* 5 (1934): p. 17.

Walters, Ronald. "The Erotic South: Civilization and Sexuality in American Abolitionism." *American Quarterly* 25 (May 1973): 155-201.

Wood, Gordon. "Conspiracy and the Paranoid Style: Causality and Deceit in the Eighteenth Century." *William and Mary Quarterly* 39 (July 1982): 401-41.

Wyatt-Brown, Bertram. "The Abolitionists' Postal Campaign of 1835." *Journal of Negro History* 50 (October 1965): 227-38.

———. "Prelude to Abolitionism: Sabbatarian Politics and the Rise of the Second Party System." *Journal of American History* 58 (September 1971): 329-35.

———. "Stanley Elkins' *Slavery*: The Antislavery Interpretation Reexamined. *American Quarterly* 25 (May 1973): 154-76.

Books

Abzug, Robert H. *Cosmos Crumbling: American Reform and the Religious Imagination.* New York: Oxford University Press, 1994.

———. *Passionate Liberator: Theodore Dwight Weld and the Dilemma of Reform.* New York: Oxford University Press, 1980.

Adams, John Quincy. *A History of Auburn Theological Seminary, 1818-1918.* Auburn, N.Y.: Auburn Seminary Press, 1918.

Ahlstrom, Sidney E. *A Religious History of the American People.* 2 vols. New Haven, Conn.: Yale University Press, 1972.

———, ed. *Theology in America, The Major Protestant Voices from Puritanism to Neo-Orthodoxy.* Indianapolis: Bobbs-Merrill, 1967.

Altschuler, Glenn C., and Jan M. Saltzgaber. *Revivalism, Social Conscience, and Community in the Burned-Over District: The Trial of Rhoda Bement.* Ithaca, N.Y.: Cornell University Press, 1983.

Anbinder, Tyler. *Nativism and Slavery: The Northern Know Nothings and The Politics of the 1850s.* New York: Oxford University Press, 1992.

Bailyn, Bernard. *The Ideological Origins of the American Revolution.* Cambridge: Belknap Press, 1967.

Banner, James M. *To the Hartford Convention: The Federalists and the Origins of Party Politics in Massachusetts, 1789-1815.* New York: Alfred A. Knopf, 1970.

Barnes, Gilbert. *The Antislavery Impulse, 1830-1844.* New York: D. Appleton-Century, 1933.

Barclay, Wade C. *History of Methodist Missions.* Vol. 2: *Early American Methodism.* New York: Board of Missions and Church Extension of the Methodist Church, 1950.

Barkun, Michael. *Crucible of the Millinnium: The Burned Over District of New York in the 1840s.* Syracuse, N.Y.: Syracuse University Press, 1986.

Behnke, Donna A. *Religious Issues In Nineteenth Century Feminism.* Troy, New York: The Whitston Publishing Company, 1982.

Benson, Lee. *The Concept of Jacksonian Democracy: New York as a Test Cast.* Princeton, N.J.: Princeton University Press, 1961.

Berk, Stephen E. *Calvinism versus Democracy: Timothy Dwight and the Origins of American Evangelical Orthodoxy.* Hamden, Conn.: Archon Books, 1974.

Billington, Ray A. *The Protestant Crusade 1800-1860: A Study of the Origins of American Nativism.* New York: Macmillan, 1938.

Blassingame, John W. *The Slave Community: Plantation Life In the Antebellum South.* New York: Oxford University Press, 1979.

Bloch, Ruth H. *Visionary Republic: Millennial Themes in American Thought 1756-1800.* Cambridge: Cambridge University Press, 1985.

Bodo, John R. *The Protestant Clergy and Public Issues, 1812-1848.* Princeton, N.J.: Princeton University Press, 1954.

Boyer, Paul S. *Urban Masses and Moral Order in America, 1820-1920.* Cambridge, Mass.: Harvard University Press, 1978.

Bozeman, Theodore Dwight. *Protestants in An Age of Science: The Baconian Ideal and Antebellum American Religious Thought.* Chapel Hill: University of North Carolina Press, 1977.

Branch, Edward Douglas. *The Sentimental Years.* New York: D. Appleton-Century, 1934.

Bremner, Robert H. *From the Depths: The Discovery of Poverty in the United States.* New York: New York University Press, 1956.

Brock, Peter. *Radical Pacifists in Antebellum America.* Princeton, N.J.: Princeton University Press, 1968.

Brumberg, Joan Jacobs. *Mission For Life: The Story of the Family of Adoniram Judson.* New York: Free Press, 1980.

Butler, Diana H. *Standing Against the Whirlwind: Evangelical Episcopalians in Nineteenth Century America.* New York: Oxford University Press, 1995.

Butler, Jon. *Awash in Sea of Faith: Christianizing the American People.* Cambridge, Mass.: Harvard University Press, 1990.

Calkins, Earnest E. *They Broke the Prairie: Being Some Account of the Settlement of the Upper Mississippi Valley by Religious and Educational Pioneers, Told in Terms of One City, Galesburg, and of One College, Knox.* Westport, Conn.: Greenwood, 1937.

Carwardine, Richard J. *Evangelicals and Politics in Antebellum America.* New Haven, Conn.: Yale University Press, 1993.

Caskey, Marie. *Chariot of Fire: Religion and the Beecher Family.* New Haven, Conn.: Yale University Press, 1978.

Cecil, Anthony C., Jr., *The Theological Development of Edwards Amasa Park: Last of the "Consistent Calvinists."* Missoula, Mont.: Scholars Press, 1974.

Cherry, Conrad. *The Theology of Jonathan Edwards, A Reappraisal.* Gloucester, Mass.: Peter Smith, 1974.

Christie, John W., and Dwight L. Dumond. *George Bourne and "The Book and Slavery Irreconcilable."* Philadelphia: Presbyterian Historical Society, 1969.

Cogliano, Francis D. *No King, No Popery: Anti-Catholicism in Revolutionary New England.* Westport, Conn.: Greenwood, 1995.

Cole, Charles C., Jr. *The Social Ideas of Northern Evangelists, 1826-1860.* New York: Columbia University Press, 1954.

Conforti, Joseph A. *Samuel Hopkins and the New Divinity Movement: Calvinism, the Congregational Ministry, and Reform in New England between the Great Awakenings.* Grand Rapids, Mich.: Christian University Press, 1981.

―――. *Jonathan Edwards: Religious Tradition and American Thought.* Chapel Hill: University of North Carolina Press, 1995.

Conkin, Paul K. *The Uneasy Center: Reformed Christianity in Antebellum America.* Chapel Hill: University of North Carolina Press, 1995.

Conser, Walter H. *God and the Natural World: Religion and Science in Antebellum America.* Columbia: University of South Carolina Press, 1993.

Clark, Norman H. *Deliver Us from Evil: An Interpretation of American Prohibition*. New York: W. W. Norton, 1976.

Crawford, Michael J. *Seasons of Grace: Colonial New England's Revival Tradition in Its British Context*. New York: Oxford University Press, 1991.

Cross, Barbara M. *Horace Bushnell: Minister to a Changing America*. Chicago: University of Chicago Press, 1958.

Cross, Whitney R. *The Burned Over District: The Social and Intellectual History of Enthusiastic Religion in Western New York, 1800-1850*. Ithaca, N.Y.: Cornell University Press, 1950.

Dannenbaum, Jed. *Drink and Disorder: Temperance Reform in Cincinnati from the Washingtonian Revival to the W.C.T.U.* Urbana: University of Illinois Press, 1984.

Davidson, Edward H. *Jonathan Edwards: The Narrative of a Puritan Mind*. Boston: Houghton, Mifflin, 1966.

Davidson, James West. *The Logic of Millennial Thought in Eighteenth Century New England*. New Haven, Conn.: Yale University Press, 1977.

Davis, David Brion, ed. *Antebellum Reform*. New York: Harper & Row, 1967.

———. *The Problem of Slavery in Western Culture*. Ithaca, N.Y.: Cornell University Press, 1966.

———. *The Problem of Slavery in the Age of Revolution, 1770-1820*. Ithaca, N.Y.: Cornell University Press, 1975.

———. *The Slave Power Conspiracy and the Paranoid Style*. Baton Rouge: Louisana State University Press, 1969.

———. *Slavery and Human Progress*. New York: Oxford University Press, 1984.

Donovan, Josephine. *Uncle Tom's Cabin: Evil, Affliction and Redemptive Love*. Boston: Twayne, 1991.

Elkins, Stanley M. *Slavery: A Problem in American Institutional and Intellectual Life*. Chicago: University of Chicago Press, 1959.

Elson, Ruth M. *Guardians of Tradition: American Textbooks in the Nineteenth Century*. Lincoln: University of Nebraska Press, 1964.

Essig, James D. *The Bonds of Wickedness: American Evangelicals Against Slavery, 1770-1808*. Philadelphia: Temple University Press, 1982.

Faust, Clarence H., and Thomas H. Johnson, eds. *Jonathan Edwards, Representative Selections*. New York: Hill and Wang, 1962.

Fell, Sister Marie Leonore. *The Foundations of Nativism in American Textbooks, 1783-1860*. Washington, D.C.: Catholic University Press, 1941.

Filler, Louis. *The Crusade Against Slavery, 1830-1860*. New York: Harper & Row, 1960.

Fletcher, Robert S. *A History of Oberlin College from Its Foundation Through the Civil War*. 2 vols. Oberlin, Ohio: Oberlin College, 1943.

Fogel, Robert William, and Stanley L. Engerman. *Time on the Cross: The Economics of American Negro Slavery*. Boston: Little, Brown, 1974.

Foner, Eric. *Free Soil, Free Labor, Free Men: The Ideology of the Republican Party before the Civil War*. New York: Oxford University Press, 1970.

Formisano, Ronald P. *The Birth of Mass Political Parties: Michigan 1827-1861*. Princeton, N.J.: Princeton University Press, 1971.

————. *The Transformation of Political Culture: Massachusetts Parties, 1790s-1840s.* New York: Oxford University Press, 1983.

Foster, Charles H. *The Rungless Ladder: Harriet Beecher Stowe and New England Puritanism.* Durham, N.C.: Duke University Press, 1954.

Foster, Charles I. *An Errand of Mercy: The Evangelical United Front, 1790-1837.* Chapel Hill: University of North Carolina Press, 1960.

Foster, Frank H. *A Genetic History of the New England Theology.* Chicago: University of Chicago Press, 1907.

Fraser, James W. *Pedagogue for God's Kingdom: Lyman Beecher and the Second Great Awakening.* Lanham, Md.: University Press of America, 1985.

Fuller, Robert C. *Naming the Antichrist: The History of an American Obsession.* New York: Oxford University Press, 1995.

Gaustad, Edwin S., ed. *The Rise of Adventism: Religion and Society in Mid-Nineteenth Century America.* New York: Harper & Row, 1974.

Genovese, Eugene D. *Roll Jordan Roll: The World the Slaves Made.* New York: Random House, 1974.

Gienapp, William E. *The Origins of the Republican Party, 1852-1856.* New York: Oxford University Press, 1987.

Goen, C.C. *Broken Churches, Broken Nation: Denominational Schisms and the Coming of the American Civil War.* Macon, Ga.: Mercer University Press, 1985.

Goodykoontz, Colin B. *Home Missions on the American Frontier, with Particular Reference to the American Home Missionary Society.* Caldwell, Idaho: Claxton Press, 1939.

Griffin, Clifford S. *Their Brothers' Keepers: Moral Stewardship in the United States, 1800-1865.* New Brunswick, N.J.: Rutgers University Press, 1960.

Guelzo, Allen C. *Edwards on the Will: A Century of American Theological Debate.* Middletown, Conn.: Wesleyan University Press, 1989.

Gusfield, Joseph R. *Symbolic Crusade: Status Politics and the American Temperance Movement.* Urbana: University of Illinois Press, 1963.

Hambrick-Stowe, Charles E. *Charles G. Finney and the Spirit of American Evangelicalism.* Grand Rapids, Mich.: William B. Eerdmans Publishing, 1996.

Hammond, John L. *The Politics of Benevolence: Revival, Religion and American Voting Behavior.* Norwood, N.J.: Ablex, 1979.

Hampel, Robert L. *Temperance and Prohibition in Massachusetts 1813-1852.* Ann Arbor, Mich.: U.M.I. Research Press, 1982.

Hanley, Mark Y. *Beyond a Christian Commonwealth: The Protestant Quarrel with the American Republic, 1830-1860.* Chapel Hill: University of North Carolina Press, 1994.

Harding, Vincent. *A Certain Magnificence: Lyman Beecher and the Transformation of Amercan Protestantism, 1775-1863.* Brooklyn, N.Y.: Carlson, 1991.

Hardman, Keith J. *Charles Grandison Finney, 1792-1875: Revivalist and Reformer.* Syracuse, N.Y.: Syracuse University Press, 1987.

Haroutunian, Joseph. *Piety versus Moralism: The Passing of the New England Theology.* New York: Henry Holt., 1932; rprt. with introduction by Sydney E. Ahlstrom, New York: Harper & Row, 1970.

Hatch, Nathan O. *The Democratization of American Christianity*. New Haven, Conn.: Yale University Press, 1989.

————. *The Sacred Cause of Liberty: Republican Thought and the Millennium in Revolutionary New England*. New Haven, Conn.: Yale University Press, 1977.

Hatch, Nathan O., and Mark A. Noll, eds. *The Bible in America: Essays in Cultural History*. New York: Oxford University Press, 1982.

Hatch, Nathan O., and Harry S. Stout, eds. *Jonathan Edwards and the American Experience*. New York: Oxford University Press, 1988.

Hedrick, Joan D. *Harriet Beecher Stowe: A Life*. New York: Oxford University Press, 1994.

Heimert, Alan E. *Religion and the American Mind from the Great Awakening to the Revolution*. Cambridge, Mass.: Harvard University Press, 1966.

Henry, Stuart C. *Unvanquished Puritan: A Portrait of Lyman Beecher*. Grand Rapids, Mich.: W. B. Eerdmans, 1973.

Hersh, Blanche G. *The Slavery of Sex: Feminist-Abolitionists in America*. Urbana: University of Illinois Press, 1978.

Hewitt, Nancy A. *Women's Activism and Social Change: Rochester, New York, 1822-1870*. Ithaca, N.Y.: Cornell University Press, 1984.

Hislop, Codman. *Eliphalet Nott*. Middletown, Conn.: Wesleyan University Press, 1971.

Hodge, Archibald Alexander. *The Life of Charles Hodge*. London: T. Nelson and Sons, 1881.

Hofstadter, Richard. *Anti-Intellectualism in American Life*. New York: Vintage Books, 1962.

————. *The Paranoid Style in American Politics and Other Essays*. New York: Vintage Books, 1967.

Holbrook, Clyde A. *The Ethics of Jonathan Edwards, Morality and Aesthetics*. Ann Arbor: University of Michigan Press, 1973.

Holifield, E. Brooks. *The Gentlemen Theologians: American Theology in Southern Culture, 1795-1860*. Durham, N.C.: Duke University Press, 1978.

Holt, Michael F. *Forging a Majority: The Formation of the Republican Party in Pittsburgh, 1848-1860*. New Haven, Conn.: Yale University Press, 1969.

————. *The Political Crisis of the 1850s*. New York: John Wiley & Sons, 1978.

Hood, Fred J. *Reformed America: The Middle and Southern States 1783-1837*. Tuscaloosa: University of Alabama Press, 1980.

Howard, Victor B. *Conscience and Slavery: The Evangelical Calvinist Domestic Missions, 1837-1861*. Kent, Ohio: Kent State University Press, 1990.

Howe, Daniel Walker. *The Political Culture of the American Whigs*. Chicago: University of Chicago Press, 1979.

————. *The Unitarian Conscience: The Harvard Moral Philosophers, 1805-1861*. Cambridge, Mass.: Harvard University Press, 1970.

Hutchison, William R. *Errand to the World: American Protestant Thought and Foreign Missions*. Chicago: University of Chicago Press, 1987.

Jedin, Hubert. *A History of the Council of Trent*. 2 vols. Translated by Dom Ernest Graf, O.S.B. London: Thomas Nelson

Johnson, Curtis D. *Redeeming America: Evangelicals and the Road to the Civil War.* Chicago: Ivan R. Dee, 1993.

Johnson, Paul E. *A Shopkeeper's Millennium: Society and Revivals in Rochester, New York, 1815-1837.* New York: Hill and Wang, 1978.

Kaestle, Carl F. *Pillars of the Republic: Common Schools and American Society, 1780-1860.* New York: Hill & Wang, 1983.

Keller, Charles R. *The Second Great Awakening in Connecticut.* New Haven, Conn.: Yale University Press, 1942.

Kelley, Brooks Mather. *Yale, A History.* New Haven, Conn.: Yale University Press, 1974.

Kerr, Hugh T., ed. *Sons of the Prophets: Leaders in Protestantism from Princeton Seminary.* Princeton, N.J.: Princeton University Press, 1963.

Kingsley, William L., ed. *Yale College: A Sketch of Its History.* 2 vols. New York: Henry Holt, 1879.

Kraditor, Aileen S. *Means and Ends in American Abolitionism: Garrison and His Critics on Strategy and Tactics, 1834-1850.* New York: Pantheon, 1969.

Krout, John Allen. *The Origins of Prohibition.* New York: Alfred A. Knopf, 1925.

Kuklick, Bruce. *Churchmen and Philosophers: From Jonathan Edwards to John Dewey.* New Haven, Conn.: Yale University Press, 1985.

Kuhns, Frederick I. *The American Home Missionary Society in Relation to the Antislavery Controversy in the Old Northwest.* Billings, Mont.: [privately published], 1959.

Kuykendall, John W. *Southern Enterprise: The Work of National Evangelical Societies in the Antebellum South.* Westport, Conn.: Greenwood, 1982.

Le Beau, Bryan F. *Jonathan Dickinson and the Formative Years of American Presbyterianism.* Lexington: University Press of Kentucky, 1997.

Leonard, Ira M., and Robert D. Parmet. *American Nativism 1830-1860.* New York: Van Nostrand Reinhold, 1971.

Loetscher, Lefferts A. *A Brief History of the Presbyterians,* 4th ed. Philadelphia: Westminster Press, 1983.

Loveland, Anne C. *Southern Evangelicals and the Social Order, 1800-1860.* Baton Rouge: Louisiana State University Press, 1980.

Mabee, Carlton. *The American Leonardo: A Life of Samuel F.B. Morse.* New York: Alfred Knopf, 1943.

McGiffert, Arthur C. *Protestant Thought Before Kant.* New York: C. Scribners Sons, 1936.

McKivigan, John R. *The War Against Proslavery Religion: Abolitionism and the Northern Churches 1830-1865.* Ithaca, N.Y.: Cornell University Press, 1984.

MacLean, John. *History of the College of New Jersey from its Origin in 1746 to the Commencement of 1854.* Philadelphia: J. B. Lippincott, 1877.

McLoughlin, William G. *Cherokees and Missionaries, 1789-1839.* New Haven, Conn.: Yale University Press, 1984.

———. *New England Dissent 1630-1833: The Baptists and the Separation of Church and State.* 2 vols. Cambridge, Mass.: Harvard University Press, 1971.

————. *Modern Revivalists: Charles Grandison Finney to Billy Graham*. New York: Ronald Press, 1959.

Marsden, George M. *The Evangelical Mind and the New School Presbyterian Experience*. New Haven, Conn.: Yale University Press, 1970.

May, Henry F. *The Enlightenment in America*. New York: Oxford University Press, 1976.

————. *Protestant Churches and Industrial America*. New York: Harper and Brothers, 1949.

Mead, Sidney E. *Nathaniel William Taylor, 1786-1858: A Connecticut Liberal*. Chicago: University of Chicago Press, 1942.

Merideth, Robert. *The Politics of the Universe: Edward Beecher, Abolition and Orthodoxy*. Nashville: Vanderbilt University Press, 1968.

Miller, Perry. *Jonathan Edwards*. New York: William Sloan Associates, 1949.

————. *The Life of the Mind in America from the Revolution to the Civil War*. New York: Harcourt, Brace & World, 1965.

————. *Nature's Nation*. Cambridge, Mass.: Belknap Press, 1967.

————. *The New England Mind: From Colony to Province*. Cambridge, Mass.: Harvard University Press, 1953.

————. *The New England Mind: The Seventeenth Century*. New York: Macmillan, 1939.

Mintz, Steven. *Moralists and Modernizers: America's Pre–Civil War Reforms*. Baltimore: Johns Hopkins University Press, 1995.

Moorhead, James H. *American Apocalypse: Yankee Protestants and the Civil War, 1860-1869*. New Haven, Conn.: Yale University Press, 1978.

Morais, Herbert M. *Deism in Eighteenth Century America*. New York: Columbia University Press, 1934.

Morgan, Edmund. *The Gentle Puritan: A Life of Ezra Stiles*. New Haven, Conn.: Yale University Press, 1962.

Mott, Frank Luther. *A History of American Magazines*. 5 vols. Cambridge, Mass.: Harvard University Press, 1938.

Muelder, Hermann R. *Fighters for Freedom: The History of Antislavery Activities of Men and Women Associated with Knox College*. New York: Columbia University Press, 1959.

Murray, Andrew E. *Presbyterians and the Negro—A History*. Philadelphia: Presbyterian Historical Society, 1966.

Nichols, James Hastings. *Romanticism in American Theology: Nevin and Schaff at Mercersberg*. Chicago: University of Chicago Press, 1961.

Nichols, Robert Hastings. *Presbyterianism in New York State*. Completed and edited by James Hastings Nichols. Philadelphia: Westminster Press, 1963.

Niebuhr, H. Richard. *The Kingdom of God in America*. New York: Harper & Brothers, 1937.

Niesel, Wilhelm. *Theology of Calvin*. Translated by Harold Knight. Philadelphia: Westminster Press, 1956.

Noll, Mark A. *A History of Christianity in the United States and Canada*. Grand Rapids, Mich.: Willilam B. Eerdmans, 1992.

———. *Princeton and the Republic, 1768-1822*. Princeton, N.J.: Princeton University Press, 1989.

——— ed. *The Princeton Theology, 1812-1921*. Grand Rapids, Mich.: Baker Book, 1983.

Nye, Russell B. *Fettered Freedom: Civil Liberties and the Slavery Controversy*. East Lansing: Michigan State University Press, 1963.

Parish, Peter J. *Slavery: History and Historians*. New York: Harper & Row, 1989.

Parker, Harold M. *The United Synod of the South: The Southern New School Presbyterian Church*. Westport, Conn.: Greenwood, 1988.

Perry, Lewis. *Radical Abolitionism, Anarchy, and the Government of God in Antislavery Thought*. Ithaca, N.Y.: Cornell University Press, 1973.

Phillips, Clifton J. *Protestant America and the Pagan World: The First Half Century of the American Board of Commissioners for Foreign Missions 1810-1860*. Cambridge, Mass.: Harvard University Press, 1969.

Phillips, Joseph W. *Jedidiah Morse and New England Congregationalism*. New Brunswick, N.J.: Rutgers University Press, 1983.

Pope, Earl A. *New England Calvinism and the Disruption of the Presbyterian Church*. New York: Garland, 1987.

Potter, David M. *The Impending Crisis, 1848-1861*. New York: Harper & Row, 1976.

Rabinowitz, Richard. *The Spritual Self in Everyday Life: The Transformation of Personal Religious Experience in Nineteenth Century New England*. Boston: Northeastern University Press, 1989.

Rammelkamp, Charles H. *Illinois College: A Centennial History 1829-1929*. New Haven, Conn.: Yale University Press, 1928.

Ray, Sister Mary Augustina. *American Opinion of Roman Catholicism in the Eighteenth Century*. New York: Columbia University, 1936.

Rice, Edwin W. *The Sunday School Movement 1780-1917 and the American Sunday School Union 1817-1917*. Philadelphia: American Sunday School Union, 1917.

Richards, Leonard L. *Gentlemen of Property and Standing: Anti-Abolition Mobs in Jacksonian America*. New York: Oxford University Press, 1970.

Richey, Russell E., and Donald G. Jones, eds. *American Civil Religion*. New York: Harper and Row, 1974.

Rorabaugh, W.J. *The Alcoholic Republic: An American Tradition*. New York: Oxford University Press, 1979.

Rowe, Henry K. *History of Andover Theological Seminary*. Newton, Mass.: Andover Theological Seminary, 1933.

Rugoff, Milton. *The Beechers: An American Family in the Nineteenth Century*. New York: Harper & Row, 1981.

Schmidt, George P. *Princeton and Rutgers: The Two Colonial Colleges of New Jersey*. Princeton, N.J.: D. Van Nostrand, 1964.

Schmidt, Leigh Eric. *Holy Fairs: Scottish Communions and American Revivals in the Early Modern Period.* Princeton, N.J.: Princeton University Press, 1989.

Scott, Donald M. *From Office to Profession: The New England Ministry 1750-1850.* Philadelphia: University of Pennsylvania Press, 1978.

Sewell, Richard H. *Ballots for Freedom: Antislavery Politics in the United States 1837-1860.* New York: Oxford University Press, 1976.

Sher, Richard B., and Jeffrey R. Smitten. *Scotland and America in the Age of the Enlightenment.* Princeton, N.J.: Princeton University Press, 1990.

Smith, Bradford. *Yankees in Paradise: The New England Impact on Hawaii.* Philadelphia: J.B. Lippincott, 1956.

Smith, David L. *Symbolism and Growth: The Religious Thought of Horace Bushnell.* Chico, Calif.: Scholars Press, 1981.

Smith, Elwyn A., ed. *The Religion of the Republic.* Philadelphia: Fortress Press, 1971.

Smith, Hilrie Shelton. *Changing Conceptions of Original Sin: A Study in American Theology since 1750.* New York: Charles Scribner's Sons, 1955.

Smith, Timothy L. *Revivalism and Social Reform in Mid-Nineteenth Century America.* Nashville: Abingdon Press, 1957.

Smith-Rosenberg, Carroll. *Religion and the Rise of the American City: The New York City Mission Movement, 1812-1870.* Ithaca, N.Y.: Cornell University Press, 1971.

Snay, Mitchell. *Gospel of Disunion: Religion and Separatism in the Antebellum South.* New York: Cambridge University Press, 1993.

Snyder, Stephen H. *Lyman Beecher and His Children: The Transformation of a Religious Tradition.* Brooklyn, N.Y.: Carlson, 1991.

Stansell, Christine. *City of Women: Sex and Class in New York, 1789-1860.* New York: Alfred A. Knopf, 1986.

Stein, Stephen, ed. *Jonathan Edwards's Writing: Text, Context, Interpretation.* Bloomington: Indiana University Press, 1996.

Stephen, Sir Leslie. *A History of English Thought in the Eighteenth Century,* 3d ed. 2 vols. New York: G. P. Putnams Sons, 1902.

Stevens, Sylvester K. *American Expansion in Hawaii, 1842-1898.* Harrisburg: Archives Publishing Company of Pennsylvania, 1945.

Stevenson, Louise. *Scholarly Means for Evangelical Ends: The New Haven Scholars and the Transformation of Higher Learning in America.* Baltimore: Johns Hopkins University Press, 1986.

Stewart, James Brewer. *Holy Warriors: The Abolitionists and American Slavery.* New York: Hill & Wang, 1976.

Sweet, Leonard I. ed. *The Evangelical Tradition in America.* Macon, Ga.: Mercer University Press, 1984.

Sweet, William Warren. *Religion on the American Frontier 1783-1850: The Congregationalists.* Chicago: University of Chicago, 1930.

———. *Religion on the American Frontier: The Presbyterians.* New York: Harper & Brothers, 1936.

Trinterud, Leonard J. *The Forming of an American Tradition: A Re-Examination of Colonial Presbyterianism.* Philadelphia: Westminster Press, 1949.

Tuveson, Ernest Lee. *Redeemer Nation: The Idea of America's Millennial Role.* Chicago: University of Chicago Press, 1968.

Tyler, Alice F. *Freedom's Ferment: Phases of American Social History to 1860.* Minneapolis: University of Minnesota Press, 1944.

Tyrrell, Ian R. *Sobering Up: From Temperance to Prohibition in Antebellum America, 1800-1860.* Westport, Conn.: Greenwood, 1979.

Valeri, Mark. *Law and Providence in Joseph Bellamy's New England: The Origins of the New Divinity in Revolutionary America.* New York: Oxford University Press, 1994.

Walters, Ronald G. *American Reformers, 1815-1860,* 2d ed. New York: Hill and Wang, 1997.

———. *The Antislavery Appeal: American Abolitionism After 1830.* Baltimore: Johns Hopkins University Press, 1976.

Weisberger, Bernard A. *They Gathered at the River: The Story of the Great Revivalists and Their Impact upon Religion in America.* Boston: Little, Brown, 1958.

Welch, Claude. *Protestant Thought in the Nineteenth Century.* 2 vols. New Haven, Conn.: Yale University Press, 1972.

Welter, Rush. *The Mind of America 1820-1860.* New York: Columbia University Press, 1975.

Wertenbaker, Thomas Jefferson. *Princeton 1746-1896.* Princeton, N.J.: Princeton University Press, 1946.

Williams, Daniel Day. *The Andover Liberals.* 1941. rprt. New York: Octagon Books, 1970.

Wood, Gordon S. *The Creation of the American Republic 1776-1787.* New York: W. W. Norton, 1969.

Wright, Conrad. *The Beginnings of Unitarianism.* Boston: Starr King Press, 1955.

Wyatt-Brown, Bertram. *Lewis Tappan and the Evangelical War Against Slavery.* Cleveland: Press of Case Western Reserve University, 1969.

Yeager, Iver F. *Church and College on the Illinois Frontier: The Beginnings of Illinois College and the United Church of Christ in Central Illinois, 1829 to 1867.* Jacksonville, Ill.: Illinois College, 1980.

York, Robert M. *George B. Cheever: Religious and Social Reformer 1807-1890.* Orono: University of Maine, 1955.

Zwiep, Mary. *Pilgrim Path: The First Company of Women Missionaries to Hawaii.* Madison: University of Wisconsin Press, 1991.

Unpublished Dissertations and Papers

Baghdadi, Mania K. "Protestants, Poverty and Urban Growth: A Study of the Organization of Charity in Boston and New York, 1820-1865." Ph.D. dissertation, Brown University, 1975.

Banner, Lois Wendland. "The Protestant Crusade: Religious Missions, Benevolence and Reform in the United States 1790-1840." Ph.D. dissertation, Columbia University, 1970.

Breitenbach, William K. "New Divinity Theology and the Idea of Moral Accountability." Ph.D. dissertation, Yale University, 1978.

Cott, Nancy F. "In the Bonds of Womanhood: Perspectives on Female Experience and Consciousness in New England, 1780-1830." Ph.D. dissertation, Brandeis University, 1974.

Davis, E. Bradford. "Albert Barnes--1798-1879: An Exponent of New School Presbyterianism." Th.D. dissertation, Princeton Theological Seminary, 1961.

Della Vecchia, Phyllis. "Rhetoric, Religion, Politics, A Study of the Sermons of Lyman Beecher." Ph.D. dissertation, University of Pennsylvania, 1973.

Giltner, John H. "Moses Stuart 1780-1852." Ph.D. dissertation, Yale University, 1956.

Hales, Jean. "The Shaping of Nativist Sentiment, 1848-1860." Ph.D. dissertation, Stanford University, 1973.

Hirrel, Leo P. "The Ideology of Antebellum Reform Within the New School Calvinist Community." Ph.D. dissertation, University of Virginia, 1989.

Keller, Ralph Alan. "Northern Protestant Churches and the Fugitive Slave Law of 1850." Ph.D. dissertation, University of Wisconsin, 1969.

Mooney, Michael E. "Millennialism and Antichrist in New England." Ph.D. dissertation, Syracuse University, 1982.

Morrison, Michael Gordon. "Conceptions of Sin in American Evangelical Thought in the Early Nineteenth Century." Ph.D. dissertation, University of Wisconsin, 1971.

Neufeldt, Harvey G. "The American Tract Society, 1825-1865: An Examination of Its Religious, Economic, Social, and Political Ideas." Ph.D. Dissertation, Michigan State University, 1971.

Rosell, Garth, M. "Charles Grandison Finney and the Rise of the Benevolence Empire." Ph.D. dissertation, University of Minnesota, 1971.

Shiels, Richard D. "The Connecticut Clergy in the Second Great Awakening." Ph.D. dissertation, Boston University, 1976.

Spurlock, John. "The Awful Disclosures of William Leete Stone: Nativism and Nationality." Presented to the Society for Historians of the Early American Republic, July 26, 1991.

Vulgamore, Melvin L. "Social Reform in the Theology of Charles Grandison Finney." Ph.D. dissertation, Boston University, 1963.

Wood, Raymond Lee. "Lyman Beecher 1775-1863, A Biographical Study." Ph.D. dissertation, Yale University, 1961.

Wosh, Peter J. "Bibles, Benevolence and Emerging Bureaucracy: The Persistence of the American Bible Society, 1816-1890." Ph.D. dissertation, New York University, 1988.

Index